BUENOS AIRES

and the best of

ARGENTINA

ALIVE

GUIDE

Arnold Greenberg
Linda M. Tristan

Harriet Greenberg, Editor

HUNTER
PUBLISHING

Hunter Publishing, Inc.
300 Raritan Center Parkway
Edison NJ 08818
(908) 225 1900
Fax (908) 417 0482

ISBN 1-55650-680-5

Maps by Kim André

Acknowledgements

To Susan Brushaber
for her persistence and uncanny ability
to "suavizar las esquinas"

To "Tete,"
our Buenos Aires insider,
whose tips are always on the mark

Table Of Contents

Maps

South America

Introduction to Argentina

Congratulations! If you are reading this introduction you are at least contemplating taking a trip to Argentina. If so, you can look forward to an extraordinary vacation, enjoying both man-made wonders and natural ones. Argentina is not yet a major tourist destination, although the number of visitors from North America has risen dramatically over the last five years. The reasons are obvious. They begin where everything begins in Argentina – Buenos Aires.

One of the world's wondrous cities, Buenos Aires is a European city in Latin America. Open the phonebook and you'll find as many Italian surnames as Spanish ones. You'll also find many British, German, Jewish and Japanese names. Much like the United States, Argentina experienced waves of immigration at the turn of the century and after the Second World War.

It is a city that hardly sleeps, with restaurants routinely serving until 2 or 3 a.m. There are no obvious slums and, unlike many U.S. cities, the "downtown" areas are not decaying. In fact, they are the heart of the city, housing the best hotels, shops and restaurants. You'll spend much of your time downtown. Soccer is a national passion; but, thanks to the British, polo is also first rate. The city has many fine museums and a world-class opera house. Shopping for fine leathers and furs can be fun and rewarding.

You can begin and end your stay in Buenos Aires, but why not see the rest of Argentina? The second largest country in South America, it covers an area of over one million square miles. If you can imagine South America resembling a lamb chop, Argentina and Chile share the bone. The country is over 2,000 miles long and only 884 miles across at its widest point. It narrows as it moves southward and its terrain varies dramatically, changing from tropical jungles and rainforests in the north, to majestic Andes peaks that are snowcapped year round along the spine and an ever-expanding glacier near its southern tip.

Argentina offers a wide range of vacation options which change with the seasons. You can combine your visit to Buenos Aires with great skiing near Mendoza or in Bariloche and, because the seasons are reversed, you can ski on July 4th weekend. Or, if you prefer to trek, hunt or fish, you can explore Argentina's National Parks in the Argentine summer and swim in Lake Nahuel Huapi on Christmas Eve. Islands inhabited only by penguins and the world's most spectacular waterfall can also be part of an Argentine vacation. See "Around Argentina" for experiences in other parts of this vast country.

Getting to Argentina

By Air

Buenos Aires is readily accessible from the U.S. and Canada, with major carriers flying to the capital city daily. They offer direct flights, usually with one stop enroute at Lima, Rio or Miami. Gateway cities include New York, Los Angeles, Montreal, Toronto and Vancouver.

See Buenos Aires A-Z for a list of the airlines that fly here.

Aerolíneas Argentinas is the national carrier of Argentina. It enjoys a fine reputation for good service both in the air and on the ground. Its private terminal at Ezeiza International Airport in Buenos Aires, complete with customs facilities, allows you to move through the entrance formalities quickly. Aerolíneas offers a host of special tours which you should investigate, including the **Visit Argentina Pass**. This is actually a booklet of four flight coupons which can, and must, be purchased at the time you buy your ticket to Argentina. The cost of the booklet is $450. Each coupon is good for one flight within Argentina; additional four-coupon booklets can be purchased for $120. All coupons, including those in additional booklets, are valid for 30 days from the date the first coupon is redeemed. You have to plan carefully since you must state the destinations you intend to use the coupons for at time of purchase (dates are open), and each connecting flight requires an individual coupon. In the United States, the toll-free number is 1-800-333-0276, with assistance available from 9 a.m. to 9 p.m. (EST) Monday through Friday and 10 a.m. to 6:45 p.m. on weekends.

In New York call 212-698-2050.

American Airlines has two daily flights out of Miami. Both are evening departures. For information and reservations call 1-800-624-6262.

United Airlines offers daily non-stop service to Buenos Aires from New York and Miami. For information and reservations call 1-800-241-6522.

Varig Brazilian Airlines, an excellent carrier, flies from New York and Miami to Rio, where you can transfer for the daily flight to Buenos Aires. Some travelers may welcome breaking up the flight with a short diversion at the Rio airport. Varig's New York number is 212-682-3100.

Canadian Pacific flies to Buenos Aires from Toronto and Vancouver. For information and reservations call 1-800-426-7000. Many other Latin American carriers fly from their home base to Buenos Aires. These include **AeroPerú**, **Avianca**, **LanChile** and **Viasa**. This takes on major importance if Buenos Aires is just one stop on a South America trip.

To get the best fares, you will have to do your homework or have an experienced travel agent do it for you. Deregulation, length of time before departure, your flight route, season of the year and a host of other factors affect fares. Make sure to explore such money saving options as package tours offered by the airlines, bucket shops, stand-by travel if your time is flexible, and assorted charter opportunities.

Overland

Buses, ferries and railroads link Argentina with countries nearby – although rarely at Buenos Aires. You can drive or hop a bus from **Chile** (no rail). The busiest crossing goes from Santiago, Chile to Mendoza, although the most exciting is from Puerto Montt through the Chilean and Argentinean lake regions. This route is particularly recommended if you can break your trip. There are bus and rail connections between **Bolivia** and Argentina; and you can hop a bus or ferry in Paraguay. The most popular crossing is the one at Iguazú. It is also the favored crossing point from **Brazil**. Keep in mind that you will still be far from Buenos Aires. **Montevideo, Uruguay** and Buenos Aires are just a hydrofoil ride apart.

See Bariloche for crossings in the Lake Region.

Entry Requirements

A valid passport is required for United States and Canadian citizens to enter Argentina. In addition, you will be issued a tourist card by your airline prior to landing which you must keep in your passport at all times. This is generally true for citizens of other Latin American and European countries. All foreign students who come to Argentina to study should check on entry requirements. No special vaccinations are necessary to enter Argentina or to return to the United States or Canada.

Climate

Argentina's climate varies by region. Located in the heart of the Pampas along the shores of the

Río de la Plata, Buenos Aires enjoys a fairly dry climate. The summer months (December through March) can be very hot and humid, with temperatures in the 80s and 90s. School vacations begin at Christmas and continue through January. The city is less crowded then and a few restaurants close.

The Buenos Aires winter is cool but relatively mild, with temperatures in the 40s and 50s. Heavy rainfall occurs during the winter months and, although rare, snow is not unheard of.

The northeastern region of the country, including Iguazú Falls, is semi-tropical and quite humid all year long. Temperatures are lowest in July and August. Bariloche is a year-round resort destination. Summer temperatures are often in the high 70s, while winter temperatures are often in the 30s. Patagonia is much colder and rainfall is heavier as well. Winds, sometimes reaching gale force, are not uncommon and the weather fluctuates greatly in a 24-hour period. Ushuaia, Tierra del Fuego is most popular in the summer when the temperature is often in the 50s.

Packing For Your Trip

Depending on the season and regions you will be traveling in, you will need to pack a somewhat varied suitcase. For Buenos Aires and the temperate regions, plan on light spring-like clothing for the summer months and don't forget your bathing suit. Make sure you have a light jacket or sweater for cool evenings and heavier clothes if you are traveling south. Obviously, if you are planning to visit Bariloche during ski season (May through September), you will need warm winter-wear. The same is true if you plan to stay in Buenos Aires during the Argentine winter. Bring a warm sweater or jacket.

The dress code relaxes in summer.

While clothing in more rural parts of Argentina tends to be casual (jeans are quite acceptable all over), Buenos Aires residents are quite fashion conscious and often dress more formally. Dressing up for dinner is an everyday occurrence in the city and is usually required when dining in the nicer restaurants or attending the nightclubs. Men should bring along a jacket and tie, and women should have at least one dressy outfit. Walking shorts are generally acceptable in the capital (but not at dinner).

Money Matters

Historically the Argentine exchange rate fluctuated sharply and suddenly – sometimes overnight. At the time of this writing, the situation appears to be much improved, with rates staying fairly constant. In 1992 the **new peso** replaced the **austral** at a rate of 10,000 australes to one new peso. The exchange rate of the new peso has since held steady at $1 U.S. to one new peso. However, do check the rate immediately prior to your departure.

It may help for you to be aware of the events leading up to the introduction of the new peso. In the 1970's Buenos Aires was one of Latin America's best buys for the dollar. A budget traveler's dream, a steak dinner at a lovely restaurant could run all of three dollars. With the advent of the "parallel market" in 1974, there was enormous variation between the parallel and the official rate, so costs depended largely on where you purchased your pesos.

Inflation soared out of sight in 1980. A cup of coffee, for example, cost $5 and a cab to the airport was over $50. In 1985 the austral replaced the peso as the unit of currency at approximate par with the dollar. Inflation continued to soar and so did the strength of the dollar. Upon his election in 1989, Argentina's current president, the Peronist Carlos Menem enforced strict austerity measures and the Argentine economy began to improve.

Today prices in Buenos Aires are comparable to those of other major cities around the world, although slightly lower than those in New York and Paris.

Dollars and travelers checks can be exchanged at banks and *cambios* (exchange houses) as well as at your hotel. At this writing there is no parallel market and the dollar and peso are accepted equally. By the way, in the years that it did exist, it was not a hush-hush thing. Parallel rates were published in daily newspapers. Stay posted.

Credit Cards - Tipping

All major international credit cards – American Express, MasterCard, Visa and Diner's Club – are readily accepted at hotels, restaurants, and shops. You should have cash and traveler's checks with you because some smaller places may not accept credit cards.

A restaurant tip of 10% is customary, plus a 5% bonus for excellent service. Taxies are not tipped.

The Language of Argentina & Buenos Aires

The language of Argentina is Spanish or "Castellano," as the Argentineans call it. However, they've flavored it with a cadence and intonation all their own. The musicality and variations in pronunciation of the Spanish spoken in Argentina, especially in Buenos Aires, set it apart from all others. Most notable is the pronunciation of the "ll," commonly pronounced "ya" as in "llama" ("yama"). In Argentina, however, the "y" becomes a combination of "z" and "sh" ("zshama").

If you speak Spanish, you'll also pick up on the use of "che" among friends, and that the 2nd person "tú" has been replaced by "vos," the 2nd person plural conjugation not used anywhere else in South America. Listen carefully and you'll also note differences in vocabulary. For example, "avocado," which in Spanish is "aguacate," is "palta" in Argentina. "Money," which is "dinero," is referred to here as "yira," while a silly person is not "tonto" but "boludo." "Barbaro!" is "fantastic!"

In some districts of Buenos Aires you're bound to hear people speaking something which sounds like Spanish but isn't. That language, or actually a dialect, is **Lunfardo.** As you know, Buenos Aires is a city of immigrants. Lunfardo arose from the need for mutual understanding among the different peoples who came to Argentina to start a new life. It is a recognized dialect; you can even buy a phrase book entitled, *Aprender Lunfardo* (*Learn Lunfardo*).

A Capsule History

"*Y allí levantamos una ciudad que se llama Buenos Aires* – And here we raised a city called Buenos Aires."

When these words were written in the 16th century, the chronicler must have been quite a visionary. At that time, the "city" had only a few hundred inhabitants. With its new port barred from commerce by its Spanish rulers, the future did not look too bright. But just a century later, Buenos Aires had become a cultural center and the heart of South America's fight for freedom from Spain. The cosmopolitan metropolis of today can be traced back to Indians who inhabited the area for centuries before the first Europeans arrived.

Before the Spanish

Argentina and Chile were the last areas of what is now South America to be inhabited by early humans. The Bering Straits formed a bridge from Asia to America during the Ice Age, providing the first group of Asians with access to the west around 25,000 B.C. The earliest settlers probably reached the southern tip of South

America by 9,000 B.C. Cave sites near the Straits of Magellan corroborate this theory. Development throughout the country was uneven, with certain groups remaining as hunters and gatherers until the arrival of the Spanish, and others progressing to advanced agricultural techniques and culture. However, nowhere in Argentina was there a unified and advanced culture like those of the Maya, Aztec or Inca.

The northwest section of what is now Argentina was the most developed because of its proximity to the culturally advanced centers of Bolivia and Peru. Around 1480 A.D. the Inca armies invaded and actually incorporated the area into its vast empire. Here, natives lived in simple stone houses in towns that sometimes reached 3,000 in size. Many of these towns were built on hilltops and were walled in for protection. Agriculture was the main source of livelihood, and irrigation and the domestication of animals, particularly llamas, were practiced widely. Ceramics, wood carvings, large stone sculptures and high quality metal tools, especially of copper and bronze, have all been found in this region.

Remains of Inca roads, storage places and forts can still be found in the area.

The area around the Central Mountains and what is today Santiago del Estero (the province) was far less developed. Hunting and gathering were the main source of food, although some agriculture was practiced. Artifacts found here were rougher and cruder. Villages, some built partially underground, were smaller.

Santiago del Estero (the city) is the oldest in Argentina.

Life in the northeast was very similar to that in the central region but, because there was access to two large rivers (the Paraná and the Uruguay), fishing became an important part of the economy.

The southernmost region of Argentina, Tierra del Fuego, experienced little cultural development. Few artifacts or examples of architecture have been found. The peoples who lived here were nomadic, moving throughout the area in search of food that could be hunted, fished or gathered. Little or no agriculture was practiced; pottery, metalworking and other crafts were virtually unknown. On the other hand, tools made of bone and stone were highly developed, reflecting a successful adaptation to the local environment. The lifestyle of these nomads remained the same for 6,000 years until the Spanish introduced agricultural techniques.

There are beautiful caves throughout the southern regions of Argentina. On their walls, the paintings of these primitive peoples are still visible. The best known of these caves is **La Cueva de las Manos**, just outside the village of Perito Moreno in the province of Santa Cruz in the Lake District. Archaeologists have identified four different periods or styles in the highly stylized drawings of animals, primarily guanacos and men portrayed as hunters. While much remains a mystery, the caves do provide some insight into the prehistoric peoples who populated the region.

Archaeologists are still trying to fill in their knowledge of the cultures and religions of Argentina's earliest inhabitants. Yet, one thing is certain. When the Spanish arrived, they encountered a wide variety of peoples and stages of cultural development.

The Colonial Period

Spurred on by the exploits of Columbus and subsequent adventurer-explorers such as Amerigo Vespucci and Ferdinand Magellan, the Spaniards (under the monarchy of King Philip II) continued to send expeditions to South America.

The city of Buenos Aires was actually founded twice, the first time by Pedro de Mendoza in 1536, and later and more definitively by Juan de Garay in 1580. The city did not immediately prosper. It was the southernmost part of the Peruvian Viceroyalty and in 1554 the King of Spain had decreed that all trade from Spain come via Panama and Peru, then south to Argentina. This effectively cut off any commercial traffic for the fledgling city on the Río de la Plata. For 200 years Buenos Aires remained a small town, peopled primarily by "criollos," Spaniards born in Argentina and "mestizos," those of mixed Spanish/Indian descent.

The major industry was smuggling Spanish goods.

It was the northwest part of today's Argentina, along with Córdoba, that experienced the greatest growth due to its proximity to Peru. Wheat, cotton, corn and tobacco were cultivated here for export. The Jesuits established a university in Córdoba in 1613 which made it a cultural center as well.

This changed in 1776 when the Spanish decided to open the Río de la Plata for transatlantic trade. They had created the Viceroyalty of Río de la Plata and named Buenos Aires as its administrative center. One immediate effect was a population explosion with 25,000 new inhabitants swelling the city to over 30,000 in just two years. As the city flourished, so did the fertile pampas surrounding it. Here vast *estancias* (ranches) were established and the *gaucho* rode into the country's folklore.

About a third of the new inhabitants were Africans brought here as slaves. Their fate is largely unknown.

Events in Europe began to affect the new viceroyalty. Spain's navy was virtually destroyed by the British during the Napoleonic wars, leaving the colonies vulnerable to attack. And attack the British did. In 1806, the city was successfully defended by a ragtag army organized by a local hero, Santiago de Liniers and again the following year. This time the British sent 8,000 men to invade the city but were once again, fought off by volunteers, including women and children who, perched on roof tops, doused them with boiling water.

The successful defense of the city by locals gave impetus to a movement that had been silently growing for several years – independence from Spain. The city's *criollo* leadership was fed up with restrictions on trade that had favored the Spanish and with being forced to play a neglible role in the growth of a nation. As elsewhere in Latin America, large landowners and clergy often brought over from Spain, formed the city's power base, effectively preventing the *criollos* from having any real influence.

Emboldened, the *criollos* formed a local council and voted to unseat the Spanish Viceroy. The council formed to rule was composed of Argentina's finest intellectuals, including Bernardino Rivadavia, Manuel Belgrano and Mariano Moreno. They wanted to create a nation based on European ideas of democracy and liberalism.

Each has an important street named in his honor in downtown Buenos Aires.

Naturally, the establishment vehemently opposed any changes in the status quo.

On May 25, 1810 the council voted to dissolve the viceroyalty and form a local government. But the definitive break from Spain would not occur until 1816. Those intervening six years were filled with political anarchy and civil war sparked by the conflicts of interest among the various factions which arose from the dissolution of the viceroyalty – revolutionary nationalists vs. royalists; *criollos* vs. *peninsulares*; and *unitarios* (supporters of a strong central government in Buenos Aires) vs. *federales* (supporters of a loose confederation of autonomous provinces). Political *juntas* came and went until July 9, 1816 when the Congress of San Miguel de Tucumán declared Argentina's independence from Spain. Two months earlier, Juan Martín de Pueyrredón had been appointed Supreme Dictator of the United Provinces of the Río de la Plata.

Although not a nation at peace with itself, Argentina did take the lead in freeing other parts of the continent from Spanish rule. Led by General José de San Martín (*El Libertador* – The Liberator), the Argentine Army crossed the Andes and joined the Chilean army under Bernardo O'Higgins to defeat the Spanish in February 1817; and then braved the 1,500-mile trip to Lima to free Peru in 1822. San Martín also inspired his northern counterpart, the Venezuelan Simón Bolívar who helped free Venezuela, Colombia and Ecuador.

After years of continued conflict between the *federales* and the *unitarios*, Bernardino Rivadavia was elected the first president of the United Provinces of the Río de la Plata in February, 1826 by the constituent congress in Buenos Aires. Rivadavia, with the backing of the unitarians, proposed that Buenos Aires be designated the federal capital of the United Provinces. A Unitarian Constitution was approved on July 19, 1826. Rivadavia also attempted to establish a land redistribution program. Yet, once again, Buenos Aires and provincial federalists, among them powerful *caudillos* (land owners), opposed reform and Rivadavia's government failed in 1827.

Shortly thereafter in 1829, Juan Manuel de Rosas was elected governor of Buenos Aires and remained in that position, except for the period of 1832-1835, until 1852. De Rosas was a fascinating character – just perfect for a Paul Newman flick. Born to a wealthy family, he grew up on an *estancia* and could ride, rope and handle a horse with any *gaucho*. He was also a successful businessman. He seemed to be the strong leader the country needed. De Rosas formed a coalition between the *caudillos* and prosperous merchants and others who supported the federalist cause, and eventually gained almost unlimited authority over Buenos Aires and the country. He led a campaign to wipe out the native Indians of southern Argentina and consolidated the federalists' power by imprisoning and killing all those who opposed him. Under Rosas, horrific methods of death and torture were made official and estimates of the number of dead are in the thousands. Putting all his energies into staying in power, Rosas succeeded in destroying the economy and wasting national funds.

By the late 1840's and early 1850's, an underground movement had begun to plot the overthrow of Rosas. A group of upper class intellectuals was led by Bartolomé Mitre, Juan Bautista Alberti and Domingo Sarmiento. Their opportunity came when Justo José de Urquiza, a wealthy *caudillo* and former Rosas supporter from Entre Ríos, turned against him in May, 1851. Urquiza raised a volunteer army, which included members of Rosas' own force. Rosas was easily overthrown on February 3, 1852.

Rosas fled to England, where he died 25 years later.

The next three decades were filled with efforts to organize a unified nation and to create governmental bodies that could formulate and implement policy. On May 25, 1853 a new Constitution closely modeled on that of the United States replaced the Constitution of 1816.

Urquiza was elected the first constitutional president of the Argentine Republic. He built banks, schools, and roads linking Buenos Aires to the outlying provinces. In 1862, Buenos Aires was named the capital of the country. Bartolomé Mitre, then governor of Buenos Aires, was elected president. He was succeeded by Domingo Sarmiento, whose term (1868-1874) saw Argentina take its place on the world stage. It was Sarmiento who ushered in the "golden age" of Argentina. It would last until World War I.

During this period immigration soared, as did exports to Europe; land was opened up; communications improved; and the nation's economy boomed. Intellectual growth occurred as well, with the founding of newspapers, political parties, a world-class opera house, and the nation's first five teacher training schools.

Modern Argentina

Although all was well on the surface, political unrest was increasing. More and more people resented being ruled by a government of wealthy landowners. Labor strikes became frequent occurrences and eventually so did other opposition groups' confrontations with the military. In the 1930's, with the onset of the worldwide depression, conditions worsened and the economy ground to a halt. The military stepped in and deposed Hipolito Yrigoyen, then in his second term as president. This was the first of several military interventions in Argentina's modern political life.

Military regimes alternated with elected governments and in the coup of 1943 a new figure emerged in Argentina and onto the world stage. Juan Domingo Perón was a career military officer who had been sent to Italy for training. There he became an admirer of Benito Mussolini, as did other Argentine officers. Upon his return he joined a secret organization that promoted these facist policies.

In 1943, Perón was appointed Secretary of the Ministry of Labor and Social Welfare. It was from this position that he built a strong power base. He enacted a series of child labor laws, job security and pension reforms that made him the hero of Argentina's working class. On October 9, 1945 Perón was arrested by the army, who feared his growing popularity. This move back-

Los Madres de la Plaza de Mayo still continue their Thursday demonstrations.

fired largely due to the efforts of Eva Duarte, Perón's consort and soon-to-be wife. Eva and Perón's followers organized large-scale demonstrations and protest marches by the working classes. The largest filled the Plaza de Mayo, where the army bombed its own people. Perón was released on October 17 and was elected president in 1946. He was bitterly opposed by the United States, who labeled him a fascist.

Eva Duarte, a relatively unknown singer/actress, became Juan Perón's second wife in 1944. Although 25 years his junior, she was an astute politician and her influence on his political rise was enormous. It was due to her urging that he made the working class and labor unionists his power base. The legislation he proposed to benefit them was greeted by their political loyalty and this support carried him to the presidency. During her husband's first term, Evita became the champion of the "*descamisados*" (shirtless ones, i.e., the workers) and a near-cult figure. The social organization she founded built schools and hospitals and, as a feminist, she even started a women's political party. She was greeted as a celebrity during a tour of European capitals. When she died in 1952 at the age of 33, she left her followers in grief and her husband without his most devoted aide and visible supporter.

Evita's remains were sent to Europe for burial after Perón was overthrown in 1955. However, upon his death in 1974 her body was reinterred in the Recoleta Cemetery. Fresh flowers are placed there daily and the crypt is guarded. Evita's epitaph, immortalized in song, reads,

"Don't cry for me Argentina, I remain quite near you."

Perón, following Mussolini's policy, took control of many industries and projects. The years following World War II were prosperous. National wealth grew and, along with it, workers' wages. Perón was overwhelmingly re-elected in 1951, but a series of droughts hurt the economy and a drop in grain prices put an end to the prosperity.

Perón began to leave important decisions to his staff and the nation slid ever deeper into a depression. The Peronist government, which had organized Argentina along fascist lines, eventually paralyzed production, discouraged investment and strengthened the armed forces. The latter ultimately rebelled and overthrew Perón in 1955. He fled to Paraguay.

The armed forces returned Argentina to civilian government in 1958, but in the following 18 years there were nine different governments and countless coups. Each government seemed incapable of solving the serious economic problems facing Argentina: inflation was extremely high; the trade deficit was unmanageable; and foreign ownership of Argentine companies had hit a high of nearly 60%. The military exercised a great deal of power during this period. Heavy use of torture and murder was not uncommon.

These repressive conditions created the proper climate for Juan Perón to stage a comeback. Perón ran by proxy in the 1973 elections and won. He made his third wife, María Estela (Isabel) Martínez, vice-president and attempted to undo some of the damage wrought in the previous 20 years. However, his efforts were cut short by his sudden death in mid-1974 and "Isabelita" was left in control. Her government, like most to follow, was marked by corruption, conservatism and an increased reliance on violence. The military seized power again in March, 1976.

Although the military had never run the country with great success, the new *junta* passed a constitutional amendment giving them both executive and legislative powers. This was to become the worst period in Argentina's history.

General Jorge Videla was chosen as the new president and he determined to attack the country's problems – strikes, corruption and minor terrorist activity – by ruthlessly attacking the "leftists" he decided were the instigators. This campaign of state-sponsored terrorism practiced against the Argentine people became known as "The Dirty War." Thousands of Argentineans simply "disappeared" and became known as "*los desaparecidos*." Included among them were priests, nuns, students, reporters, and professors. Entire families simply vanished. Anyone suspected of anti-government activities was tortured and killed, rather than arrested and tried for treason. Estimates of the numbers of dead range from 10,000 to 20,000. Those unfortunates are still turning up in shallow graves all over the country. Their disappearances led to a moving ceremony every Thursday in the Plaza de Mayo, where hundreds of "mothers" march and demand information about their missing loved ones.

Conditions remained the same under Videla's successor, General Viola, and did not change until Lieutentant General Leopoldo Galtieri rose to power in 1981. To take the population's mind off The Dirty War and the economic stagnation, he rallied the country to war. They would take back their South Atlantic islands, Las Malvinas, from British control. Britain had controlled the islands, which they called the Falklands, since the 19th century – much to Argentina's dismay. The rise of strong nationalistic fervor was quickly dispelled when Britain decided to fight to keep the islands. Outclassed, the Argentine "war" effort was over in two months. Galtieri was forced to resign and was replaced by yet another military man.

But the humiliation felt by the people over this defeat heightened their dissatisfaction with military rule. Massive demonstrations took place in the Plaza de Mayo and pressure for a change to civilian rule increased. In the election of 1983 a civilian, Raul Alfonsín, was elected. Alfonsín re-instituted the independent legislative branch, stopped censorship of the press and encouraged free enterprise. He also proceeded to prosecute the military leaders for their part in The Dirty War.

Unfortunately, the new liberalism and freedom in Argentinean life did not cure the economic problems. Inflation rose to an annual rate of 1,000% shortly after Alfonsín took over. He reacted by freezing wages and prices, and changed the currency from the peso to the austral – a bold plan that initially helped greatly to reduce inflation, yet was less successful in stimulating the economy.

The lack of economic growth, dissatisfaction with Alfonsín's austerity plans, which included wage freezes and heavy taxes on gasoline and electricity, ultimately led to the increased appeal of the Peronist party, the Justicialistas. Their candidate, Carlos Saul Menem, in a campaign designed to appeal to the traditional supporters of the Peronistas, the poor and the working class, was elected president in 1989.

With the economy crumbling, Alfonsín stepped down five months early. Menem, cultivating both his playboy image, with appearances both on the racetrack and basketball court, and a free market economy, began an economic program of privatization of inefficient government industries combined with wage-price pacts between labor, business and government. Though times were tough in the beginning, the Argentine economy has improved under his policies. The economic success of his programs is apparent and at this writing the Argentine economy is flourishing. Prices are stable and the peso is on a par and trading freely with the U.S. dollar. At present President Menem is seeking to change the law only allowing him to serve one six-year term in order to run for a second term in 1995.

The Argentine Population

Who are the Argentineans of today? They are the descendants of the Spanish colonists and of Sicilian farmers, Portuguese sailors, British adventurers, Greek traders and Lebanese merchants. They may be refugees from a war-ridden land or the privileged heirs of a cattle empire. Their immigrant experience is the history of Argentina, as it has been of all the Americas. The doors were open, the country was ripe for the picking, and they came from everywhere.

The national constitution contains a paragraph describing the Argentinean as "... anybody in the world who wishes to reside in Argentina...." It may not be so simple nowadays, but it was at one time. The 32 million people in Argentina all have roots in far away places; but most of them can claim Europe as their motherland. The strong influence of Spain remains just beneath the surface in many *porteños*, as residents of Buenos Aires are known. Others can trace their roots to Italy, Germany, Britain and France. Wars have always instigated mass migrations to Argentina, where hopes of peace and prosperity could be fulfilled. That hasn't changed – you will find a surprising number of Southeast Asians in Argentina today.

Buenos Aires is the center of the nation and has a population of more than 12 million. The burden of this intense concentration of people has compelled the government to take drastic measures. Housing projects offering affordable shelter and jobs have been generated in the interior of Argentina to lure people away from Buenos Aires. This policy has enjoyed only moderate success. Another idea that has been in the works for too many years to mention is the shifting of the capital from Buenos Aires to a town called Viedma in the southeastern region of the country. An attempt to create another Brasilia has yet to prove successful and Buenos Aires seems reluctant to give up its title.

It's an undeniable truth that Argentineans have a strong identification with their place of birth, their family and their fellow man. Strolling around the city, one can't help but be overwhelmed by monuments, statues and plaques that remind the locals of their history at every turn. This translates into patriotism, and it's a mighty force in this country.

The Culture

Buenos Aires has been called the "Goliath's Head" because of its colossal urban concentration. Many of the 12.5 million people who live in Greater Buenos Aires left the *pampas* and the other provinces to enter a city where the night is always young, and commerce and culture stand shoulder to shoulder. The city is a spawning ground for a vibrant cultural life.

Porteños like to boast that their city is home to over 300 theaters, 100-plus art galleries, at least 70 museums and hundreds of bookstores. Furthermore, there are 50 magazines and 12 daily newspapers. Night has a strong hold on everyone here. The general public mills about Corrientes – the street that never sleeps – taking in a movie, a pizza, and a bit of local gossip, while intellectuals haunt the all-night bookshops.

Lavalle is the famed "cinema street," with its bright billboards advertising the latest releases, local, foreign, and Hollywood. You can walk either of these streets at all hours of the day or night – one of the special pleasures of Buenos Aires.

Culture is everywhere: in the tango parlors and music halls of San Telmo; in the open-air Caminito theater; in La Boca, where the side streets are decorated with murals and sculptures by local artists; in the aristocratic residences of Barrio Norte. Most of all, culture is in the people: the slightly built Indians singing folksongs from Jujuy on the corner of Florida and Viamonte, or the rough old *porteño* with a gold tooth and fedora spilling out his soul in a version of "Sur," a traditional tango of the port city. Theater, opera, ballet, modern music and dance are deeply rooted in the Argentine. This is evident not only in Buenos Aires, but in the passionate devotion to the arts that exists in the smaller towns and communities.

Many Buenos Aires churches are architecturally important and/or contain beautiful statuary and museums. They are detailed in the sighseeing section.

Theater and Film

Theater has a history in Argentina that dates back to 1778, with the "Teatro de la Ranchería." Today the theater is an established art form, with the Teatro Colón, the Cervantes, and the General San Martín Theater Complex in the vanguard of all that is new and novel or time-honored and classic. **The Teatro Colón Opera House** has a brilliant past and a shining future. It's really a theatrical world unto itself. **The Cervantes Theater**, founded in 1921, is the home of the *Comedie Nationale*, the National Theater Ensemble. Here the audience is treated to plays about the *gaucho*, plays by European masters like Pirandello and Molière, zarzuelas (Spanish light opera), and slice-of-life dramas depicting everyday life in Argentina.

Argentinians love the Spanish playwright Federico Garcia Lorca whose **Bodas de Sangre**

(Blood Wedding) is usually playing in one of the theaters around town. Adaptations of novels by Kafka and Dostoevsky also reach the stage in this city. Shakespeare and Sophocles are given equal time, while experimental theater from Eastern Europe, Africa and the Third World has been getting a great deal of exposure in recent years. Corrientes is Buenos Aires' "Broadway." Theaters stand alongside *parrillas* and cinemas. The entertainment here might range from a version of "Porgy and Bess" starring a major media star to a visit by the Russian Kirov Ballet Troupe.

Cinema has always been a favorite medium among Argentineans. Of the 200 or so first-run films shown annually, about 30 are produced in Argentina. Ever since the ousting of the military government in 1983, Argentine cinema has achieved a measure of worldwide recognition. In 1986, films like **La Historia Oficial** *(The Official Story)* won academy awards and brought to light the suffering caused by The Dirty War that plagued the country in the late 1970's and early 80's.

Music and Dance

Argentineans are proud of the old saying: "The Mexicans descended from the Aztecs, the Peruvians from the Incas, but we descended from boats." Their music, melody and harmony have roots in these diverse pasts. European influence has always been a strong component of Argentine music. Jesuit missionaries in the 17th century were already composing and teaching music. The works of **Alberdi, Alcorta**, and **Blas Parera** (composer of the national anthem) all demonstrate a markedly European style. Later composers like **Boero, de Rogatis** and **Gaito** veered only slightly from the accepted traditional style.

Not until the likes of **Alberto Williams, Buchardo** and **Ugarte** was there an attempt to incorporate native Argentine music into the generally European framework. **Juan José Castro, Luis Gianneo** and **Alberto Ginastera** stressed the content as much as the music, making new inroads in the caliber of composition. Argentina has many musical artists of international standing: **Bruno Gelber, Martha Argerich, Alberto Lysy, Delia Rigal,** and pianist **Pia Sebastiani** are but a few.

Popular music, old and new, has been an important form of expression for the country. The truly native music of **Atahualpa Yupanqui** and **Mercedes Sosa** have their roots in the high country. **Gato Barbieri** and **Chick Correa** are contemporary jazz age gurus, while **Pimpinela** and **Marilena Ross** draw mainly young audiences with their slick yet totally Argentinean pop songs.

In ballet, **Liliana Belfiore** and more recently **Julio Bocca** have mesmerized audiences with their talent and grace. Bocca stands at the threshold of ballet immortality in the manner of Nureyev and Baryshnikov. The National Ballet Company at the Teatro Colón has brought many national luminaries to the attention of the world and has been a popular stage for international dancers throughout the decades.

Literature

"Buenos Aires es un hombre/Que tiene grandes las piernas/Grandes los pies y las manos/Y pequeña la cabeza."

In these lines from her poem "Buenos Aires" the Argentine poet Alfonsina Storni compares the immense city to a man with long legs, large feet and large hands, and an amusingly tiny head. She is using the metaphor to describe the way the city grew from a tiny hamlet, spreading outwards until it lost all sense of proportion. The tiny head of Buenos Aires exists only in this fanciful imagery. In actuality, Buenos Aires has a grand tradition of great minds. In its relatively short history, Argentina has produced an enviable body of literature and poetry. Argentina's (and Buenos Aires') literary history can be traced back to the first great politicians and statesmen like **Echeverría** and **Sarmiento**, men who were excellent writers in their own right. Sarmiento was a leader in establishing free, compulsory and non-denominational schooling. He also wrote a brilliant novel, *Facundo,* based on the life of an early pioneer in the new land of Argentina.

The definitive start of literary history lies with the timeless **Martín Fierro**. Published in 1878, this epic poem based on the life and times of the original *gaucho* was written by José Hernández, a politician and writer, and is considered one of the foremost examples of Argentine literature and a manifesto of the Argentine character. The "*gaucho* genre" came into its own and soon other writers such as **Hilario Ascasubi** were expressing themselves in this singularly Argentine way.

In the early 1900's Latin American literature went through a metamorphosis. The Modernist Movement was to change the face of Argentine literature. The new prose and poetry became more centered around city life, as the pampas receded into the people's imagination and opportunities grew within the city limits. **Leopoldo Lugones, Evaristo Carriego, Baldomero Fernández Moreno** and **Alfonsina Storni** appeared on the scene.

The young writers of the 1920's formed a group called the "Martinfierristas" after the literary review they joined forces to publish. One of the most cerebral members of the group was the late **Jorge Luis Borges**, the brilliant essayist-writer who died several years ago at the age of 86. Borges was a unique mind, deeply searching and refreshingly inventive. Many of Borges' titles are on bookshelves around the world. *Ficciones* and *Laberinto* are two excellent collections of his short stories. Other prominent names in the early modernist period are **Eduardo Mallea** and **Ricardo Güiraldes**, author of *Don Segundo Sombra*, a classic depiction of the life of an ordinary Argentine farmhand. Poets and writers of that period, including **Martínez Estrada, Nale Roxio, Macedonio Fernández,** and **Molinari,** contributed greatly to the literary scene.

Post-Modernists included Mujica Láinez, Silvina O'Campo, Adolfo Bioy Casares, Silvina Bullrich, Julio Cortázar and Ernesto Sabato, whose *Autopista del Sur* is a modern masterpiece. Sabato is the quintessential Argentine writer; a student of physics, his works test new territories of the psyche.

Even more recently, the novels of **Manuel Puig** have become known to the non-Spanish-speaking world. His novel, **Kiss of the Spider Woman** was turned into one of the most interesting films of the 1980's and is currently being performed on Broadway. When one speaks of literature, the name **Victoria O'Campo** often comes up. She was a maverick in the Modernist Movement, a female Maxwell Perkins in her ability to find talent and promote it. She came from an immensely wealthy family and used a great part of that fortune to pursue her first great love, publishing. She became an ardent publisher of Argentine literature in her own country and abroad. *Sur*, her literary review, was among the first to introduce the writings of Borges and Sabato.

Already mentioned elsewhere are the hundreds of bookstores in Buenos Aires, several open 24 hours (sheer heaven for vacationing bookworms). Many are on Corrientes, including shops featuring imported books. The publishing industry is alive and kicking in Argentina, one of the three biggest such industries in the Spanish-speaking world. Over 21 million books are published annually. Argentina exports about 50% of these books throughout Latin America and has over 200 publishing houses and more than 3,000 printing shops. These facts and figures attest to the Argentine love for the printed word.

Religion

Argentina is 87% Catholic. The original name of the city as the Spanish explorers christened it is **Nuestra Señora de Buenos Aires** (*Our Lady of Good Airs*). Despite this, Argentinians do not wear religion on their sleeves. They do go to church on Sunday and during the holidays, and will often cross themselves at the shrine of a patron saint, but the country is secular as far as politics and the populace are concerned. Freedom of religion is a firm tenet of the Constitution. Article 14 clearly states that all Argentinians have the right to freely profess their religion.

Apart from Catholicism, many other religions are widely practiced. There are over three million non-Catholics in Argentina. About one million follow the Evangelical religions, which are divided into various subgroups or sects. There are approximately 300,000 Jews, an equal number of Muslims, and approximately one million Argentineans belong to the Russian, Greek and Syrian Orthodox churches, the Armenian church or various Spiritualist religions.

Dining in Argentina

Rest assured you will not go hungry in Argentina. There are wonderful dining options throughout the country, with the finest, most elegant dining rooms in Buenos Aires. Restaurants are small and many augment their space by adding a sidewalk café. Weather permitting, these tables fill up first. Dinner in Buenos Aires is more formal than in the United States and

porteños dress in casual chic attire. You never see shorts, even Bermuda style, at night. Restaurants in resort areas such as Bariloche and Ushuaia are far less formal.

Dining hours are 12 to 3:30 p.m. for lunch and 8 p.m. to 2 a.m. for dinner. Reservations are not required but are practical on weekends, unless you don't mind waiting for a table.

You can eat well and inexpensively in Argentina without resorting to fast foods. Obviously, eating in the country's finer restaurants will add to the pleasure of your trip and you will sometimes want to do so.

Alive Price Scale

To give you an idea of price before you set out, we have devised this price scale based on three courses (appetizer, entrée, dessert), excluding drinks.

Expensive	*$40+ per person*
Moderate	*$25+ per person*
Inexpensive	*under $20 per person*

The Taste of Argentina

When asked for the first word that comes to mind for Argentina, many people would respond with *gaucho* or *pampas*. The taste of Argentina is largely related to these two words. The *pampas* or plains have vast *estancias* (ranches) where cattle and sheep are raised. These are tended by the legendary *gauchos* (cowboys) who wear distinctive attire and are excellent horsemen. The grasses of the *pampas* are so rich in nutrients that no chemical supplements are required as feed. The meat is less marbled with fat and therefore is lower in cholesterol. It has a unique flavor and is buttery soft. *Bife* reigns supreme here and appears on lunch and dinner plates in a variety of cuts and preparations. Virtually no part of the animal is discarded. Chewy and slightly charred *chinchulines* (cow intestines), chunky ribs and *morcillas* (blood sausages) accompany other meats as part of the renowned *parrillada*, a steaming platter of prime beef and sausage served on a brazier. A real treat is to visit an *estancia* (some are within a two-hour drive of the city) for a typical *asado*, which is an Argentine barbecue. A typical *asado* appetizer is *matambre*, a pounded flank steak stuffed with hard boiled eggs, spinach, pieces of ham and vegetables, then rolled jelly-roll style. Marinated in red wine and slowly baked, it is sliced and served with *chimichurri* sauce. *Chimichurri* is a condiment made with oil, vinegar, garlic and peppers. It comes "hot" or "hotter."

Matambre is served cold.

Empanadas are mouth-watering finger foods. Crusty baked dough shells encircle such ingredients as spicy ground beef with black olives, chunks of chicken, ham and cheese or vegetables. Delicious.

Churros are long, thin, hollow pastries that are fried like donuts. They are often sugared or filled with jelly. *Medias lunas* (half moons) are particularly popular at breakfast, when they are served with butter and jelly. They are similar to croissants but are less buttery and flakey. Pastries are delicious and offerings include German-style strudels, Italian-style cannoli and

French-style tarts. These are often served at high tea or with a *cortado*, an espresso that is cut *(cortado)* with steamed milk. Argentines never take their coffee and dessert together. The sweets are eaten before or after and are often accompanied by a glass of water.

Pizzas are very popular here and they are excellent. Toppings include cheese, olives, anchovies, ham, meatballs, sausage and others. One restaurant offers 50 different varieties. *Panchos* are beef hot dogs usually sold by street vendors. You add the condiments. *Fiambres* are toasted sandwiches with a selection of ingredients.

What To Drink

Any Argentinean will tell you that the only drink that does justice to beef is good Argentinean red wine. The excellent vineyards in the Mendoza region produce the grapes that become first class wine. The regions of Cuyo, San Juan, Cafayate, Salta and Catamarca supply the entire country with premier wines. These local wines are inexpensive, as are the excellent carbonated mineral waters. The many *whiskerías* and bars in town dispense drinks into the wee hours.

Argentine scotch is quite good, so there is no need to order the imported brands, which are triple the price at the very least. *Los Criadores* (Breeder's Choice) is one brand to try, and it's as good as anything from the Scottish highlands. Argentina is the only place where you can find an after-dinner drink called Legui. It's a cordial named after one of Argentina's most illustrious jockeys. Most bars stock Legui, and it makes a wonderful gift. Stash a bottle in your suitcase before you leave the country.

A non-alcoholic beverage that you might enjoy is a "submarino." It's a glass of cold milk with a spoonful of chocolate syrup sunk to the bottom. Argentines don't stir it. They drink a little milk, lick some of the chocolate off the spoon and continue this process until the glass is empty.

Buenos Aires

More than any capital city we've ever visited, Buenos Aires is the heartbeat of Argentina. On the *pampas*, in the *campo* or in the remote corners of Patagonia – all of Argentina's roads eventually lead back to Buenos Aires. One of every three Argentineans live within its borders. The city is at once an anomaly and a reflection of the Argentineans. Where the pace of the rest of the country is calm and unhurried, Buenos Aires is energetic and fast-paced. It offers a charming combination of European tradition and Latin attitude. The city most resembles Paris. Many of its imposing buildings were built in French style and its wide tree-lined boulevards are dotted with colorful sidewalk cafés. Fashionably dressed *porteños* (people of the port, as residents are called) move briskly along pedestrian promenades lined with boutiques selling fine leathers and furs or browse in chic art galleries.

The city's pace is daunting and you will have to reset your inner clock. Most restaurants don't even begin to serve dinner until at least 9 p.m. and *porteños* linger over espresso till the wee hours. Most restaurants serve until 2 a.m. week nights and even later on weekends; while nightclubs are in full swing until 4 or even 5 a.m.

Argentina is known for the quality of its beef and thick juicy cuts of lean beef are served in restaurants throughout the city. *Bife* is grilled on huge skewers over a hardwood fire. Sample a *parrillada*, a mélange of different cuts brought to the table on a mini-grill. It includes a variety of sausages and organ meats, and is usually served with a sliced tomato and onion salad, along with a huge platter of *papas fritas* (French fried potatoes).

The **Teatro Colón**, the refurbished world-class opera house in which Caruso sang, is a popular night stop, as are the many theaters and night-clubs throughout the city. These run the gamut, and we'll leave it to you to find your niche. However, no visit to Argentina would be complete without a visit to a tango club. Tango is Argentina's contribution to the popular music scene. Born in clubs, music houses and bordellos in the late 19th century, tango mixes the candomble rhythms of Africa with the haunting melodies of Southern Spain and Italy. At its peak after the Second World War, interest waned in the 1960's and 1970's. Fortunately, the intricate dance steps and sultry melodies are once again very popular.

If Buenos Aires is your only Argentinean destination, we suggest a daytrip or overnight to the nearby *pampas*. While only an hour's drive or train ride from center city, the world of the *gaucho* has rolling pastures, corrals of cattle and sprawling *estancias* (ranches) which are often home to priceless collections of silver and other treasures. If the fabled *gaucho* no longer exists, don't tell the Argentineans. The lore and legends are kept alive by city and country dweller alike. The *gaucho*, erect astride a handsome horse, a *maté* gourd in one hand and his *boleador* (lariat) in the other, is the personification of the country's pioneer spirit, courage and dogged independence. He is loyal to nature and true to himself, a romantic and an idealist – in short, an Argentinean.

Buenos Aires, a familar place south of the equator, yet closer to Madrid and Paris than a map would indicate, has absorbed its European sons and daughters and borrowed the best of their cultures, architecture and savoir faire. It is the city that inspired its native son Jorge Luis Borges to write: *"A mi se me hace cuenta que empezó Buenos Aires. La juzgo tan eterna come el agua y el aire."* (It seems to me that there has always been a Buenos Aires. She is as eternal as the water and the air.")

From the Airport to the City

International flights land at **Ezeiza International Airport** which is about 45 minutes from the heart of Buenos Aires. It is modern, sparkling clean and organized with baggage claims, customs officials, car rentals and money changing facilities *(cambios)* all readily accessible. There is also a duty free shop where you can buy cigarettes, liquor, perfume and other goods at bargain rates. You are permitted to take your purchases with you into Buenos Aires. Pick up maps and literature, including a current copy of *Where*, Buenos Aires' monthly magazine at the **Secretario de Turismo** office.

You then play roulette with Customs' red light/green light system. You press a button and if the green light flashes you simply pass through. However, if the light flashes red, you may have to go through a perfunctory search of your luggage. After passing through customs, head left towards the **Transportes** sign where you can make arrangements for transportation into the city, as well as book accommodations or confirm your hotel reservation if you already have one. Give the government clerks at the desk a list of our suggestions and they'll book you a room and give you a sheet listing the name and address of the hotel as well as the rate.

The **Manuel Tienda Leon buses** are your best bet for getting downtown. The fare is $14 and they stop at the major hotels throughout the city. Another option is a fixed fare or **remis cab**. The fare should be $45 to $50. A final option is public bus #86 which leaves from in front of the International Hotel. The fare is $1 and it will drop you at the downtown bus station an hour and a half later, where private cars will take you to your hotel free of charge. Hang on to your bus ticket since you will have to give it to the driver of your car. Baggage, especially if you have a lot, can be a problem.

Getting Around

By Taxi

TAXI

Looking like beetles scurrying through a grassy field, the small black and yellow cabs of Buenos Aires are readily available, except during the morning and evening rush hours. Taxis can be hailed on the street or called by telephone. Cabs have meters which register distance and time. (Occasionally, if rates have risen and the meters have not yet been adjusted, at the end of the ride, the driver will show you a chart on which the appropriate fare will be listed.) Fares are reasonable and since cabs are a convenient way to travel from the center of the city to the outlying *barrios*, you'll probably use them often. Hosts at most nightclubs or restaurants (occasionally for a small charge) will usually call a cab for you. Or, you can call yourself – **Pídalo S.A.** is a 24-hour service at 093-4991/1142. Day or night, drivers do not expect a tip, but you should round out the fare.

The raised flag and lighted top means the cab is free.

By Subway

Even faster and cheaper than taxis, the *Subte* deserves kudos for efficiency, economy and speed. Even the aesthetics are a welcome surprise. The glazed tiles that line the subterranean walls were baked by artisans in Spain and France and the brightly colored and luminous tunnels are art galleries in their own right. The system dates from the 1920's and costs little more now than it did then. You can explore Buenos Aires from Retiro to Palermo and transfer along the way. There are five separate lines that intersect at various points. Trips rarely take more than 25 minutes. The wait for a train is seldom more than a few minutes.

The Peru Station on Linea A is just as it was in the 1920's.

The **Primera Junta** or **A** line runs from the Plaza de Mayo to Primera Junta. The **B** line runs from L.N. Alem to Federico Lacroze. The **C** line runs from Constitución to Retiro with transfer points at Avenida de Mayo (for the A line) and 9 de Julio (for the B and D lines). The **D** line runs from Catedral to Palermo and has transfer points at Florida (for the B line) and 9 de Julio (for the B and C lines). The **E** line, which has no transfer points, runs from Bolívar to Plaza de los Virreyes. The lines connect the center city with the terminus stations of the two suburban railroads, one at Constitución and the other at Retiro.

For complete subway details, pick up a Peuser map at one of the kiosks.

The *Subte* system is clean, fast and relatively safe. Trains stop running at 11:30 p.m., at which time a bus or taxi is your best alternative.

Buses

Called *colectivos*, buses are an extremely popular way for *porteños* to move through the city. We give them a less enthusiastic vote than the *Subte* because there are so many lines that it is easy to become confused. Since buses are often overcrowded, it is hard to see where you are going.

Definitely get a Peuser map if you intend to use the buses.

A word of advice: make sure the driver knows exactly where you want to go. If you don't make a point of telling him and you are the only passenger for your destination, forget it! The bus will keep on moving. Practice just enough

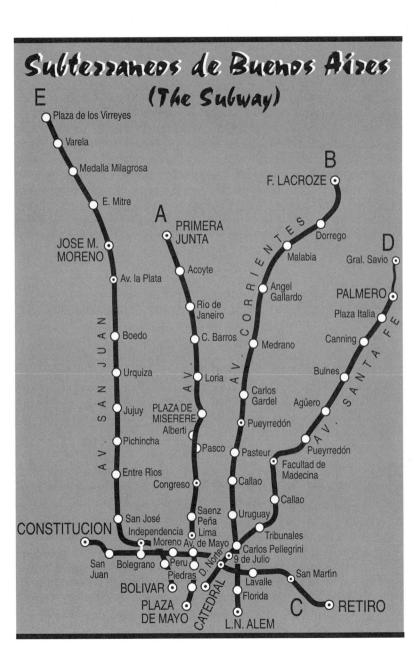

Spanish to say "I am going to..." and you won't be sorry.

Bus stops in central locations often have a map outlining the individual route of each bus that stops there. It is a good idea to become familiar with these. The following is a list of the most important bus lines: the #10 stops in Palermo; the #11 stops in Belgrano; the #17 takes you into the heart of Recoleta; the #24 and #25 make the rounds from Recoleta to La Boca and environs; the #44 and #55 take you to the Barrancas (Belgrano); and the #60 takes you all the way to Tigre (see the excursion section for Tigre).

There are also buses that run back and forth between the city and Ezeiza Airport – namely the #86 and #138. However, it is generally impractical to take your luggage onto one of these inevitably overcrowded buses.

City Tours

For an overview of the city's sites and sights you may want to sign up for a half-day city tour. Virtually every hotel has an arrangement with a local tour operator. You will be picked up at your hotel and, for the most part, guides speak English. Reliable agencies include **Buenos Aires Tur** at Lavalle 1444 or **Teletour** at Corrientes 579.

A Note On Safety

You can feel comfortable walking through the downtown area of Buenos Aires even late at night. Streets are well lit and restaurants and clubs are open till the early hours, meaning that there are always people in the streets. Violent street crime is not the major problem here that it is in many other big cities. It is usually eclipsed by petty thievery.

Use the same common sense you would at home. Leave your finest jewelry behind or store it with your passport in your hotel's safety deposit box. Carry a photocopy of your passport with you. Don't carry large sums of cash. Use traveler's checks instead.

Unescorted women will inevitably be the beneficiaries of the *piropo*, a well-honed come-on that is second nature to men here. Don't take it seriously and don't act pleased by the attention. Politely ignore it. Women traveling solo (or without a male companion) are still an unusual occurrence here. In fact, some bars and nightclubs will not admit unescorted women. If you stick to bars and clubs in hotels you will feel comfortable.

Orientation

Buenos Aires is quite flat and streets, laid out on straight lines, cross at straight angles forming mini-plazas, which are often spots of greenery. The city's "downtown" area is not large and can be walked easily. Both a commercial and cultural center, it is bordered loosely by Avenida Libertador (N), Paseo Colón (E), Avenida Belgrano (S) and Entre Rios (W). The downtown area is encircled by interesting neighborhoods (*barrios*) which, while not technically part of downtown, are an integral part of the inner city.

Porteños rarely use the words calle (street) or avenida (avenue).

Downtown Streets & Landmarks

Although you will spend little time on it, **Avenida Rivadavia** is a key orientation street in this downtown grid. A particularly long street, Rivadavia cuts through the city from east to west, creating large north and south sectors. Chances are that you'll spend most of your time in the northern sector, for that is where the hotels, restaurants, and shops are located. Avenida Rivadavia is also the point at which street names change and the numbering system begins. Blocks are numbered in hundreds. For example, Calle Florida in the northern section runs for 11 blocks from Avenida Rivadavia to the Plaza San Martín. #960 Calle Florida is on the 10th block north of Avenida Rivadavia. #960 south of Avenida Rivadavia is on the 10th block of Calle Peru. Important downtown streets follow:

North of Rivadavia/South of Rivadavia
Reconquista/Defensa
San Martín/Bolívar
Florida/Peru
Maipú/Chacabuco
Esmeralda/Piedras
Suipacha/Tacuari

Streets running parallel to Avenida Rivadavia (E-W) do not change names in the downtown area.

Plaza de Mayo

The Plaza de Mayo, the city's oldest square, dates back to the second founding of Buenos Aires in 1580 when it was designated the Plaza Mayor, the city's principal square. At one time it was a large marketplace and at another it was home to a hangman's gallows. This lovely green oasis, surrounded by important government buildings, has been the site of nearly all the important political and social events in Argentina's history. Surrounding the plaza are the **Casa Rosada**, the seat of the executive branch of the Argentine government; the **Cabildo**, the colonial town hall; and the **Metropolitan Cathedral**, where Argentina's national hero General San Martín is buried.

Plaza del Congreso

This is a wide expanse marked by interesting sculptures, including Rodin's *The Thinker*, and gurgling fountains. It is actually three mini-plazas that encircle the Congress building, seat of the legislative branch of government. The Plaza del Congreso is also the "kilometer 0" point on all road maps of Argentina, a real life example of the saying "All roads lead here."

The Thinker (El Pensador) is one of only two existing copies of this statue.

Avenida de Mayo

The first official street in the city, Avenida de Mayo links the two plazas above. Take note of the various architectural styles of the buildings lining the street. Some were considered skyscrapers in the late 18th century when they soared to five stories. South America's first subway was built beneath it.

Avenida 9 de Julio

At 450 feet across, 9 de Julio is the world's widest street, created by knocking down the buildings that ran through its center. It is actually composed of three streets. The outer streets are **Cerrito/Lima** on the west and **Carlos Pellegrini/Bernardo de Irigoyen** on the east. The central strip, 9 de Julio, does not change its name for its entire length. Occupying center stage is the towering **Obelisco** (obelisk) at the **Plaza de la República**, which commemorates the country's 400th anniversary.

Calle Florida

Calle Florida, a pedestrian promenade, is the liveliest street downtown. Along its length are posh boutiques, the Galerías Pacífico shopping mall, a branch of Harrod's department store, scratch bands, classical guitarists, hot dog vendors and lots of *porteños* who work and shop here. It runs 11 blocks from Avenida Rivadavia to the Plaza San Martín.

Avenida Corrientes/Calle Lavalle

Avenida Corrientes, which runs east to west, is known as the "street that never sleeps." A wide thoroughfare, it is home to cinemas, fast food places and late night clubs and restaurants, along with a large number of bookshops that stay open well past midnight. Adjacent to Corrientes, **Calle Lavalle** mirrors it on a smaller scale. Closed to traffic, it comes alive at night when the streets are crowded with movie-goers and diners headed to the many moderately priced restaurants here.

Avenida Santa Fe/Avenida Callao

Avenida Santa Fe, lined with attractive shops and art galleries, is another fine shopping area.

Airline offices and provincial tourist boards are located here. Avenida Callao is at the heart of the trendy cinema/eaterie area in the near north side of the city.

Plaza San Martín

One of the few higher areas in a very flat city, this plaza is actually dominated by a large park. In earlier times this hilly spot was called *El Retiro* for the monastery there, which later served as an army barracks. When Sarmiento became president he built a monument to honor General San Martín and planned the park around it. The lower park retained the name which it shares with Buenos Aires' large railroad station. The nearby clock tower was a gift from Argentineans of British ancestry. Its plaza, formerly called Plaza Británica, was renamed Plaza Fuerza Aérea following the Malvinas Conflict (The Falklands War).

Retiro means retreat.

Most porteños still refer to this as the Plaza Británica.

Barrios

Much like New York, Chicago and Vancouver, Buenos Aires is a melting pot created by millions of immigrants, who, while Argentinean to the core, have remained sentimentally attached to their ethnic origins. The city has approximately 50 *barrios*. Some, built around a plaza and church, reflect a specific ethnic group, while others are fashionable or working class residential neighborhoods. The *barrios* are a jumble of old and new, with modern apartment buildings adjacent to older ones whose glass-lined French doors open onto plant-filled wrought iron balconies. You will want to explore such key *barrios* as **Recoleta**, **San Telmo**, **La Boca**, and **Palermo**.

Recoleta

Although the proper name is **La Recoleta**, *porteños* simply refer to it as Recoleta. Located in the northern part of the city, Recoleta is the city's most fashionable residential area. It has elegant restaurants, deluxe hotels and fine shops, as well as several interesting museums. Key streets are **Avenida Alvear** and **Avenida Quintana.** One of its best known attractions, the **Recoleta Cemetery** is the resting site of Eva Perón and other well-known Argentineans.

San Telmo

In the southern part of the city, San Telmo was established in the 16th century when it was the heart of the city. Wealthy residents fled the area when a yellow fever epidemic hit and immigrants moved in. Badly run down, it has undergone a refurbishing and its colonial buildings now house art galleries and antique stores. The city's best flea market is held in Plaza Dorrego on Sundays year-round and the tango clubs clustered here are key to the neighborhood's popularity in the evenings. **Calle Defensa** is the area's main street while **Carlos Calvo** is restaurant row.

La Boca

A picturesque area populated by working class Italians, La Boca has the feel and mouthwatering aroma of a Southern Italian village. Cobblestone streets are lined with colorfully painted small homes that have remained unchanged for a century. Inexpensive restaurants and lively clubs that open late and close early in the morning have made La Boca popular after dark. **Ne-cochea** is the main street here.

Palermo

While the other *barrios* we've mentioned are urban, Palermo, a large *barrio* north of the city, has a suburban flavor. It can be reached by commuter railroad. It is home to **Los Bosques de Palermo**, a huge park which is a popular weekend destination for bikers, joggers and small boat enthusiasts. The **City Zoo**, **Botanical Gardens** and **Planetarium** are also here, as are the *hipódromo* (race track) and **National Polo Fields**.

Buenos Aires Hotels

Travelers to Buenos Aires are lucky when it comes to hotel accommodations. The hotels here are modeled on European standards, with large rooms and attractive public areas. Accommodations run the gamut from huge 500-room hotels to smaller places with 30 rooms or fewer, where everyone gets to know you on the first day.

Argentine hotels operate on a star system in which five is the highest and one is the lowest. All of the hotels selected have at least a two-star rating. Extra stars usually mean pools, shops and room service. All two- and three-star hotels provide the fundamentals: clean rooms, private baths, fresh linens and civility.

Four-star hotels generally provide the niceties that make hotel visits a pleasure. These include a telephone in every room, mini-bars, television and room service. Five-star hotels are self-contained worlds, with an array of shops in the lobby, several restaurants, at least one bar and a disco. Some also have pools, health clubs and beauty parlors. If you are concerned about being understood, note that five-star hotels have multilingual staffs, thus eliminating any language barriers.

This should not, however, steer you away from the smaller, more personal places if price is a consideration. The hotel tradition in this city requires that the staff speak enough English to get their point across and to understand you as well. Many employees also speak French, Italian and Japanese. Remember to make the most of the people who work in your hotel. They can be good sources of information, and the concierge is usually happy to obtain opera and theater tickets for guests and will arrange excursions.

Occasionally there is a shortage of hotel rooms in Buenos Aires, especially when there are a number of conventions in town or a championship football game. Fortunately, with the addition of several new hotels, this does not happen too often. Nevertheless, it is a good idea to book in advance whenever possible, especially when you have a specific hotel in mind.

The hotels we have included are centrally located. Very few are far from the downtown area and you should be able to walk to the city's major attractions. Since most are in a central area of the city, there are some sections which you may want to avoid, as they can be quite noisy, even at night. Corrientes, Lavalle and even Florida are examples of high-decibel-level spots where a hotel room, especially if it's facing the street, can be less a pleasure than a nightmare.

The Alive Scale

Our price scale is designed to give you a ballpark figure around which to plan your budget.

It is based solely on prices for a double room. Single rooms are generally about 20% less.

Deluxe	*$175+*
Expensive	*$100+*
Moderate	*$60-100*
Inexpensive	*$35-60*
Budget	*Under $35.*

Hotels are listed by order of preference within each price range, although the star rating is included as well. All hotels accept major credit cards unless otherwise noted. Most offer a buffet breakfast, the cost of which is included in your rate.

Deluxe Hotels

PARK HYATT BUENOS AIRES ☆☆☆☆☆
Posadas 1088
Tel 326-1234
Fax 326-3032
157 rooms
The new Park Hyatt offers all the five-star amenities you've come to expect from a Hyatt Hotel anywhere in the world. Located at the end of 9 de Julio just a few blocks from Recoleta, several restaurants have opened around it. Not far from the banking center, the Hyatt caters to business travelers, offering them fully-equipped conference facilities and two floors reserved for traveling executives. A health spa/fitness center with an indoor pool, sauna and beauty salon and formal as well as informal dining options round out a stay at the Hyatt.

ALVEAR PALACE HOTEL ☆☆☆☆☆
Avenida Alvear 1891
Tel 804-7777
Fax 804-0034
200 rooms, 9 floors

This is surely one of the loveliest of the five-star hotels. Its European style and ambience and cozy suites have made it a long-time favorite of discriminating people. **La Bourgogne Restaurant** serves haute French cuisine in elegant surroundings. Rooms have a decidedly Parisian flair and many feature French period furnishings with elegant touches such as candle sconces, escritoires and brass lamps. All have direct dial phone service, central heating, air conditioning and color television.

CAESAR PARK ☆☆☆☆☆
Posadas 1232/46
Tel 814-5151
(In U.S.A., call toll-free 1-800-228-3000)
Fax 814-5148
152 rooms

An excellent location in Recoleta across from the Patio Bullrich Shopping Center is one of the many reasons for choosing the Caesar Park. Fine dining is another of the highlights at this Westin Hotel. The cold buffet, featuring patés, terrines, mousses and other delicacies at the **Café del Plata** is perfect for lunch or a late supper. The complimentary breakfast buffet served here is equally fine. Sushi and Japanese cuisine are featured at **Midori.** High tea with scones, tortes and assorted pastries is served every afternoon in the Lobby Bar and the traditional English bar, **Cheers**. Finally, for a refined candlelight dinner, you needn't venture further than **Il Cesare**, the hotel's formal restaurant.

The Caesar Park also has modern fitness facilities, state-of-the-art conference rooms, consummate service and immaculate accommodations.

**THE BUENOS AIRES SHERATON
HOTEL AND TOWERS** ☆☆☆☆☆
San Martín 1225
Tel 311-6311
(In U.S.A. call toll-free 1-800-325-3535)
Fax 311-6353
800 rooms, 23 floors
The Buenos Aires Sheraton, located near the new IBM Plaza, is a home away from home for North Americans. It is sleek, well run and boasts the highest view in town from its rooftop lounge, the **Atalaya** (Watchtower). It has everything you would expect a five-star hotel to have: an Olympic-size pool, tennis courts, a health club and a shopping mall featuring fine leather shops, boutiques and a branch of H. Stern Jewelers. Restaurants include **La Pampa** (24-hour coffee shop), **Cardinale** (Italian cuisine), and the formal **El Aljibe**.

Rooms are spacious and modern, many with fine views of downtown. Ample closet space, separate dressing rooms, well-equipped bathrooms and plush towels are the hallmarks of this first-class hotel. Color television, direct dial phones and mini-fridges are additional luxuries.

THE MARRIOT PLAZA HOTEL ☆☆☆☆☆
Florida 1005
Tel 311-5011
(In U.S.A. call toll-free 1-800-522-2588)
Fax 313-2912
390 rooms

A member of the Leading Hotels of the World, The Plaza was only recently acquired by Marriott. This should not compromise its quality in any way.

Located in the heart of one of the best shopping districts in South America, the old world Plaza Hotel keeps a firm grip on the good reputation it has enjoyed for decades. Over the years it has attracted the crème de la crème of Argentinean, European and American travelers, all of whom appreciate being surrounded by the finer things in life. Renovations have kept what are quite old-fashioned rooms in pace with the changing demands of modern travelers. Many have wonderful views of the Plaza San Martín, so be sure to request one. There is a small pool.

LIBERTADOR KEMPINSKI ☆☆☆☆☆
Avenida Córdoba and Maipú
Tel 322-2095
(In U.S.A. call toll-free 1-800-426-3135)
Fax 322-9703
200 rooms, 22 floors

Avenida Córdoba is a wide, bustling thoroughfare.

Located just a few blocks from Avenida 9 de Julio, the Libertador is a comfortably large hotel with well-furnished rooms that are clean and spacious. Three extra deluxe suites are the pride of this hotel, along with two fine dining rooms: **The Grand Bourg** and **La Pergola**, which has been one of the city's top international eateries for quite a few years now.

There is a swimming pool and sundeck under a sliding glass roof on La Terraza, the top floor of the hotel.

THE CLAIRIDGE ☆☆☆☆☆
Tucumán 535
Tel 314-8634
(In U.S.A., call toll-free 1-800-223-5652)
Fax 322-8022
160 rooms, 14 floors

The Clairidge ranks among the premier hotels of the city and has been refurbished, adding even greater luster. The decor, with its Greco-Roman columns of white marble at the entrance and timeless interior, is decidedly English. The Clairidge maintains an extensive wine cellar and four distinctive salons. These unique rooms give the Clairidge much of its refined atmosphere. The Reading and Tea Rooms are decorated with an English country flavor full of warm wood, flowers and leaded tudor windows.

The Clairidge is a member hotel of the Steinberger Reservation Service and a popular choice for weddings.

HOLIDAY INN CROWNE PLAZA ☆☆☆☆☆
Carlos Pelegrini 525
Tel 326-6111
Fax 393-6570
205 rooms, 18 floors
The five-star Crowne Plaza is nothing like the Holiday Inns you pass along the interstate. Facing the Obelisk and the Teatro Colón, the Crowne Plaza towers above its neighbors, offering first class accommodations along with executive services, a swimming pool and exercise room. The restaurant, **Tomo** I, has earned a well-deserved reputation as one of the finest restaurants in Buenos Aires. It moved to the second floor in 1993.

HOTEL INTERCONTINENTAL BUENOS AIRES ☆☆☆☆☆
Moreno 809
Tel 345-6202
Fax 345-6204
(In U.S.A., call toll-free 1-800-327-0200)
310 rooms, 19 floors
As we went to press, this brand new (Jan. 1995) hotel was just opened. Located downtown, a

block and a half from Av 9 de Julio, it should be a popular stop for business travelers. We were unable to visit it for this edition, so let us have your comments.

Expensive to Moderate Hotels

ETOILE HOTEL ☆☆☆☆☆
Roberto M. Ortiz 1835
Tel 804-8603
Fax 805-3613
100 rooms, 15 floors
Despite a marked lack of notoriety, the Etoile is a very fine five-star hotel which features primarily suite-style accommodations. Perhaps the absence of advertising is what has permitted management here to keep prices below those of our earlier selections. Its Recoleta location is definitely a plus. Facilities include a modern gym, an indoor/outdoor pool, and sauna. Although it is not as showy as other five-star hotels, guests here do not lack for comfort.

CARSSON HOTEL ☆☆☆☆
Viamonte 650 (between Florida and Maipú)
Tel 322-3551
Fax 322-3551
100 rooms, 5 floors
Argentineans and other South Americans have come in droves over the past years to this clubby hotel located in one of the busiest parts of town. Inside, however, quiet reigns supreme and the deep red velvet and dark leather give it a handsome old world feel. Rooms are attractive and comfortably furnished. A bar, coffee shop

and convenient location near Calle Florida are all the reasons you'll need to stay here. Reserve well in advance.

GRAN HOTEL COLON ☆☆☆☆
Carlos Pellegrini 507
Tel 325-0717
Fax 325-4567
182 rooms, 12 floors
If you want to stay in the heart of Buenos Aires, the Colón, right across from the Obelisk on Avenida 9 de Julio, should be at the top of your list. Rooms, many facing the Obelisk, are attractively furnished. The rooftop pool, though far from ostentatious, is a nice extra.

THE GRAN HOTEL DORA ☆☆☆☆
Calle Maipú 963, near Paraguay
Tel 312-7391
Fax 313-8134
100 rooms
The Dora is a traditional favorite whose popularity has never flagged. Many guests return time and time again, making advance reservations often a necessity. All rooms have air conditioning, direct dial telephone and central heating. If you want a television, you may have to request it. The busy bar is often packed with neighborhood residents. The hotel also has a restaurant and a 24-hour snack bar. A sister hotel is recommended in Mar del Plata.

HOTEL PRESIDENTE ☆☆☆☆
Cerrito 850 (far side of 9 de Julio)
Tel 325-5985
Fax 372-5081
30 suites, 42 apartments with kitchenettes, 178 rooms, 18 floors

The modern Presidente is at the high end of our expensive price scale. Furnishings here are very modern and comfortable. 24-hour room service, a gym with paddle court and sauna, and a beauty salon are the extras you'll enjoy here.

ROCHESTER HOTEL ☆☆☆☆
Esmeralda 542
Tel/Fax 326-5220
160 rooms
The Rochester is centrally located and most of its rooms offer grand views of the busy Calle Esmeralda. Furnishings are tasteful and functionally plush.

HOTEL BRISTOL ☆☆☆☆
Cerrito 286
Tel 35-5400
Fax 35-0061
130 rooms
Reasonably priced with all the standard amenities of a four-star hotel. Set on the far side of Avenida 9 de Julio, the location is splendid.

Moderate Hotels

POSTA CARRETAS ☆☆☆☆
Esmeralda 726
Tel 394-1625
40 rooms
This beautiful country-style hotel offers rooms that are simply furnished in natural wood and earth tones to create a warm and relaxing atmosphere. Wooden beams, lanterns and russet tones make the hotel restaurant just as inviting as the hotel itself.

HOTEL CONTINENTAL ☆☆☆☆
Avenida Pte. Roque Sáenz Peña 725
Tel 49-3251
200 rooms
A lovely hotel in the *centro* area, harmony is the byword for the service and ambience here. The deep burgundy velvet of the lobby, massive wood furnishings, brass in the elevators, and revolving doors make the Continental stand apart from the rest.

Rooms are delightful. Most have two full closets, a balcony overlooking Sáenz Peña, large bathroom, a television and mini-bar. High French windows let in plenty of bright morning light. Late sleepers needn't fret. There are also heavy curtains and shutters to block out the sun. Typical Argentine entertainment is often featured in the second floor salon.

THE HOTEL REGIDOR ☆☆☆☆
Tucumán 451
Tel 392-9939
100 rooms
The Regidor takes an impressive approach to decor, individualistic and more Argentinean than most other hotels in the city. There is an *estancia*-like coziness to the public areas, with murals in the breakfast room, Flanders Gobelin tapestries in the lounge, Sèvres porcelains and sculptures in the main hall, and plenty of fireplaces throughout.

Guest rooms, though not as elaborate, do have personal touches. All are carpeted and air conditioned. Reasonable rates and a pleasant atmosphere keep this hotel popular with savvy travelers.

GRAN HOTEL BUENOS AIRES ☆☆☆☆
Marcelo T. de Alvear 767
Tel 312-3001
Fax 311-1347
90 rooms, 10 floors
Near the Plaza San Martín, the location of the Gran is excellent. A tightly-run, family hotel, there are a number of impressive touches such as the newspaper in your language which is delivered to your room every morning. Rooms are immaculate, spacious, and bright, and they overlook a vine-covered courtyard.

GRAN HOTEL DEL TUCUMAN ☆☆☆☆
Tucumán 570
Tel 393-4576
Fax 393-4786
90 rooms
A sparkling lobby, covered with mirrors and dramatically lit, greets you before you reach the reception desk. Service, no less bright, is terrific, thanks to a friendly and efficient staff.

Large, modern rooms are designed for convenience, with radio, telephone and light switches built right into the headboards. The color scheme is grey and white and the baths are fresh and airy.

HOTEL PRINCIPADO ☆☆☆☆
Paraguay 481
Tel 313-3022
Fax 313-3952
88 rooms, 11 floors
Located on busy Calle Paraguay, this hotel offers intimate atmosphere on a street that is chock full of wonderful boutiques and shopping experiences. The Principado's decor is

partly Spanish colonial and quite attractive. Rooms are individually decorated, some a bit better than others. The nicer rooms face the street.

HOTEL SALLES ☆☆☆☆
Cerrito 208
Tel 35-0091
Fax 36-0754
90 rooms
A refined atmosphere and quiet elegance make this a popular choice of visiting scholars and scientists. Rooms, though not quite spectacular, are clean and nicely furnished.

Inexpensive Hotels

VICTORY HOTEL ☆☆☆
Maipú 880, near Paraguay
Tel 314-8415
This 10-story hotel is located near the Plaza San Martín and features a courteous staff and homey decor. All rooms are air conditioned and have direct dial telephones as well as modern bathrooms. A good value.

HOTEL CASTELAR ☆☆☆
Avenida de Mayo 1152
Tel 383-5001
Fax 325-6964
200 rooms
The familiar faded splendor of the Castelar is reminiscent of Paris and Vienna. Though it has seen better days, the marble hallways and leather furniture are still elegant. Rooms are large and comfortable.

HOTEL REGIS ☆☆☆
Lavalle 813
Tel 393-5131
85 rooms
A fine budget choice, rooms fill quickly, so reserve ahead.

HOTEL EIBAR ☆☆☆
Florida 328, between Corrientes
and Sarmiento
Tel 325-0969
100 rooms
The centrally located Eibar offers modern, spacious doubles and singles. The cafeteria is more than adequate and the service is friendly and bilingual. Remember to request a room that does not face the street.

Buenos Aires Restaurants

Buenos Aires has a wonderful assortment of restaurants. The overwhelming number of them are steakhouses serving grilled meats, but beef is well represented on restaurant menus throughout the city. In steakhouses beef, lamb and pork are cooked on huge skewers over coals from local *quebracho* trees. Buttery soft and lower in fat content than beef in the United States, the meat has a unique flavor. Chunks of it are often brought to your table on small grills that keep them hot. The amalgam of people from more than a dozen different countries, each arriving with grandma's favorite recipe or two, has resulted in restaurants that cater to a multitude of palates. So, whether you get an urge for ravioli, sushi or paella, you'll find a restaurant – in fact, you'll find several – to satisfy you. In a business that is notoriously fickle, with restaurants opening to great fanfare and fading quickly, there are many that have remained popular for over 20 years and you can dine in any number of exceptional establishments in all parts of the city. There are scores of restaurants where first rate food, intimate atmosphere and impeccable service make dining a definite pleasure. But, on an evening when your mood is far more casual, you'll find an even larger number of eateries where you can enjoy delicious food in informal and unconventional surroundings.

Our selections are subjective, of course, but we have tried to recommend the city's top choices as well as fine dining spots in all parts of the city serving a variety of foods and in a wide price range. Pruning the list was not an easy task and we know you'll discover many great dining options we didn't include. We hope you'll write and share them with us and with the readers of the next edition of *Buenos Aires Alive*.

Alive Price Scale
(per person)
Expensive: $40+
Moderate: 25+
Inexpensive: under $20

Dining Hours

Whether it's a *parrillada* you're sharing with friends or a heaping plate of pasta in the La Boca section of town, dinner is practically an all-night affair. Restaurant ovens aren't even warm until 8 p.m. and 10 p.m. is prime time for families and singles alike to crowd into eateries that serve until 2 a.m. or later. It is quite possible to order a full course meal at an hour when most of the world would be asleep. You'll have to alter your inner clock a bit. *Porteños* take a "coffee break" in the late afternoon rather than in the morning. You'll find a late day snack will keep you from being famished by dinner time.

Service & Tipping

Unlike many U.S. restaurants, even expensive ones, where service is perfunctory at best, service is taken very seriously here. Restaurant patrons are treated with respect as if they were guests in one's home. Even inexpensive restaurants have starchy tablecloths, uniformly dressed waiters (who are almost always male) and printed menus. Some restaurants, often the steakhouses, add a service charge to the bill but an additional 10% gratuity is the norm. Other restaurants do not add a service charge and therefore you should tip as you would at home.

Hotel Dining

The city's five-star hotels house excellent restaurants. In most cases these are run independently, such as **Tomo Uno** in the Crowne Plaza PanAmericano and **La Bourgogne** in the Alvear Palace. The most famous hotel-run restaurant in the city is the **Plaza Grill** in the Plaza Hotel. It is one of the city's most elegant dining spots and a well-known meeting place. With that exception we have not detailed hotel restaurants on the premise that eating where *porteños* eat is more fun than eating with other visitors – but the option does exist.

Plaza Grill serves continental food. Jacket required.

Dining in Recoleta

Recoleta, the most fashionable residential *barrio* of the city, is also the mecca for those who enjoy dining well in elegant yet "informal" surroundings. A two-block traffic-free promenade is lined with sidewalk cafés and fine restaurants where people watching has been raised to an art form. Although side-by-side, these restaurants are crowded each night and it is not unusual to wait for a table at midnight. Restaurant fare varies from Japanese to German to Continental and the decor and ambience vary enormously as well.

Informal means casual chic.

We have not listed every restaurant on the promenade. There are many others. Check the menus posted outside.

Favorites with Argentineans are the outdoor dining areas on the promenade that each restaurant maintains. Covered with water-proof tarps and heated when necessary, alive with flowers and hanging lamps, these are the most sought-after locations. Diners on a tighter budget can eat in Recoleta as well. A new upscale food court (not fast food) has opened near Pilar Church. All the restaurants that follow accept major credit cards. Reservations, while not necessary, are a good idea, particularly on weekends. Open seven days except where noted, most open for lunch from 12 noon until 3:30 p.m. and dinner from 9 p.m. Brunch is popular on weekends.

CABAÑA LAS LILAS
R.M. Ortiz 1813
Tel 804-3410
Grilled meats
Moderate

The owners of Cabaña Las Lilas have decorated their walls with humorous drawings of chickens, cows and pigs at play and they have extended the light touch to the floral tablecloths and napkins. The humor stops with the decor, however, because they are very serious about the fine meats served here. Owners of an *estancia* where they've bred their own cattle for 70 years, they are proud of the low fat levels and unique flavor of the beef. Start with a select-your-own salad from the score of salad fixin's offered. Although virtually all your neighbors will be eating grilled meats, there are a number of pasta dishes on the menu as well. Dinner is served till 1 a.m.

HARPER'S
Junín 1763
Tel 801-7140
Continental
Expensive to moderate

Harper's, a perennial Buenos Aires favorite
since it opened in 1979, looks like a restaurant
that would be at home in New York's Soho
district. A brick wall, highly polished wooden
floors and a carved oak bar where singles congregate add to the trendy ambience, as do the
works of art by local artists. The food, which
includes chicken sautéed with chestnuts, trout
and salmon with delicate sauces as well as the
house specialty *cordero del diablo* (lamb with a
spicy sauce), is first rate. Start with a leafy salad
and leave room for dessert, which appears at
your table on a cart.

LA BOURGOGNE
Ayacucho 2037 (Alvear Palace Hotel)
Tel 805-3857
French
Expensive

Having opened a wildly successful French restaurant in Punta del Este, Uruguay in 1980, Relais Gourmand chef Jean Paul Bondoux took his
show on the road and opened La Bourgogne in
1993. Among the most formal and elegant dining rooms in the city, the restaurant is decorated
in pastel shades with plush-backed armchairs at
each table and pink candles and flowers everywhere. A central table displays the special salads prepared for that meal as well as suggested
wines. The menu changes frequently so as to
use the freshest ingredients, but if large shrimp
with sesames is on the menu you should try it.
Chateaubriand with bearnaise sauce and roast

*Many restau-
rants list a vari-
ety of salad
ingredients and
you choose
what you'd like.*

duck with cassis wine sauce are excellent. Try a light dessert such as sorbet or fruit tart.

French food in less formal surroundings.

Less formal in decor and serving lighter food, **La Cave** on the lower level is also special. It has country French furniture and the cave-like effect comes from its low ceilings with hanging wine racks and long crusty breads. Enjoy a steaming bowl of onion soup covered with melted cheese, or garlicky escargot, smoked salmon and salads. It has the same owners as La Bourgogne. Take-out cheeses and gourmet foods are available as well.

GATO DUMAS COCINERO
Junín 1745
Tel 806-5801
Nouvelle
Expensive

Since Gato is a celebrity in his own right, his restaurant draws many well-known patrons.

Carlos "Gato" (The Cat) Dumas is arguably Argentina's most famous chef. His dishes, using organically grown vegetables, delicate herbs and spices and light sauces, have won him international awards for creativity. Dumas has been the chef/owner of some of the finest restaurants in the city. He opened this restaurant in 1992. It is starkly modern and occupies several floors. There are celebrity photos in the foyer and ornately carved sofas in the bar area. Among the specialties (which change frequently) are warm shrimp and salmon salad, dishes made with black pasta and flakey tenderloin of beef with caviar. Honey flavored ice cream or crèpes in a coffee liquor top off a special meal.

CLARK'S
Junín 1777
Tel 801-9502
Eclectic
Moderate
With a menu that ranges far and wide, appealing to many tastes, Clark's remains a favorite of *porteños* and visitors to the city. It usually boasts an outstanding chef (Gato Dumas worked here) and the menu and decor are carefully planned.

Clark's II (downtown) is also highly recommended.

An Edwardian ghost would surely feel at home amid the rich wood paneling, old brass mirrored walls, stained glass and plush seating. A favorite here, the green salad with mushrooms, avocado, palm and scallions, is enough for two. Loin of pork, salmon blinis and a filet mignon that needs little chewing are a few temptations. Of course, the menu changes frequently and, while you may not find the dishes above, you can be sure that what you do find will be delicious.

SENSU
R.M. Ortiz 1815
Tel 804-1214
Japanese
Dinner only
Moderate
Sensu is a Japanese steakhouse. Diners sit at communal tables, the centers of which are the *teppans* (hot grills) on which the food is prepared. The chef artfully wields his sharp knife – cutting, dicing and chopping filet mignon, salmon or chicken – which are served with rice and noodles. All meals start with soup, grilled shrimp and a salad. Your bill reflects the main course you've selected.

The decor is simple, with light woods on the walls and floors. One exception is the elegant embroidered samurai robe in the front window.

LOLA
R.M. Ortiz 1805
Tel 804-3410
Continental with French leanings
Expensive

If a contest were held to find the city's most attractive restaurant, Lola would be at the top of many lists. Tables are widely spaced and topped by floral cloths and impeccably folded napkins. Although the dishes are continental, many lean to French and Italian. Duck with fruit sauces that vary or stuffed with truffles, trout with watercress in a light red wine sauce and chunks of salmon served with pasta are good choices. We recommend you eat lightly here because there are over 30 desserts to choose from, including crêpes and chocolate mousse with nuts. Ask for a table on the ground floor.

HAPPENING
Guido 1931
Tel 805-2633
International
Moderate to inexpensive

The original Happening is on Costanera Norte.

One block from the promenade, Happening has a glass-enclosed roof that gives the bi-level dining area an open, airy look. The light woods, hanging plants and attractive fabrics on the chairs make this a popular dining spot. Its rear wall is glassed and the kitchen is visible behind it. The grill is busiest here, with beef and lamb kebobs as well as fish and special treats. Happening is a popular yuppie hang-out.

MORA X
Vicente Lopez 2152
Tel 803-0261
French
Closed Sunday
Moderate

One of the most unusual restaurants we've ever seen, you'll either love Mora X or loathe it. It has one huge dining room on the main floor and a smaller upper level. The room is divided into areas by wooden planters with spiky plants and the covered bar is a focal point. Although the decor is starkly modern, the food is surprisingly traditional French. Salmon mousse, terrines of vegetables and crêpes are popular choices.

Not on the promenade. Turn right when you pass the cemetery.

LA GOMERIA
Vicente Lopez 2134
Tel 803-6170
Inexpensive

Just down the street from Mora X, La Gomería draws a less trendy younger crowd, who enjoy the pizzas and burgers and the cold beer on tap. Very large, with red lacquered walls and widely scattered tables, La Gomería is open till 6 a.m. There's a show nightly at 11:30 p.m., usually a musical group. MTV-type videos are shown on scattered TV monitors.

HENRY J. BEAN'S
Junin 1749
Tel 801-8477
Bar and grill
Inexpensive

Henry J. Bean's, a newly opened "saloon" on the promenade between Gato Dumas and Harpers, is standing room only at this writing. Serving American-style foods, such as baby back ribs and great chili, apple pies and brownies, and lots of beer, Henry Bean's is drawing the yuppie crowd. The noise level is high, especially at happy hour. Posters, old license plates and photos are the decor. Light foods, lots of fun.

Plaza Del Pilar Dining

Just downhill from the Cultural Center, you'll find the new art and design building where the city's finest decorators and architects have their showrooms. The ground floor houses a dozen restaurants which serve lighter fare than those listed previously. Less expensive, they draw a younger and family-oriented crowd. Open for lunch and dinner every day, the restaurants offer several dining options. Each has indoor tables and arcade-covered dining areas, and they all share an open terrace. All have waiter service but some allow you to select and pay for your food and carry it to the outdoor tables. Among our favorites, **Moliere Café** is a charming *confitería* serving sandwiches, pastries, and drinks. **Mummy's** serves burgers and brew, while **Romanacci Co. Pizza** serves pies with all manner of toppings and pasta. It has a salad cart (waiter served). **Fishy Bar**, part of a local chain, lets you select your fish platter or paella and take it to a nearby table. **Munich de Pilar** serves German specialties and **Café Rix** whips up luscious crêpes. There's good food here and it's a nice area to spend an evening.

Trendy food court. No fast food here. These restaurants do not close after lunch.

Sidewalk Cafes

Anybody who is anybody in Buenos Aires and even wannabes head to **La Biela Café** and its neighbor **Café de la Paix**, which face each other across Avenida Quintana at the Recoleta Promenade. They are the hottest meeting and greeting places in town. Weather permitting, choose an outdoor table.

Downtown Dining

The sights and sounds of downtown Buenos Aires will be familiar to those of you who live in a big city. There are streets crowded with smartly dressed working people rushing to their offices, lots of cars, buses, taxis and well-stocked stores filled with shoppers. Here, too, are the historic areas of the city. The city fathers have attempted to make the area people-friendly. The major shopping street, Calle Florida, is a pedestrian promenade, as is Calle Lavalle, where many cinemas and restaurants are found. You'll spend many of your Buenos Aires days and nights here. Restaurants run the gamut from among the city's finest to fast food stops and everything in between. Here you can dine well and inexpensively. Restaurants accept major credit cards and many stay open all afternoon.

LA CABAÑA
Entre Rios 436 (at Belgrano)
Tel 381-2372
Grilled meats
Lunch 12 noon-3 p.m. Dinner until 3 a.m.
Expensive
Founded in 1935, La Cabaña is a first-rate steakhouse and a landmark *parrilla* or grill, famous for its buttery baby beef. Many consider these giant sirloins the best beef north or south of the

Portions are huge. Skip afternoon tea. Arrive hungry.

Rio Grande. It may be disconcerting, considering the fare, to pass a large steer in the entrance foyer. The restaurant has several dining areas, all panelled with dark wood. Tables are widely spaced but you'll immediately notice that your fellow diners are speaking English, Japanese or German as well as Spanish. That is because many a VIP guest to Argentina has been escorted here and many an Argentinean businessman trying to impress brings guests here as well. Celebrity diners include Richard Nixon, María Callas, and the King of Spain.

Have your photo taken by the house photographer. A great souvenir, it is delivered to your hotel.

While beef is king here, the lamb chops and grilled chicken served with mountains of *papas fritas* and a tomato onion salad are also excellent. As you sip your house red and absorb the aroma of the sizzling *parrillas* nearby, you'll realize that in Buenos Aires it doesn't get any better than this.

TOMO I
Carlos Pellegrini 525
(Crowne Plaza Panamericano Hotel)
Tel 326-6310
Italian/Continental
Lunch served weekdays only; closed Sunday
Expensive
For 23 years, Ada Cancaro and her sister Ebe operated their splendid Tomo I restaurant from an elegant brownstone setting on Calle Las Heras, but in 1993 they decided to move to a more modern setting in the Panamericano Hotel. The move has been successful and it hasn't hurt the food one bit.

While the names of the Continental and Italian dishes will be familiar to you, each will have an unusual ingredient or seasoning that makes it special. The raviolis stuffed with spinach were served with either a tomato-based sauce or a buttery one. There were pasta dishes on the menu that included olives, shrimp, anchovies and vegetables in their sauces. Chicken with huge mushrooms, lamb with herbs and sliced sweet and sour pork dishes were all lightly sauced. There is a fixed-price menu (different at lunch and dinner), which includes an appetizer, main course, wine and coffee. Service here is exemplary.

CATALINAS
Reconquista 875
Tel 313-0182
Brit-style French cuisine
Expensive
Calle Reconquista in the Retiro section of downtown is crowded during the day with executives who work in this busy area. So, it is no surprise that Catalinas is a popular lunch spot. Many an important deal has been discussed and closed over the seafood specialties here. What is a surprise and a distinct credit to the terrific food, conceived and prepared under the direction of Chef Ramiro Rodriguez Pardo, is that Catalinas is also very crowded at night when the area is quiet. The ambience is British, with fine Villeroy and Bach table settings, linen cloths and several antique chandeliers. There are two dining areas and the one on the ground level is the nicer of the two. The terrine of salmon is superb. The *sopa del mar* (seafood soup) features crabmeat, lobster chunks, tender mussels and the freshest fish in the Paraná River, all swimming in a light cream sauce. The *steak Tiber de queso atuel con tomate y albahaca fresca* (steak with cheese, to-

mato and fresh basil) is a tasty alternative for landlubbers. Price-fixed menus are available.

LONDON GRILL
Reconquista 455
Tel 311-2223
British
Noon-midnight, daily
Inexpensive

British in style and cuisine.

The London Grill is the most popular British eaterie in a city with many Brits. This was one of Borges' favorite haunts – the blind poet savored classical English cuisine just as locals do today. Turkey, leg of lamb and the roast beef with Yorkshire pudding are specialties at the grill. Britain puts its best foot forward with this warmly inviting pub. There is an oyster bar here as well. Another popular British pub, **Downtown Matias** is at 979 San Martín (tel. 312-9844). Specialties here are the hot chicken curry and the meat and kidney pies. Closed weekends.

LA ESTANCIA
Lavalle 941 (near 9 de Julio)
Tel 326-0330
Grilled meats
Open daily, noon-3 a.m.
(less crowded at lunch)
Inexpensive

La Estancia has become a legend for the leagues of people that have been well-fed at these tables. Its location on Lavalle, in the hub of the downtown area, makes it a mecca for tourists, but that shouldn't deter you. Its stellar reputation is well deserved and, in spite of many tourists, the majority of your fellow diners are *porteños*. The quality and freshness of the meat is unsurpassed and, as you wait in line for a table on a busy night along with many other hungry people, you can watch the *gaucho*-clad chefs preparing the meats over wood-burning fires in the front windows. Although the tables are close together and the waiters have large sections to serve, they manage to provide friendly service. The *parrilladas* – which are most popular – are served sizzling and are enormous.

CLARKS II
Sarmiento 645
Tel 325-1960
Continental
Closed weekends
Moderate

This sister restaurant to Clarks of Recoleta is even more attractive. Located in what was once a fashionable tailor shop, it was converted to its present day elegance in 1978. Many of the interior decorative elements were preserved, such as the original wood paneling and the stained glass. The antique bar is a real eyeful. You can have *asado* , grilled salmon, or glazed duckling anytime. Or you can select lighter fare. The house specialty is a buttery cut of beef encrusted by a crispy shell.

ZUM EDELWEISS
Calle Libertad 431
Tel 382-3351
German
Noon-6 a.m. daily
Inexpensive

Weiner Schnitzel anyone? If you enjoy such German specialties as *choucroute garni, eisbein* (pigs knuckles), or *leberwurst with pickles*, head to this attractive restaurant, which is a favorite among theater people, performers and specta-

Another German-style eaterie, Otto is at Sarmiento 1679.

tors alike. It's a short two blocks from the Teatro Colón. There are non-German specialties as well. Do try their dessert pancakes. They're delicious.

ROMA PIZZERIA
Lavalle 888
No credit cards
Inexpensive

Roma's huge dining room is always crowded but particularly so at lunch and after the last show at the nearby cinemas. There is waiter service at the tables and counter service in the front. Roma has the best and least expensive *empanadas* in the city. One *empanada*, its crusty dough stuffed with ground beef, ham and cheese or chicken chunks, is enough for lunch. Also terrific are the pizzas, which are served by the slice at the counter and by the pie if you're seated. Toppings include anchovies, ham, onions and olives.

LAS NAZARENAS
Reconquista 1132
Tel 312-5559
Grilled meats
Open noon-2 a.m. daily
Inexpensive

Especially attractive if you are staying at the Sheraton or Plaza Hotels, this restaurant is a brisk walk from the center of town. A two-story colonial-style building, it is easily recognized by the cheery flags that hang from its exterior. The interior is cheerful as well, with brightly painted yellow walls and matching cloths, hanging chandeliers and green plants everywhere. Las Nazarenas' high quality *parrilladas*, *bife de lomo*, brochettes and special salads are enough to lure all discriminating tastebuds. The beef in particular is always superlative.

EL PALACIO DE LA PAPA FRITA
Lavalle 735
Lavalle 954
Tel 393-5849
Inexpensive

Don't let the silly name of these sister restaurants turn you off. "The Palace of the Fried Potato" delivers the goods. Palatial? Maybe not. Comfortable? Certainly. What it lacks in decor it makes up for in the friendly service you receive, the freshness of food, the large selection of entrées and the generous portions served. All of the chicken dishes are excellent and you may appreciate the switch from beef. Try the chicken Valenciana with a salad, simply roasted in its own juices with herbs – it was perfect.

And don't miss the flaming desserts. The waiter will happily flambé cherries, bananas, or any other seasonal fruit right at the table, and serve it to you warm in a silver bowl.

BROCCOLINO
Esmeralda 776
Tel 322-9848
Italian
No credit cards
Inexpensive

Broccolino, a family-owned restaurant, would be right at home in a small town near Naples. It has red checkered tablecloths, with wine bottles and posters providing the decor. The pizza is superb and is very popular with Argentinean families. There are many pasta dishes as well. The sauces are red and hearty.

YING YANG
Paraguay 858
Tel 311-7798
Natural foods
Breakfast and lunch only; closed Sundays
No credit cards
Inexpensive

Yes Virginia! some *porteños* eat brown rice, vegetable pies, fresh salads and fish. Many of them head to Ying Yang which serves natural foods in its small restaurant and is a popular take-out mecca too.

EL IMPARCIAL
Hipolito Yrigoyen 1201
Tel 383-7536
Spanish
Inexpensive

Friends tell us that El Imparcial is the oldest restaurant in Buenos Aires, having opened in 1860 – yes 1860! It must be doing something right and, since there is no decor to speak of, it must be the food. Spanish specialties include paella with shellfish and a spicy *arroz con mariscos* that has chunks of shrimp and mussels. There are meat dishes on the menu as well.

These restaurants are near Plaza del Congreso.

EL GLOBO
Calle Salta 98
Tel 381-2926
Spanish
Inexpensive

A virtual newcomer, having been here only since 1908, El Globo is another eaterie serving Spanish specialties. Serrano ham is always on the menu and the paellas and *pucheros* (hearty soups) are very popular.

Fast Food/Light Dining

Fusion Café at Tucumán 839 is a comfortable restaurant where you can enjoy breakfast and lunch. They offer breakfast specials and fresh salads and sandwiches at lunch. **Bompler**, Calle Florida 491, serves French-style fast food which means that sandwiches arrive on croissants or baguettes and there is always hot onion soup. **Quick**, Calle Florida 130, is similar. **Pumper-nic** has branches on Calle Florida 532 and elsewhere in the city. Burgers are the best selling item here, but **McDonald's** has become even more popular and ubiquitous, with branches throughout the city. The menu is familiar, but many have salad carts where you select items and a waiter serves them to you. Salad is sold by weight. **La Lecherísima**, which serves such items as yogurt, fresh fruits and cereals, has branches scattered all over town. Two convenient locations are at Avenida Corrientes 839 and Avenida Santa Fe 726.

Confiterías

European-style coffee houses, many with sidewalk cafés, are located throughout the downtown area, in fact throughout the city. Although they vary in ambience, they nearly all serve identical foods and beverages. Small finger sandwiches, delicious croissants and pastries are excellent choices, while drinks range from alcohol to exotic coffees and teas. The service is always formal, with tea arriving in its own pot. Many serve breakfast and some stay open well into the night and offer entertainment. They are most crowded in late afternoon (4-5 p.m.) when *porteños* take a coffee break. Two legendary *confiterías* are the **Gran Café Tortoni** at Avenida de Mayo 825 (see "Buenos Aires After Dark"), which is over 100 years old and was formerly a barber shop, and **Confitería Ideal** at Suipacha 384. Ideal has live music daily starting at 5 p.m. Other favorites include **Florida Garden** at Calle Florida 899; **Queen Bess** at Avenida Santa Fe 868; **Young Men's** at Córdoba 784; and **Del Molino** at Avenida Rivadavia 1801 near the Congress Building.

Barrio Norte "Sud"

The up-and-coming near north side.

Slightly off the beaten track and not centered around a specific site, the restaurants that follow are, for the most part, newcomers on the Buenos Aires dining scene. They are largely scattered, which means you cannot walk from one to the other easily, but they are all within walking distance of downtown and Recoleta. The heart of the area we've dubbed "Northern Barrio-South" is Avenida Callao where it joins Santa Fe, Arenales and Juncal. Lots of cinemas and shops are here and the main streets are alive with people well into the night. The area is up and coming, with lots of new buildings and renovated ones. It reminds us of Soho in New York and the Gaslight District of San Diego. Restaurants are informal, as is the dress code.

AU BEC FIN
Vicente Lopez 1825
Tel 801-6894
French
Dinner only; closed Sunday
Expensive

Au Bec Fin is neither a newcomer on the city dining scene nor is it trendy and informal. It is, however, the top dining spot in this area, particularly if you enjoy French food. The restaurant occupies all three floors of what was an elegant home in the 1920's. It changed hands several times until Au Bec Fin opened in 1983. There are several dining rooms, some so small that they only hold three or four tables. The dim lighting, elegant tableware and relative privacy makes Au Bec Fin a romantic dining experience. Friends raved about the mousse, which is made with shrimp as well as liver. The fish dishes are terrific and not heavily sauced, and the beef is stuffed with mushrooms and other ingredients. They offer a four-course price-fixed dinner.

BANANA
Ayacucho 1425
Tel 812-6321
Pizza
Closed for lunch; open till 2 a.m. nightly
Moderate to inexpensive
As you step over the threshold of this contemporary restaurant, you'll feel as if you've left Argentina and landed in an exotic Amazon village. The large, vividly painted room is filled with palm trees and lots of hanging fruit – particularly (you guessed it) bananas. You expect Tarzan to plop down on your table at any point. If you are anticipating wild boar steaks or piranha stew, guess again. Banana is a pizzeria and the pizza is terrific. Topped by all kinds of ingredients, it arrives with cheese and bubbling hot. Pastas are also served. The atmosphere is noisy with people and live music that starts at 10:30 p.m. Perfect for after the theater or a movie. Its upstairs partner, **Como** (on the sec-

A wild and crazy place.

ond level) is subdivided in decor with exposed brick walls and deep blue cloths on widely spaced tables. It looks like a converted loft. It too serves pizza and pastas but the larger menu includes salads, carpaccio and ribs. Enter through the door to the right of Banana.

LAS TEJAS
Arenales 1934
Tel 814-3585
International
Moderate

An attractive dining spot, Las Tejas is covered by a glass roof that allows the light to come in and makes you feel as if you are dining outdoors, sans traffic noise. It has brick walls and hanging lamps over each wooden booth. There are tables as well. The menu roams the globe and includes homemade pastas, chicken with oriental spices and vegetables and the house specialty, *pincho gaucho,* a kebab that has pork, beef and chicken as well as vegetables. Unhurried service. Good choice.

LOS INMORTALES
Callao 1165
Pizza
Inexpensive

The Lavalle branch of this near-elegant pizzeria has been an institution in Buenos Aires for years as the photos of the V.I.P. munchers can attest to. But the Callao branch is less crowded and more comfortable, with its leather-backed settees and director's chairs. Menus are the same; steak and chicken dishes join a list of over 50 different pizza choices. The *empanadas,* another house specialty, are large and crusty. Either branch (and there are others) is fine to eat in.

Largest branch is at Calle Lavalle 746.

LA ESQUINA DE LAS FLORES
Montevideo 823 (near Avenida Córdoba)
Natural foods
Inexpensive
As you approach this "Corner of Flowers" and spot the vividly painted exterior with red, blue and yellow flowers, it seems natural that it serves healthy foods. The foods, freshly made on the premises, change daily, but you'll often find vegetable lasagna, vegetable and cheese stuffed *empanadas*, pizzas and pastas, plus a help-yourself salad and fruit bar. There's a take-out store and bakery as well. The interior is very basic, with weathered tables and chairs and worn linoleum. The food's the thing here.

RODIZIO III
Avenida Callao 1290
Brazilian steakhouse
Moderate
In a city with scores of outstanding steakhouses, what can be unique at Rodizio? The difference is that Rodizio is a Brazilian-style steakhouse and that means that the waiters roam through the restaurant with grilled meats displayed on large sword-like skewers. They stop at each table and carve off a chunk of whatever you desire. You can sample beef (of different cuts), lamb, pork, chicken and a variety of sausages and you can keep sampling them until you beg for mercy. The price is fixed. The restaurant itself is sprawling and has several dining rooms, all with whitewashed walls, floral prints and Brazilian cowboy gear.

PIEGARI
Posadas 1042
Italian
Moderate

Modern in decor, with light woods and recessed lighting, Piegari has one large dining room divided into three serving areas by wooden banquettes. There is a bar area at center stage. Specialties are Italian and Piegari makes terrific risotto with chicken, mushrooms and shellfish. Pastas are served, as are pizzas. Portions are good sized.

These restaurants are in the Calle Posadas Arcade.

EL BOULEVARD DE POSADAS
Posadas 1054
Tel 326-6994
French and Italian
Moderate

A more formal-style dining room with dark green floral cloths, the Boulevard of Posadas has both French and Italian specialties. Dijon steak is served with ratatouille and grilled trout or salmon have almondine sauces. It has a good dessert menu and some outdoor tables on a terrace.

EL MIRASOL DE LA RECOVA
Posadas 1032
Tel 326-7322
Argentinean
Moderate

Grilled meats, *empanadas* and other Argentinean specialties are served in this informal eaterie, which is down a few steps from the main floor of the arcade. Outdoor tables.

CALLAO PARRILLA Y PASTAS
Avenida Callao 1033
Moderate
The larger café serves burgers and triple-decker sandwiches while the restaurant (on the right as you enter) serves grilled meats and pastas. The big lure here is a $12 four-course lunch. Comfortable. Best for lunch or tea.

THE EMBERS
Avenida Callao 1111 (near Santa Fe)
Inexpensive
For a light late-night snack head to The Embers, which looks like an old-fashioned ice cream parlor complete with counter. Waffles, pancakes, sandwiches and omelettes are the biggest selling items.

The Carritos of Costanera Norte

Costanera Norte is a waterfront promenade that runs along the River Plate. At different points enroute, run-down dock areas have been converted into shopping malls, modern sports facilities and private clubs. River Plate Stadium and Aeroparque Jorge Newbury are in this area, but the most notable attractions are the *carritos* that line a stretch of one inlet, Avenida Rafael Obligado. The *carritos* of today are popular restaurants that serve Italian, *parrilla* and seafood specialties. The name *carrito* is derived from the time several decades ago when this area was largely unpopulated. On weekends, when *porteños* came here to fish or enjoy the waterfront, the only food to be had was supplied by the men in horse-drawn carriages (*carritos*) who sold sausages and sandwiches. Side by side, the restaurants here are big, filled with talk, laughter, music and large family groups – particularly on weekends. You can "*carrito* hop" and pick the one that most appeals to you, but you will have to wait for a table unless you make a reservation.

A Few Favorites:

A Nonna Immaculata (tel. 782-1751) is the "mother of all carritos," with two huge dining rooms and walls lined with old family photos. Noisy and a lot of fun, it specializes in Italian food. *Moderate.*

Hereford (tel. 782-7447) specializes in grilled meats. It has two levels, but ask to sit downstairs. Decor is *estancia* -style. *Moderate.*

Happening (tel. 787-0666) is the most attractive restaurant on the strip, with leather chairs and lots of hanging plants. A rear walk opens onto a garden and an outdoor terrace overlooking the water. Very popular. Grilled meats and fish. Good food. *Moderate.*

El Padrino (tel. 781-4110) is quite modern looking with low whitewashed ceilings and exposed wooden beams. It serves both grilled meats and pastas. *Moderate.*

Los Años Locos (tel. 783-5126) has a huge cold buffet with both meats and salads. They also serve hot grilled meats. Young lively crowd. *Moderate.*

Gardiner (tel. 788-0437) is not a typical *carrito*. It is dimly lit and starkly modern in decor. It has an eclectic menu offering mixed salads, pastas, grilled fish, meats and special dishes such as *cordero Patagónico* (Patagonian Lamb). *Moderate.*

Dining in San Telmo

For lunch stops around Plaza Dorrego see the "Exploring San Telmo" section in "Sunup to Sundown." The restaurants that follow are more formal and can be considered for a relaxed dinner or pre-tango show evening.

EL REPECHO DE SAN TELMO
Carlos Calvo 242
Tel 362-5473
Continental
Dinner only; closed Sunday
Expensive
Tucked behind a whitewashed gate in a Spanish colonial house built in 1807, El Repecho de San Telmo is luxurious and quite formal inside. The dining room is colonial with whitewashed walls and graceful arches leading from one room to another. The white linen cloths are spotless and starchy, as are the tuxedos of the staff. In keeping with the restaurant's formality, most diners wear coat and tie here. The food served is Continental, with many traditional Argentine dishes served as well. These are prepared in the style of the early 20th century and are not grilled meats.

LA CONVENCION DE SAN TELMO
Carlos Calvo 375
Tel 361-6200
Dinner only 8 p.m.-2 a.m. Sunday Brunch
Closed Monday
Moderate

Clearly less formal both in decor and in fare but extremely attractive in its own right, this is a bi-level restaurant which has exposed brick walls and deep red tablecloths offset by red brocade trim everywhere. Interesting are the black and white photos of old Buenos Aires scenes and of famous tango performers. The menu is simple, with roast chicken and fine herbs, good steaks with fries and sautéed trout in a black butter sauce with capers that is terrific. Lots of lighter foods such as salads are served too.

ANTIGUA TASCA DE CUCHILLEROS
Carlos Calvo 319
Tel 361-7237
Grilled meats
Lunch 12 noon-4:30 p.m. daily; dinner 8 p.m.-2 a.m. except Sunday
Inexpensive

Here's your chance to enjoy traditional Argentine *parrillada* in a typical Argentine colonial building. The restaurant menu, which gives the history of the building, says it was built in 1729. Today it has several dining areas and an outdoor patio. The whitewashed walls and graceful archways give it an open, airy look. Grilled meats are the main attraction, but there are pastas and such dishes as chicken cazuela, which is closely akin to cacciatore. Pleasant dining.

LA CASA DE ESTEBAN DE LUCA
Defensa 1000
Inexpensive
Sort of a saloon/restaurant, this is also in a historic building which was reputedly an arms factory. The bar is popular here and the food leans to burgers, omelettes and salads. Good for lunch and pre-tango show dinner, but not for an entire evening.

TABERNA BASKA
Chile 980
Tel 383-0903
Inexpensive
Although they have been part of Spain for centuries, the northern Basque provinces continue to fight for their independence. Their foods are quite different from those served in traditional Spanish restaurants and they use lots of garlic and unusual shellfish and squid. Basque food is popular in Buenos Aires and if you'd like to sample some you should head to Taberna Baska (Basque Tavern). It serves the best known dishes and is very old world in decor. Another Basque eaterie nearby with many of the same dishes is **Laurek Bat** at Belgrano 1144 (tel. 381-0682). No credit cards here.

Dining in La Boca

Hearty foods, Southern Italian style, are served in generous portions at La Boca's *cantinas*. Best known for the singing, dancing and fun, the food is secondary. All the *cantinas* are on Necochea Street and you can easily walk from one to another. **Il Piccolo Vapore** serves good pastas, while **Spaddevecchio** is favored by tour groups. Other choices include **La Fragata, Gaviotta** and **Tres Amigos.** All are inexpensive.

Dining in the Suburbs

If you'd like to visit a Buenos Aires suburb or want to stay for dinner after the races and enjoy a fabulous meal, then head out to the legendary Avenida Dardo Rocha in the Martínez area opposite the San Isidro Racetrack.

Reservations recommended.

There are two restaurants that are packed with locals, attesting to the excellent fare. Expect to wait a bit for a table, particularly on weekends.

Most popular is the **Rosa Negra**, Dardo Rocha 1910 at the corner of La Paz (tel. 798-7685). It is expensive. A spectacular bar area, similar to that at Harper's, separates the two dining rooms accented by red brick walls and tile floors. Valet parking is available. New to the neighborhood and already considered a "must" by residents is expensive **La Candelaría** at Dardo Rocha 1810 (tel. 792-2207). Rich wood decor and a vaulted ceiling create a lovely setting for an evening after the races.

For good *parrillada,* try the moderate Brazilian-style **Rodizio** at Pardo Rocha 2568 (tel. 793-6556), an all-you-can-eat steakhouse, or **La Herradura**, Dardo Rocha 1260 (tel. 798-5962).

A cab will cost about $15 U.S. each way and will take you through all the suburbs in about half an hour. You can also take the Bartolomé Mitre Railroad from El Retiro Station to Acassuso and hop a cab to the restaurant of your choice.

Buenos Aires Sunup to Sundown

A t their core, most capital cities in South America are Spanish colonial. Not so here. Buenos Aires has a decidedly modern European flavor – so much so that it has often been called "the Paris of the Americas." It's easy to see why. The city has wide tree-lined boulevards and cobblestone promenades. It has flower stalls, sidewalk cafés and lots of bookstores. A soaring obelisk is its Eiffel Tower and, while a river doesn't run through it, the Río Plata is always nearby. Strolling along, you'll notice traces of British, Portuguese and Italian styles of architecture, as well as clear adaptations from the French Renaissance. The inner city is composed of distinctive *barrios* (neighborhoods), each adding a unique flavor to the whole. Fine museums, excellent restaurants, chic shops, and open-air fairs are not clustered in one area but can be found in each key *barrio*. You'll want to explore the city on foot. It is a veritable walker's paradise since it is quite flat and has small plazas where you can rest. But with lots of new construction and underground cables being laid to modernize the telephone, television and transportation systems, the sidewalks are badly broken. Repairs have not caught up. Stay alert!

Citywide Pleasures

Whether you are a dedicated shopper or an indifferent one, you will enjoy browsing along Calle Florida, Avenida Santa Fe and the attractive shopping malls where the *porteños* spend their pesos. It will take power to walk away without a stunning leather coat or designer handbag. Those readers who love a bargain will enjoy "Once," a small shopping area akin to New York's Orchard Street, where haggling is an art form.

Sports enthusiasts can play squash, tennis or golf and, weather permitting, can even sail or windsurf near town. Argentineans are great sportsmen and spectator sports take place at a high level. Tennis matches, horseracing, polo, "pato" matches, and soccer games are always scheduled. Soccer, called *fútbol* , is a national passion. Try to see a game while you're here.

Pato (duck) is a game resembling basketball on horseback.

"Noshing" is another part of a Buenos Aires day. You'll be sorely tempted by *empanadas*, *panchos* with "the works," and especially the scores of *confiterías* (coffee houses) displaying delicious pastries, finger sandwiches, teas and coffees. With dinner usually eaten after 9 p.m., you can indulge yourself and still be hungry for dinner.

The city hosts special events each month. The hotel concierge will advise you of them if you

Neighborhoods of
BUENOS AIRES

1. Recoleta
2. Barrio Norte "Sud"
3. Downtown
4. San Telmo
5. La Boca

N

inquire and they will be listed in the *Buenos Aires Herald*. They include international book fairs, art exhibits, polo championships and Davis Cup tennis matches.

Buenos Aires is a sophisticated, cosmopolitan city with a wide range of activities. Enjoy!

Exploring Downtown

Plaza De Mayo

A good place to start is the **Plaza de Mayo**, an attractive tree-lined oasis in the heart of downtown Buenos Aires and the historical heart of the city. As previously noted (see History), the city was founded twice. A tiny settlement was started early in the 16th century by a Spanish explorer, Pedro de Mendoza. He named it "Puerto de Nuestra Señora de la Santísima Trinidad y Ciudad de Nuestra Señora de Santa María de los Buenos Aires." Quite a mouthful! Eventually the name was whittled down to Buenos Aires or "Good Breezes." Mendoza had promised to honor the Virgin (she is the patron saint of navigators) if the ships in his fleet were brought safely to shore. Mendoza and his men moved on and it wasn't until 1580 that the city you see today was founded. Juan de Garay marked off a square section of land and called it the Plaza Mayor. Around the square he designated areas for the *Cabildo* (Town Hall), a church, and a fort. Houses for the 63 people who had accompanied Garay took up the rest of the space. Adjoining the square, a Jesuit mission was established, as was a military garrison. Garay's Plaza Mayor did not immediately flourish – for years it served as a market place, a bullfight arena and even the site of a gallows. The church he envisioned was started a half-dozen times to no avail and today's cathedral was not begun until the late 17th century. The fort on the eastern flank of the plaza was never attacked and gradually fell into disrepair. In 1880 it was replaced by the stunning **Casa Rosada** (Pink House), which you can visit. The **Cabildo** (Old Town Hall) is the only building still standing that had its origins in Garay's time.

A wall of this fort has been unearthed and can be seen behind the Casa Rosada.

Many important events in Argentina's history have been played out in this plaza. In 1806 it was the site of a fierce battle between British forces and local soldiers during the British attempt to wrest control of the city from the Spanish. It was also here that the local junta formed the nation's first native government on May 25, 1810. This event gave the plaza its current name – Plaza of Mayo.

The Plaza de Mayo has served as a public podium for people expressing their opinions and an arena for demonstrations, both organized and spontaneous. In recent years, the plaza has seen the anguish of the "Madres de la Plaza de Mayo," a group of women wearing white kerchiefs who march around the square every Thursday with photographs of their lost children pinned to their chests. These children are among the *desaparecidos* (the disappeared ones) who vanished during the years of military oppression and The Dirty War. Visitors to the plaza will never forget the sight of these women silently gathered to remind everyone of their lost loved ones. Other demonstrations here are

Downtown

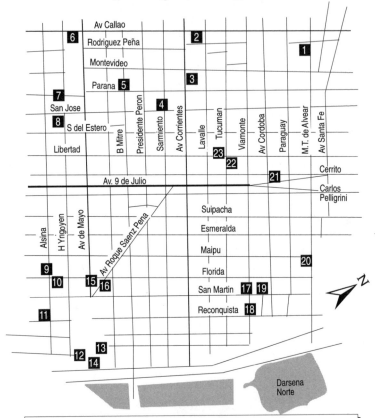

1. Consejo Nacional de Educacion
2. Catedral Metropolitana
3. Teatro Presidente Alvear
4. Centro Cultural General San Martin
5. Iglesia de la Piedad
6. Monumento a Los Dos Congresos
7. Edificio de la Inmobiliaria
8. Edificio Barolo
9. Museo de Motivos Argentinos
   "José Hernandez"
10. Honorable Consejo Deliberante
11. Museo de la Ciudad de Buenos Aires
12. Museo de la Casa de Gobierno
13. Casa de Gobierno
14. Monumento a Cristobal Colon
15. Diario La Prensa
16. Palacio Municipal
17. Galerias Pacifico
18. Templo de la Congregacion Israelita Argentina
19. Circulo Naval
20. Museo de Armas de la Nacion
21. Teatro Nacional Cervantes
22. Monumento a Carlos Maria de Alvear
23. Palacio de Justicia

often noisy, helped along by large bass drums and loudspeakers or megaphones.

As you relax on one of the benches or stroll around the plaza, be sure to take note of its two monuments. The original **Piramide de Mayo**, constructed of wood and plaster, dates back to May, 1811, when it was unveiled to commemorate the first anniversary of the May Revolution. After several restorations, it was moved to its current position at the center of the plaza in 1912. An equestrian statue of Manuel Belgrano, creator of the Argentinean Flag and a hero of her independence fight, stands in front of the **Casa Rosada**.

Look for the soldiers on horseback in the Plaza. They wear the same colorful uniforms worn by San Martín's regiment in the war for freedom from Spain.

Though dominated by banks and office buildings, the plaza is still home to three historic buildings that are open to the public. They are the **Casa Rosada,** the **Metropolitan Cathedral,** and the **Cabildo.**

The **Casa Rosada** (so named for its pinkish hue) was built between 1873 and 1894 on the site that was originally a fort as well as the city's Customs House and Post Office. Today it is home to the executive branch of the government and is often referred to as the *Casa de Gobierno.* Ask a *porteño* about the Casa's pink color and you'll hear quite a story. It seems that in the last century, following the Civil War of the Federal and Unitario Parties, President Sarmiento issued the decree that the colors of each party be blended as a symbol of cooperation. The colors were red and white, hence the rosy blush of the Casa Rosada.

The Pink House serves the same function as White House in Washington D.C.

Take a close look at the ornate first-floor balcony and nearby portico with red geraniums blooming in every niche. The Peróns stood here often, stirring the masses with their nationalistic rhetoric. One memorable rally took place in 1945. Organized by Eva Perón, it was designed to protest her husband's incarceration. It succeeded. The Peronistas were bombed at a giant rally held here in 1955 while protesting the ousting of Juan Perón. It was from this balcony that President Galtieri announced the invasion of the Malvinas/Falkland Islands in 1982. He reappeared only a few months later to admit defeat – just a few days before resigning from power.

The Lowering of the Flag at 7 p.m. each night is fun to watch, as is the Changing of the Guard by the colorfully clad Grenaderos every other Saturday at 11 a.m. Lots of pomp!

The many palm trees and fountains in the patios around the Casa Rosada create a tropical feel while providing cool shade and an inviting place to stop. By the way, the Casa Rosada has a small but choice museum which you enter from Hipolito Yrigoyan 211. Admission is free on Saturday; it is closed on Wednesday.

If you continue around to the back of the Casa Rosada, you'll see **Parque Colón**, where there is an exquisite sculpture of Christopher Columbus by the Italian sculptor Arnoldo Zocchi.

The **Banco de La Nación Argentina** on Avenida Rivadavia facing the Plaza houses a Numismatic Museum. The first Teatro Colón once occupied this spot.

You'll easily recognize the **Metropolitan Cathedral** if you look for the oversized torch to the right of the main entrance. It remains lit at all times and honors Argentina's most revered national hero who lies buried within, General José de San Martín. The very first chapel in Buenos Aires stood here in 1585. By 1622, after several failed attempts, the site was consecrated and construction began. It wasn't actually completed until 1791, and even then the portico would not be constructed for another 30 years. By that time Argentina had moved from the Spanish-dominated colonial period to the more French-inspired period of Enlightenment following the May Revolution. Two Frenchmen, Prosper Catelin and Pierre Benoit, were chosen to design the portico and are responsible for the row of 12 Corinthian columns. Resting above the columns is a sculpture pediment by Joseph Dubourdieu, "Jacob meets his son Joseph in hands of Egypt," which represents the reconciliation between Buenos Aires and the provinces.

The cathedral is a treasure trove of historical riches. Spanish mosaic floors, a barrel vaulted ceiling and five naves of Renaissance design that house priceless icons, sculptures and religious relics. Most noteworthy are: the Rococo-style **main altar**, made by Isidro Lorea, one of the best carvers of the colonial period; the statue of **Santo Cristo de Buenos Aires**, located on the left arm of the transept, which is the oldest image of Christ made in the River Plate and considered by some to be the most beautiful in Buenos Aires; and the **Virgin de los Dolores** (Virgin of Grief), imported from Cádiz, Spain in 1752.

Visitors to the church will not be admitted if they are wearing shorts, mini skirts or other clothing deemed inappropriate by the guards.

The **Mausoleum of San Martín** is in the nave to your right as you enter. Alongside the general's tomb are those of his commanders and the tomb of Argentina's Unknown Soldier. San Martín's ashes are stored in a red marble vessel at the foot of the monument dedicated to his military feats. The Grenaderos guard this nave.

In the cupola, a depiction of the Inca Sun pays homage to the Indian civilization that flourished on the continent. The victory flag carried by San Martín bears the name and image of Buenos Aires' patron saint, Martin of Tours. This Hungarian saint lived, died and was later canonized in France, his adopted country. The city's early settlers thought that a Spanish saint would be appropriate for this Spanish city, and a "scientific" method of drawing saints' names out of a hat was employed. Every slip of paper picked revealed the name of Martin of Tours so the frustrated Argentineans accepted Saint Martin as the protector of the city. To this day, the law states that the President of Argentina must be a Catholic. A beautiful garden adjoins the cathedral.

President Menem, born to the Muslim faith, converted to Catholicism.

The last historic site in the plaza and the one most closely associated with the city is the **Cabildo**. It functioned as the Town Hall in colonial times and served as the working offices of the Spanish Viceroys who governed here for hundreds of years. It was the headquarters for the first independent government of Argentina as well. The Cabildo museum contains exhibits of artifacts from the colonial period and documents and memorabilia related to Argentina's independence.

Plaza De Los Dos Congresos

A dozen short blocks separate the executive branch of government from the legislative one.

The most direct walk is to follow **Avenida de Mayo**, the oldest official avenue in the city. Inaugurated in 1894 and designed to link the two plazas, the street became a magnet for lavish edifices, including five-story buildings considered "skyscrapers" in the 1880's. South America's first *Subte* (metro) line, a five-mile run inaugurated in 1913, was built beneath the street.

Peru Station is an original. Note the wrought iron token booths and hanging gas lamps.

Along Avenida de Mayo look for the offices of Argentina's internationally known newspaper, *La Prensa*. The cupola atop the building serves as the paper's logo. **Café Tortoni** at number 829 is the oldest and most literary café in Buenos Aires. Local celebrities and foreign stars have all tipped elbows at the Tortoni (see Nightlife). As you cross Avenida 9 de Julio, look for the gaunt and picturesque sculpture of Don Quixote, a gift to the Argentine people from Queen Sofia of Spain. Another important intersection is Calle Salta, which was once home to the Avenida Theater. Built in 1808, it was the first theater in Latin America to stage Garcia Lorca's immortal play *Bodas de Sangre* (Blood Wedding). Unfortunately, this important landmark was destroyed by fire several years ago.

As you near the National Congress Building you'll find yourself strolling through a series of *plazoletas* (small plazas), each featuring a beautiful statue or an enormous fountain. You'll recognize the Rodin statue, *The Thinker*, one of several casts by the Rodin studio, placed here in 1907. The **Monument of the Two Congresses** was completed in 1914 to commemorate the 1813 Assembly that banished slavery and the 1816 Congress that officially proclaimed Argentina's independence. At night the statue is illuminated by an intricate lighting system that makes the waters seem as if they are dancing.

The **National Congress Building** will remind North Americans of the Capitol Building in Washington D.C. It was completed in 1906, designed in an Italian classical style with Greek touches. Four stories high with a pavilion at either end, it is encircled by a Corinthian colonnade. Victor Meano, yet another Italian architect, was responsible for the design. At the top of the peristyle (on the portico) is a gorgeous bronze statue of a chariot and on the corners are winged victories with trumpets.

You can visit the interior of the Congress. If you do, be sure to see the Senatorial Chamber and the octagonal Salón Azul (Blue Room). It has marble floors, baccarat chandeliers and a circular balcony, from which the dome and cupola can be seen.

Avenida 9 de Julio/Teatro Colón

Sandwiched by Avenidas Lima/Cerrito on the west and Irogoyen/Carlos Pellgrini on the east, 9 de Julio has no buildings on it.

This avenue is one city block wide – a total of 425 feet across – the widest street in the world. With many small plazas running through its center and its length of over 26 blocks, this is a lovely place to stroll and people-watch. There are also numerous cafés and *confiterías* along both sides of the avenue. 9 de Julio is a main artery of the city and thus the location of several city landmarks, such as the Obelisco, the 9 de Julio Fountains, and the Teatro Colón at the Lavalle intersection.

A huge, elegant building, the **Teatro Colón** takes up nearly the whole block at Cerrito and Tucumán. The main entrance is at the Plaza Lavalle, a lovely tree-filled park full of statues of dancers commemorating the members of an Argentinean ballet troupe who perished in a plane crash in the 1960's. The Colón is one of the world's premiere opera houses and draws international artists. It is home to its own opera and ballet companies as well as a symphony orchestra. Tours of the theater are offered year-round.

A few blocks away at the **Plaza de La República** (at Corrientes) stands the city's most visible landmark, the **Obelisk**. Two hundred and twenty feet high, it was constructed in 1936 to mark the 400th anniversary of the city's founding. In addition, there are two lovely fountains here which are illuminated at night and are visible for blocks – a beautiful sight.

Calle Florida/Plaza San Martín

Calle Florida, a pedestrian-only walkway, stretches for 11 blocks from Rivadavia to the Plaza San Martín. It was for many years the city's premiere shopping street and for sheer quantity and variety it still is. The quality of the goods sold has fallen off a bit because many of the shops formerly on the street have relocated to shopping malls. Still, there are over 500 shops along Florida, many of them tucked away in mini-arcades called *galerías*. The shops sell just about everything imaginable from fine furs and leathers to inexpensive jewelry and shoes.

Numbers rise on Florida from Rivadavia to the Plaza San Martín.

You can spend hours browsing and shopping on this vital street. Its cobblestone walkway is

More about Calle Florida in the Shopping section.

crowded with shoppers, office workers, newspaper kiosks, *pancho* carts and pick-up musicians and artists hoping for some spare change. In addition to the shops, Calle Florida has fast food eateries and several confiterías. The best known is the venerable **Richmond**, which attracts *porteños* who enjoy the clubby atmosphere and the non-stop chess games on the sub-level.

Keep in mind that the finer quality shops are closer to Plaza San Martín, with the most elegant in the 800 and 900 blocks. A standout is the stunning **Galerías Pacífico**, a multi-level mall on the 700 block, which opened in 1992 in an Italian-style building formerly the headquarters for the Buenos Aires-Pacific Railway. The dome, painted by five well-known Argentinean artists, is spectacular.

The Plaza is now part of the Marriott chain.

At the foot of Calle Florida, where it meets the Plaza San Martín, stands the **Plaza Hotel**, an elegant five-star where many VIP visitors to the city have been entertained.

Another premiere shopping street, Avenida Santa Fe branches off the plaza too.

Plaza San Martín, marked by an equestrian statue commissioned by President Sarmiento, is enveloped by a park that extends downhill to Avenida Libertador, the wide thoroughfare that heads to the northern areas of the city. This part of town is called **El Retiro**, as is the massive railroad station at the base of the park. Plaza San Martín is one of the few elevated areas in a city that is extremely flat. Today the park is crossed by winding pathways amid flowering *palos borrachos*, palm and rubber trees. It has children's playgrounds; young lovers enjoy the grassy slopes; and it is one of the most pleasant spots in the city.

El Retiro (The Retreat) is named for the San Sebastian Hermitage, which was located here.

On the Libertador side of the park a recent monument honors those Argentineans killed during the Malvinas War. Much like the Vietnam Memorial, the names of the fallen are engraved on a black stone wall, marked by an eternal flame and guarded by an honor guard.

A distinctive building overlooks the park. The **Kavanagh Building**, now a 30-story residential tower, was the tallest building in all South America when it was built in 1934.

If you spend some time in the park you're sure to hear the distinctive chimes of a clock marking each hour. The clock, a replica of London's Big Ben, was a gift of Buenos Aires' British community. The plaza was called Plaza Británica until the Malvinas conflict, when the name was changed to **Plaza Fuerzas Aéreas** (Air Force). Also nearby, a carved totem pole stands in **Plaza Canada**. Carved by Kwakiate tribesmen, it was a gift from the Canadian government.

These plazas face Retiro Station on the far side of Libertador.

Exploring Barrio Norte

Broadly speaking, Barrio Norte stretches from the Plaza San Martín to the suburb of Palermo. That encompasses a lot of geography, so the *barrio* is divided into smaller enclaves. **Recoleta** is of most interest to visitors. It is a fashionable residential area with a mingling of modern apartment dwellings and colonial-style mansions. There are museums, exclusive social clubs, posh boutiques, gourmet restaurants and lively night spots. It is fun to visit during the daylight hours as well as at night and you'll want to spend some time here.

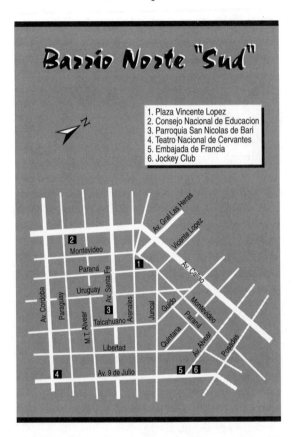

Barrio Norte "Sud"

1. Plaza Vincente Lopez
2. Consejo Nacional de Educacion
3. Parroquia San Nicolas de Bari
4. Teatro Nacional de Cervantes
5. Embajada de Francia
6. Jockey Club

Palermo Chico is another exclusive residential area, with several foreign embassies. Many diplomats live here as well. While the architecture is stunning, there is little else of interest to visitors.

A third area within the district has recently started to emerge as a magnet for young professionals and singles. Clustered between Avenida Santa Fe and Córdoba (on the Cerrito side of 9 de Julio) and extending to Avenida Callao, trendy, moderately-priced restaurants and late night stops have recently opened. A late night favorite, **La Plaza**, is in this area, as are many cinemas. Crowded late into the night, it is much like New York's Tribeca section. For want of a distinctive name, we've dubbed it "**Barrio Norte Sud**."

Recoleta

Beautiful people far out-number the Recoleta friars who gave this area its name. They established a convent here, named it for the Virgin of Pilar, and started construction of the church in 1716. Their neighbors, poor fishermen, washerwomen and butchers, called it the *Convento de los Padres Recoletos* or *La Recoleta* for short. The convent was closed in the 1820's and its orchard became Buenos Aires' first public cemetery.

In the 1870's, a yellow fever epidemic spread through the southern districts of Buenos Aires and those who were able to do so moved to the north. They built lovely "Belle Epoque" homes and "mini-palaces," now embassies and politicians' residences that look as if they were shipped directly from the Champs Elysées. Avenida Alvear even has lamposts that were donated by General Charles de Gaulle because he found the street uncomfortably dim on a visit to Buenos Aires many years ago. This style prevailed until the 1940's, when the modern urbanization process began and the middle class made Recoleta its home. With that new source of money came the restaurants, cafés, galleries and antique shops you see today.

La Recoleta

1. Tourist Information Center
2. Facultad de Ingenieria
3. Museo Roca
4. Cementerio de la Recoleta
5. Centro Cultural Recoleta
6. Basilica de Nuestra Señora del Pilar
7. Museo Nacional de Bellas Artes
8. Centro Municipal Exposiciones
9. Salas Nacionales de Cultura

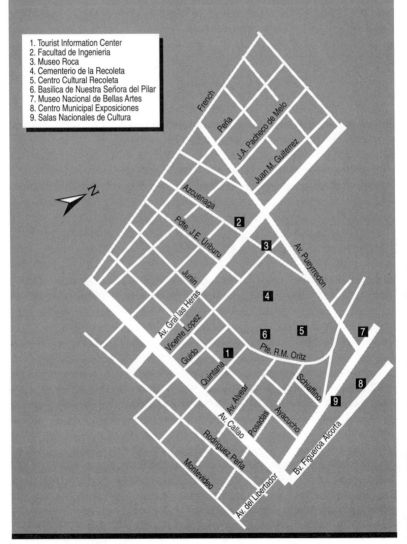

Getting There: Buses #17, 61, 62, 93, 101 and 108 all head to Recoleta from the downtown area. A taxi will take less than 10 minutes. You can easily walk to Recoleta from the Plaza San Martín. It will take about 30 minutes unless you stop enroute, which you'll probably want to do.

If you take a taxi, ask to be let off at La Biela Cafe.

Orientation

Avenidas Alvear and Quintana -Recoleta's main streets lead from Carlos Pelligrini Square to the cemetery, Basilica and convent (now a cultural center) at the heart of the district. Both streets are home to fashionable shops, hotels, night spots and lovely homes.

Calles R. M Ortiz and Junín - The finest restaurants in Buenos Aires are found on these streets, which are closed to traffic. Sidewalk cafés on the promenade are the most popular meeting spots in town.

Alvear Public Square - Adjacent to this grassy square are the cemetery, basilica and convent that are the heart of historic Recoleta.

Plaza Carlos Pelligrini - At Calle Libertad, this square houses the city's finest private clubs and foreign embassies. It is the traditional border of Recoleta and downtown Buenos Aires.

Plaza Francia - Home to the Museum of Fine Arts, the best museum in Buenos Aires.

Historic Recoleta

The Recoleta Cemetery, the Basilica of Our Lady of Pilar, and the Convent of the Recoletos form the triumvirate that sits atop the gently sloping

The Basilica is a favorite place to get married in the city. Saturdays are most popular.

hill behind the Alvear Public Square. **The Basilica of Our Lady of Pilar** sits to one side of the cemetery. The church dates back to 1716 and was completed in 1732 under the direction of Jesuit architects Andrés Blanqui and Juan Prímoli. Its beauty lies in its simplicity. Its single tower rises on the left side of the church and is partially covered in tile that was added later. There is a belfry with a double arch located on the opposite side, crowned by a colonial-era clock tower that sits between two pear-shaped ornaments.

Pilar is a splendid example of Argentinean colonial architecture. Inside, there is a main altar which is itself a great piece of Baroque art. Note the Virgin of Pilar, placed in a central niche in the altar. The Altar of Relics (*Altar de las Reliquias)* is made of mahogany with brass appliqués. The basilica, however, is not only a Baroque jewel with a valuable collection of religious art; it also served as a relief station for the British during the invasions of 1806 and remains the only church in Buenos Aires to keep its cemetery. It was declared a National Historic Monument in 1942.

The old **Convent of the Recoletos** at Calle Junín 1930 is now the **Centro Cultural de la Ciudad de Buenos Aires**. The convent occupied this site from 1732 until 1822, and was used as a home for the reclusive monks. After 1822 it served a number of different purposes. Among other things, it was an old peoples' home called the *Hogar General Viamonte*, a jail, a hospital, and an army barracks. In 1979 the city decided to house its cultural center here. The center boasts an excellent collection of 20th-century Argentine

The Eduardo Sivori Art Museum, open daily 4 p.m. to 8 p.m., tel. 46-9664.

art and offers workshops on photography, art restoration and other interesting topics. Special art exhibits are held here as well. Check schedules.

As the saying goes, "You ain't seen nothing yet." The most interesting site in La Recoleta is the **Cementerio de La Recoleta** (Recoleta Cemetery), marked by a majestic neoclassical portico and entrance. The cemetery opened in 1822 on the site of the old convent's orchard.

The Cemetery is at the corner of Junín and Qintana and is open from 8 a.m. daily.

Many of Argentina's famous citizens are buried here. The graves are spread over 10 acres of land and total an incredible 7,000. In addition to the facts, there are some quaint and hard-to-believe tales relating to some of the dead. Ask the groundskeeper about the grave of Señorita Rufina Cambaceres and he will lead you to it. The unlucky lady is said to have been mistakenly buried while in the midst of a cataleptic fit. After the burial she succeeded in escaping her casket with terrific effort, only to die at the gates of the cemetery of a heart attack. Rufina was 15 years old when she died in 1909. There may actually be a factual basis to this awful tale. The enemies of her politician father were accused of masterminding the plot and the cataleptic attack that led to her demise.

Dr. Pedro Arata's tomb is certainly one of the most unusual. It is a replica of an Egyptian pyramid and remains incomplete to this day. There are several graves with Egyptian motifs in Recoleta, recalling the obsessive fascination with the afterlife. Dr. Federico Leloir's grave is the most expensive one. There is space within for 60 coffins and the interior of the dome is covered with pure gold tiles.

Isabel Walenska was rumored to be the granddaughter of Napoleon Bonaparte. Although her grave is entered in the Recoleta registry, there is no mark on her burial place. Many bodies, in fact, are listed in the registry but do not appear anywhere in the cemetery, largely due to the remodelling that has gone on over the years. These persons lie anonymously in forgotten vaults. Remedios Escaleda de San Martín, wife of the Liberator, lies in a small and simple grave that General San Martín designed himself.

La Recoleta Cemetery is a world unto itself – a world of the dead. The people interred in these vaults of neoclassic splendor were the best and brightest or the wealthiest of the land. Recoleta was the elite place to be laid to rest in this country that reveres the dead to a near-fervent degree. Seventy of these mausoleums have been declared national monuments. The tall twisted trees that lend their shape to the sleeping citizens of Recoleta Cemetery are ancient magnolias over a century old.

Try to find a groundskeeper and ask him where the most notable persons are entombed. He will be happy to lead you to all the most interesting final resting places. Eva Duarte Perón is to be found here in the Duarte mausoleum, which is actually one of the most modest in the entire cemetery. Evita's vault is usually well attended, with visitors leaving behind bunches of roses and lilies at the foot of the tomb. Flowers are woven into the wrought iron doors of many of the flagrantly grandiose tombs, some of which include framed faded photographs of the deceased. Evita's tomb bears a plaque which proclaims her "the champion of the working classes."

You'll find it virtually impossible to fully appreciate the artistry represented in this place – it's too plentiful and too close together. Focus instead on a part of the cemetery. You will see that every portion of earth is covered with monuments to the heroes who lie beneath them: the tomb of José Paz with the imploring angels facing the heavens, the neoclassical Aramburu mausoleum (the plaque tells how one Aramburu seized power from Perón in 1955 and was subsequently kidnapped and killed by the communists) and the tombs of Yrigoyen, Saavedra, Dorrego Guillermo Brown. The names begin to sound familiar if you've been in Argentina any length of time.

The many Italians in the cemetery, including the Spineto family, are interred in mausoleums copied from ones in the famous cemetery in Genoa. Carrera marble and special stones were shipped from Italy to construct the incredible graves you see today. The Spineto grave features a bronze filigreed door with representations of St. George and the Dragon.

Facundo Quiroga's request was certainly one of the oddest. He asked to be buried in a standing position. His wishes were followed, and his coffin is supported by two pillars and walled in place with a haunting statue called "Sorrowing Mary" standing as a sentinel. The figure may, in fact, represent his grieving widow. You will see similar statues of weeping mothers and wives incorporated in the design of other graves as well.

Recoleta Today — A Walking Tour

Follow Avenida Libertador to Calle Libertad. Start at **Carlos Pelligrini Square** which is the site of **The Jockey Club**. The city's most prestigious club, it was founded by President Pelligrini and his statue stands in the middle of the square. The mansions around the square are now occupied by embassies of singular beauty. The Brazilian Embassy sports vividly painted ceilings and the delicate white mansion on the concrete island in the middle of traffic is the French Embassy.

Stop by Freddo's on Avenida Quintana at Ayachucho for ice cream.

Calle Posadas, which leads from this square, passes the five-star Caesar Park Hotel and the Patio Bullrich Shopping Center. It is a quiet block to stroll along. **Avenida Alvear**, which also leads from this square and the next parallel street, **Avenida Quintana**, are the main arteries of today's Recoleta. Here the French-, Spanish- and Italian-style mansions begin to mix with the modern steel and glass edifices of the 20th century. The streets are rife with designer clothing shops and fine furniture and antique stores. The intersection of Avenida Alvear and **Avenida Callao** has some of the city's best art galleries. You can spend hours exploring these two streets, which also boast some of the city's finest eateries and night spots. If you stop for lunch at one of the sidewalk cafés you can observe the social scene of upscale *porteños*.

You'll soon find yourself in the heart of historic Recoleta, the spot where the Recoleta Friars built their convent and church. Two important plazas lie just outside the grassy hill: **Intendente Alvear Square** and **Ramón Cárcano Public Square**. The former is marked by a statue of the Argentine Patriot, Carlos María de Alvear. Built with bronze and marble, its wide staircase affords a view of the entire area. This tree-lined, shady spot was born spontaneously when the people who attended funerals started to gather there. The kiosks they set up were the forerunners of the weekly open-air market that operates here. **Ramón Carcano Public Square** faces the gate of the Recoleta Cemetery.

The Cemetery is at the corner of Junín and Quintana and is open from 8 a.m. daily.

Stop for a light lunch or late afternoon tea at **Plaza de Pilar**, an upscale "foodcourt" in the lower level of the Recoleta Design Building. Here, you'll find a series of restaurants serving everything from burgers to pizza to pasta. You can eat indoors or out. More about Plaza de Pilar dining options in "Restaurants."

Museum buffs should keep in mind that Buenos Aires' finest museum, **Museo de Bellas Artes** (Museum of Fine Arts), is at Avenida Libertador 1473 in the Recoleta section (see Museums). It is adjacent to the beautiful **Plaza Francia**. The wonderful monument in its plaza, by the French sculptor Peynot, was a gift from the French community on the centennial of Argentina's first native government. Every Sunday afternoon Plaza Francia is the site of an outdoor flea market. It's Woodstock Recoleta-style. Young men with ponytails and girls with love beads around their throats sell silver jewelry, miniature ceramic houses in colonial style, small earthen pots and gaily painted animals. Many quaint items that don't cost much can be found here.

Palermo Chico

For a peek at Palermo Chico follow **Avenida Figueroa Alcorta**. This is primarily a residential area with stunning homes and foreign embassies. There are few shops or eateries. Here, the streets wind in through one of the few parts of Buenos Aires where the grid pattern doesn't exist. Two museums in Palermo Chico are the **José Hernández Museum** for displays of Argentine crafts and *gaucho* lore and the **Museum of Oriental and Decorative Arts**. Stop at **Café Tabac** for tea and pastries.

Both museums are covered in the Museums section.

Exploring Buenos Aires' Southern Quarter

When Juan de Garay founded the city of Buenos Aires in 1580, he brought 63 families with him. As the city grew, most of the settlements were near the Plaza Mayor (now Plaza de Mayo) or to the south of it. Beautiful homes and churches were built, businesses were opened and the area prospered. In the 1870's the city was hit by an outbreak of yellow fever. Blame for the epidemic was placed on the thick fog which rolled in from the nearby Riachuelo River. Wealthier families and anyone able to leave deserted this quarter for the northern parts of the city. The homes they left behind were filled by poor immigrants who were arriving in Argentina in large numbers. Many of these immigrants were Italian. The southern quarter of Buenos Aires became run down. The lovely homes closed, as did many businesses. Conditions remained the same until the years after the Second World War, when artists, writers and intellectuals moved into the quarter looking for inexpensive housing. They started to restore the old homes, plant small gardens and open shops and restaurants. Now the southern quarter is picturesque and charming to visit – both during the day and at night. While not trendy like Recoleta, the *barrios* of **San Telmo** and **La Boca** are fun to visit.

San Telmo

Because the government has protected San Telmo by passing strict zoning and preservation laws, this *barrio* is the most historically interesting part of the city. As you stroll along its narrow sidewalks and cobblestone streets and peek into the lovely tile courtyards, you'll see remnants of the 18th and 19th century. Most of the area has remained unchanged since the turn of the century. While many homes have been renovated of late, the facades have been retained. There are several historical museums in San Telmo. These are described in the "Museums" section that follows. The 20th century is represented by famous *tanguerías* (tango parlors), jazz clubs, antique shops and a don't-miss flea market. The *tanguerías* are detailed in "Buenos Aires After Dark." See "Dining in San Telmo" for fine dining options in this area.

El Viejo Almacen, the city's oldest and most popular tango hall, was closed at this writing. Check to see if it has reopened.

San Telmo

1. Museo Historicol Nacional
2. Monumento Pedro de Emndoza
3. Iglesia Ortodoxa Rusa de la Santisima Trinidad
4. Parroquia Inmaculada Concepcion
5. Ferias de Antiguedades de Plaza Dorrego
6. Iglesia Dinamarquesa
7. Casa Esteban de Luca
8. Canto al Trabajo
9. Facultad de Ingenieria
10. Museo Historico del Traje
11. Casa de Liniers
12. Templo Presbieriano San Andres
13. Museo Etnografico "Juan B. Ambrosetti"
14. Museo de la Ciudad de Buenos Aires
15. Colegio Nacional de Buenos Aires
16. Museo Motivos Argentinos "José Hernandez"
17. Honorable Consejo Deliberante
18. Diario La Prensa
19. Palacio Municipal
20. Museo de la Casa de Gobierno
21. Monumento a Cristobal Colon
22. Casa de Gobierno

Av. Caseros
Av. Brasil
Av. Juan de Garay
Cochabamba
Av. San Juan
Humberto 1
Carlos Calvo
Estados Unidos
Av. Independencia
Chile
Méjico
Venezuela
Av. Belgrano
Moreno
Alsina
Hipolito Yrigoyen
Av. de Mayo

Defensa
Balcarce
Av. Paseo Colon
Chacabuco
Peru
Bolivar

Getting There

San Telmo is just south of the Plaza de Mayo. **The Plaza Dorrego**, site of a wonderful Sunday flea market and the heart of the *barrio* is less than a dozen blocks away. You can walk directly between the two plazas along Calle Defensa in under 10 minutes. You can also plan a leisurely stroll from either plaza along the most interesting streets, stopping at a few historical sights. In either case, be in Plaza Dorrego when the fair is in full swing. A taxi from downtown hotels to Plaza Dorrego will take five minutes and under 15 minutes from Recoleta.

History

When the city was founded at the Plaza de Mayo in 1580, a small settlement grew up near the fledgling port on the Riachuelo. The area was known as "Alto de San Pedro" and the earliest residents clustered around a square called the Plaza de la Residencia for the Jesuit residence nearby. Now called **Plaza Dorrego**, it is the city's second oldest square. The plaza became a popular rest point for ox carts and horses enroute from the port to the city and from Buenos Aires to the interior of the country. Lots of small saloon/grocery stores were set up.

The original residents of this small port "town" were fishermen and dock workers; mostly Italians, Irish, Creoles and blacks. The presence of blacks in the area had more than a coincidental impact on the birth of the tango in that same area. The rhythm and beat of the first tangos were distinctly African-influenced. The blacks did not remain in Argentina for very long, but the unique cultural influence they brought with them did.

For a time in the late 18th and early 19th centuries a great number of wealthy homes were built to accommodate the prominent moving to the area. Generals Liniers, Manuel Belgrano and Lavalle lived in San Telmo at different times. The majority of the homes were Spanish colonial with wrought-iron adornments on the doors and windows, and Andalusian-style balconies that were handmade for distinguished families. These flat-roofed two-story houses overwhelmed the older Romanesque structures that featured slanted roofs, ample use of tiles, inner patios and long, spacious rooms.

The street now called **Defensa** was originally called Mayor and it was here that the *aguateros* or water vendors would slowly ride on their horse-driven wagons, sitting among large casks of fresh water that they sold house-to-house. The ladies of the house would collect the wash and deliver it to the washerwomen who would follow Mayor down to the river to do the laundry.

The streets were often flooded and muddy. Occasionally a puddle would be so deep that a small animal would drown in it. This may account for the yellow fever epidemic that hit San Telmo, forcing the wealthier residents to flee. Most did not return and the grand houses turned into tenement-style dwellings for the immigrants who were arriving in large numbers.

For a time San Telmo lost much of its sparkle, but in the last three decades the district has experienced a rebirth.

Orientation

Plaza Dorrego - Located at the intersection of Calles Defensa and Humberto I, Plaza Dorrego was and is the social center of San Telmo. Not a leafy retreat, this square has always been an important commercial center. The *pulperías* (saloon/grocery stores) of yesterday were the forerunners of the wall-to-wall stores, cafés, shopping arcades and restaurants we see today. Architectural styles include Spanish colonial, French and Italian.

Calle Defensa - The most direct route from the Plaza de Mayo to Plaza Dorrego. Many historic churches and buildings are on or near it. Near Plaza Dorrego, it contains the city's finest antique shops.

Calle Balcarce - Balcarce, one block east of Defensa, is an alternate route. While it meanders a bit, it does offer the opportunity to pinpoint the city's best known *tanguerías*.

Calles Carlos Calvo/Humberto I - Plaza Dorrego is sandwiched between these two streets, which are interesting in their own right. Humberto I has several important historic buildings, while Carlos Calvo has San Telmo's best restaurants, all in renovated historic quarters.

Pasaje Giuffra/Calle San Lorenzo - Two cobblestone streets, alleyways that cross Calle Balcarce (on either side of Ave. Independencia), also retain traditional San Telmo flavor. Giuffra and the blocks adjoining it are peppered with nightclubs and bars that have the added attraction of being housed in some of the district's more gracious buildings. These were converted into tenements after the yellow fever plague. Many of San Lorenzo's houses have been adapted into art galleries by their artist landlords. Numbers 319 and 389 are good examples. As interesting as the art on the walls are the walls themselves, a style that is forever gone.

San Telmo Today

Dorrego Fair – always on Sunday, from 10 a.m. to 5 p.m. Smaller fair Saturdays from October to April.

Plaza Dorrego is the place where everything begins and ends in San Telmo, especially on Sunday when the flea market/tango fest takes center stage. There is a smaller market every Saturday (October-April), but it pales next to the Sunday version, which operates year round.

On Sunday merchants set up stalls (numbered) and peddle their wares. These range from antique watches on chains (they work), to rare and used books, religious articles, copper pots and pans, *gaucho* gear, glassware and clothing. Bargaining is intense and, even if you don't understand the words, watch the body language. All the while, street musicians (called buskers) perform. Some are paid by the market organizers and, while they are dressed to the nines and beautiful to watch as they glide across the cement dance floor, it's a job. Head instead to the street performers who work different points of Calle Defensa. An older duo, the singer wiffed and dressed to look like Carlos Gardel, are really intense, as are the dance teams on Humberto I. Just a few centavos keep them going.

The market is not the only place to shop near Plaza Dorrego. There are several mini-arcades in and near the plaza to explore. **Galería El Solar de French** on Calle Defensa overlooking Plaza Dorrego has over 30 shops. Although a few sell antiques, most sell contemporary clothing and gifts. It's in a lovely historic building as well. Just south of Humberto I, you'll find **Galería Ponte Vecchio** at Defensa 1135 and nearby **Pasaje de la Defensa** at 1179. The latter is more attractive and is ensconced in a multi-level historic building. **La Botica de Vichy**, shop #3, has terrific antique clothing (hats especially) that is all the rage with U.S. teens.

Specifics on antique shops in Shopping.

Light Dining Options

You can take in the scene from any number of small eateries. The best views are from **Café French** in the Galería El Solar. Windows open onto the plaza and some tables are set on a small terrace enclosed by a wrought-iron rail. Burgers, omelettes, and the like are served with tango music (sometimes live) as an accompaniment.

Cafe is on the second floor.

Another good choice, **Plaza Dorrego Bar** is at Humberto I. Dark indoors with wooden tables scarred by cigarette burns, the floor is ankle-deep in peanut shells. Tables are set on the plaza when weather permits. Also in the plaza are **Café del Arbol** at Humberto 422, where locals read their Sunday papers and munch on *medias* *lunas* and steaming cups of coffee, and **Pizza Plaza** at 427 which serves pies and pastas.

There are fine dining establishments in San Telmo. These are detailed in "Restaurants."

San Telmo Sights

Iglesia San Pedro Gonzales Telmo, at Humberto I 340, is just a half-block from the plaza. Telmo was the name of a Neopolitan saint who is the patron of sailors. Construction on the church and the adjoining cloister began in the 1730's. They were designed by a Jesuit architect, Father Andrés Blanqui. When the Jesuits were expelled in 1767, construction stopped so the church wasn't completed until 1850. The dome and cloister are all that remain of Blanqui's design. Look for the special image of the Virgin of Bethlehem that was brought from Spain and a marble slab used as an operating table in the first city hospital. The British actually used San Telmo Church as a stronghold during their second incursion into Buenos Aires. The clock was donated by the soldiers who sought refuge there and were spared after the British were badly beaten.

The cloister that adjoins the church at #378 now houses a small and lackluster museum, the **Museo Penitenciario** (Penitentiary Museum), so named because at one point it housed the Women's Correctional Prison.

As you leave the plaza, you'll want to stroll through the surrounding streets. Calles **Carlos Calvo** and **Balcarce, Pasaje Giuffra, Calle San**

Lorenzo and others are what give San Telmo character. Look for the ceramic plaques posted on buildings. They identify those with historic significance. A good example of this is the **Casa de Esteban de Luca** on Calle Defensa at Carlos Calvo. Now a saloon/eaterie, it was once the home of a revolutionary poet and reputedly an arms factory and weapons arsenal.

Continuing north along Calle Defensa, you'll see exclusive antique shops and near Avenida Independencia you'll see the defunct **Cine Cecil**, now a funky antiques market. You have to know your stuff here. It reminds us of an antique shop sign we once saw in Singapore – "We buy junk and sell antiques."

Just beyond Independencia, you'll find yourself at **Calle Chile**, which was once a stream and the traditional border of San Telmo. The small area between Chile and the Plaza de Mayo is alternately called **Catedral al Sur** or **Montserrat**. In fact, these traditional lines have blurred and the entire area from the Plaza de Mayo south to Lezama Park is considered San Telmo.

Historic Montserrat.

The corner of Calle Defensa and Calle Venezuela is known as "Death Corner" because of the vicious fighting that took place here between the British and the *criollos*. The building at Defensa 628 has the dubious distinction of being the very spot from which Argentineans poured pots of boiling water and oil on the heads of the passing British troops in the early 1800's.

The **Santo Domingo Church**, also called the **Basílica Menor del Santísimo Sacramento**, is located at the intersection of Calles Defensa and Belgrano. This church's past has been severely marked for posterity by the British. During the second invasion in 1807 they used it as a fortress; if you look up at one of its two towers you can see the pockmarked surface, created by the bullets shot in the battle for the reconquest of Buenos Aires. Inside the church are a collection of flags and banners confiscated from the British troops and kept in a shrine in the Altar of the Blessed Virgin of the Holy Rosary. Generals Belgrano and Balcarce have found their final resting places here in the atrium of the church.

Another impressive old church, the **Basílica de San Francisco** and the smaller **Capilla San Roque** are at Calles Defensa and Alsina. At first a modest chapel, San Francisco, built in 1754, became the headquarters of the Franciscan Order, which made its first foray into the area in 1538. San Roque predates San Francisco and is part of a building that was erected in 1602. The present buildings, however, are much more recent, although they were built on the old foundations. The church was badly looted and even partially burned in the riots that preceded the fall of Juan Perón in the 1950's. Today the basilica houses a multitude of priceless items: paintings, rare books (in the Basilica Library), manuscripts dating back to the Middle Ages and ecclesiastical artifacts.

Across Calle Defensa you'll see the **Museo de la Ciudad** (Municipal Museum) at Calle Alsina 412. Yes, it is up that steep flight of stairs. The governors of the museum also manage the San Telmo market (see Museums). The **Estrella Pharmacy** *(Farmacia Estrella)* on the ground floor, was built in the 19th century and is part of the museum.

San Ignacio Church on Calle Alsina at Calle Bolívar (one block west of Defensa) is another of the city's oldest buildings. Named the "Temple of the Company of Jesus," but known as San Ignacio, it was constructed in 1710. Brother Juan Krauss designed it to follow a typical Jesuit church with a central nave and upper galleries. The main altar, made of carved and gilded wood with baroque details, is quite beautiful. The image on the left nave of the altar is the oldest in the city; it depicts our Lady of Sorrow, who is actually the Virgin Mary. San Ignacio is known for its beautiful stained glass windows and magnificent baroque facade.

The church was occupied by invading British forces and by the forces of General Belgrano in 1811. This last was known as the "Long Hair Rebellion." Believe it or not, the whole struggle began when the soldiers rebelled against an order to have their hair cut, as long hair was no longer in fashion. Eight soldiers were executed in the Plaza de Mayo for their stubborness.

The Jesuits constructed many important cultural institutions in this area. Among them were a public library, a Jesuit college and university and several churches. You can still read the inscription marking the site of the university on Calle Alsina at Calle Peru. This area became the city's cultural center and a local newspaper dubbed it **Manzana de las Luces,** "The Square of the Enlightenment."

The Enlightenment is referred to as the Siglo de las Luces in Spanish.

Virtually all the Jesuit buildings were connected by a series of tunnels and catacombs. These were unearthed during later construction projects.

The southernmost border of San Telmo is marked by the **Parque Lezama**. This park, which once stood in a pastoral setting and is now surrounded by big city traffic and noise, has seen better days. The land was once reserved for use by the King of Spain but he never visited his colony. It passed through many hands until it was purchased by an American, Carlos Home, as a gift for his Argentinean wife. They purchased adjoining property and built the mansion that was the finest in the city.

Eventually the grounds were purchased by José de Lezama who gave it his name. He too enlarged the grounds which he filled with statues, monuments and fountains. Many still stand today. His two-story home sported a high watch tower from which he and his wife could look out over the entire area.

In 1884 the municipality purchased the land and the house, transforming the first into a public park and the second into the **National Historic Museum** (see Museums). Lezama Park once boasted a cinema, a circus and even a boxing ring. These no longer exist.

The Russian Orthodox Church of the Holy Trinity located at Brazil 315 at the north end of the park, is a curious building. The church was built in Buenos Aires by architect Alejandro Christophersen, based on designs by Mihail Timofeivich Preobrazensky of St. Petersburg,

Russia. The design followed a strict Byzantine line and the church opened its doors to the relatively small Russian Orthodox congregation in 1904. Later, during the reign of the Russian royals, Czar Nicholas II and Czarina Alexandra sent 50 boxes filled with religious objects of great value to the young church. The gifts included the stars you see on the domes, made to represent the stars in the sky, and the chains which join these domes together, used in Russia to protect the domes from wind and snowfall.

The main altar of the church is gold and the floor is covered with Persian carpets. It is often closed to visitors, so if you want to attend a service or visit, ring the intercom located at the side entrance. Someone is usually inside and they will tell you when the church is open. Weekday mornings seem to be the best times.

La Boca

No part of Buenos Aires is more fun to visit than La Boca. Its wide raised sidewalks and brightly painted homes, set three feet above the ground, were designed because the area often flooded when the Riachuelo River overflowed its banks. In fact, *porteño* friends told us this happened so often that the sailors and fishermen who were the district's first residents, kept a canoe tied to their front doors as a precaution.

When Buenos Aires was growing to the north of this district, few people chose the mouth of this small river as home. But it did become home to thousands of immigrants, particularly those from Genoa, Italy. Their spirit is alive in the

La Boca

1. Vuelta de Rocha
2. Ferias de Artes Plasticas Caminito
3. Caminito
4. Museo Bellas Artes Al Aire Libre "Caminito"
5. Museo de Cera de la Boca
6. Museo de Bellas Artes de la Boca de Artistas Argentinos
7. Teatro de la Ribera
8. Estadio de Boca
9. Buque Museo Corbeta A.R.A Uruguay
10. Parroquia San Juan Evangelista
11. Puenta Nicolas Avellaneda

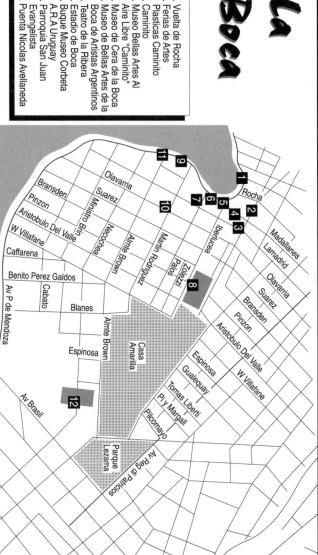

lively cantinas that open each evening, serving delicious Italian food and playing tarantella music. The life of the local fishermen takes on a distinct importance in the preparation of the "catch of the day," which is literally "of the day."

Art and Italians naturally walk hand in hand. The people that gave us Michelangelo and Fra Angelico adapted to their circumstances in a colorful way. You will understand this when you walk past **Caminito Street**, the dirt-paved alley that isn't much of a street at all. The corrugated tin shanties here have been painted in all colors of the palette and the outdoor artists' market echoes the lively scene in many of the paintings and watercolors for sale here. Caminito even lends its name to one of the most heart-wrenching tangos ever heard.

Some Background

The name of the district, "La Boca," means "The Mouth," stemming from its location at the mouth of the Riachuelo (Little River) that flows into the Río de la Plata. Some say this was the city's first port and it has functioned since the beginning of the city's history. A few revisionists point to this area as the initial founding spot by Pedro de Mendoza in 1536.

While the Riachuelo sounds romantic, its waters are dirty and polluted from the boats.

Mendoza's name lives on in the *barrio*'s main thoroughfare, but there is scant evidence that the city really started in La Boca. Not much is known about the district before 1800, when the first boatloads of immigrants arrived here. These European settlers found a land that was basically rural, made of country estates, farms and orchards. It was clear from that time on that the open spaces were not going to last very long, as the settlers saw vast opportunities, particularly near the river.

Warehouses sprang up along the riverside, and meat packing plants and curing houses replaced the grassy banks. The dry goods warehouses in La Boca purveyed their goods to all the boats that came to the Buenos Aires ports and soon business was thriving. A tramway installed in the 1870's served as the first link between the suburb and the central city and had a strong impact on La Boca's development.

La Boca was doomed to small time status, however, so long as the harbor was only capable of docking small vessels. In 1883 this minus was turned into a plus when a local engineer devised a plan for dredging the river and building a canal that could handle large overseas vessels. The first transatlantic steamer to dock there the following year was, appropriately enough, the *Italia*. By 1885 scores of Genovese had arrived with their families in tow. They liked the area and ships like the *Galileo*, overflowing with immigrants, kept on coming. Edmundo de Amicis, a writer of note, was one of these immigrants. In one novel he refers to La Boca as "a small district somewhat Genovese in nature." This reference was certainly true in Amicis' day, when over one million Italians populated the district.

They gave the area its unique look. The men worked building the warehouses, docks and bridges we see today. They came with empty pockets, and lived in ramshackle lean-tos constructed from odds and ends left over from community projects. The houses were built on piles to protect them from floods, which occurred frequently. The government allowed them to keep whatever paint was left over as well. Often the paint was only enough to cover one wall of the house, so another color was used to paint the doors and still another for the window frames. Color co-ordination was a mere coincidence.

The multi-colored houses and *cantinas* of today mimic these early dwellings. The plaster walls are painted in pastel tones – with three or four colors applied to each. The streets are built up, so the houses are well above ground level to avoid the flooding when southwesterly winds blow. These houses remain, but this area of La Boca is shrinking. Much of it contains modern apartment buildings and street-level sidewalks. You will want to spend your time in the distinctive waterfront area.

In addition to the houses, other La Boca sights include the **ships cemetery**, anchored vessels, some still navigable, others rusting away into ghosts of their former selves; a **weekend art fair**; and a **fine arts museum**. No-frills *cantinas* in the wildly painted buildings are open for lunch but roar into life at night. They are family-run restaurants with a limited menu and unlimited entertainment - part of which is supplied by you if you join in the tarentella dancing and singing. More about *cantinas* in "Buenos Aires After Dark."

La Boca is one of the few areas in Buenos Aires that is not safe to wander through at night. If you intend to dine and dance here, take a cab to and from Nicochea Street.

The Daytime in La Boca

Whether you arrive by bus, bicycle or taxi, your first acquaintance with La Boca will likely be by way of **Avenida Pedro de Mendoza**. This circuitous road extends from Avenida Brasil, near the Parque Lezama, and follows the course of the Riachuelo. It also bypasses the "Catalina Sur" complex, a relatively new development of 1,800 much-needed apartments in a modern self-contained mini-city. Beyond this complex you enter vintage La Boca, greeted at the outset by the Fine Arts Museum of La Boca.

The museum is open Wednesday to Friday from 8 a.m. to 6 p.m., weekdays from 8 a.m. to 12 noon and 2 p.m. to 6 p.m.

The Artists' Museum of Fine Arts of La Boca, located at Pedro de Mendoza 1835, is also called the Benito Quinquela Martín Museum, in honor of the illustrious artist who lived at this spot. The museum and children's school were founded in 1936 after Quinquela had collected numerous works through both donations and purchases. Today the museum contains over 800 paintings, sculptures, drawings and other works of art. Only works by Argentinean artists may be displayed by the terms of Quinquela's will.

Almirante is the Spanish word for admiral.

A few blocks away at the intersection of Pedro de Mendoza and Avenida Almirante Brown you will see the maritime museum called **Museo Corbeta A.R.A. Uruguay**. The ship displays nautical items. It is open from 1 p.m. to 6:30 p.m., weekends and holidays.

Just opposite Avenida Almirante Brown you'll see the enormous **Avellaneda Bridge** spanning the Riachuelo. The bridge provides the area with a wonderful view over the city, the river and the other side of Avellaneda district. Lovers enjoy the solitude up there, especially on a Sunday when the escalators aren't running and you have to walk about four flights to reach the top-level walkway.

There are actually two bridges at this site. The old Nicolas Avellaneda Bridge, now called the **Black Bridge**, was a transport bridge that served the locals for years. Pressing commercial requirements made the bridge obsolete, so a heavier duty bridge was erected in 1940 to link Buenos Aires with the populous suburb of Avellaneda. The bridge, by the way, weighs over 1,000 tons and is made of steel and cement.

Avenida Pedro de Mendoza follows the turn in the river that marks its mouth. It was here that the original port began and here too is the ships cemetery. The small village square, located between Pedro de Mendoza and Dr. Del Valle Ibarlucea Street, is called **Vuelta de Rocha** because the land was formerly owned by a wealthy gent named Antonio Rocha. The monument here, a mast, rudder and anchor standing on a mound of rocks, pays homage to the sailors lost at sea. If you look across the water from the Vuelta you can see the opposite bank where Almirante Guillermo Brown, Argentina's greatest naval hero, had **La Maestranza** shipyard built. Ships fighting in the battle for independence were repaired here. Owing to this, the Vuelta de Rocha square also has a bust of Almirante Brown in its center.

Fronting the Vuelta you will see **Caminito**, a short lane only one block long, located between Calles Magallanes and Lamadrid. Caminito

Caminito hosts a weekend art fair/flea market year round.

was originally a side track for the local railway and later Benito Quinquela Martín and other La Boca residents convinced the city to remove the rails and pave the alley. The initiative resulted in the picturesque street you see today. Caminito has no sidewalks or doorways but it does have outlandishly colored walls and balconies and windows decorated by the artists and writers that live in the area. Among them was Juan de Dios Filiberto, a poet and lifelong Bohemian who made Caminito his home for years. He immortalized this street in his well-known tango *Caminito*.

Every Saturday from 12 noon to 6 p.m. and every Sunday from 10 a.m. to 6 p.m. there is a flea market/art fair on Caminito. Artists paint colorful La Boca scenes and denizens. These original works of art (oils, pastels, and charcoal) are available in all price ranges and will remain favorites long after you return home. At the entrance to the street, you will see the sculpture by Roberto Capurro called *San Martín and his People*. There are other works here by Ibarra Garcia, Vergottini, Marisa Krause, José de Luca and others. In addition to the open-air art market, remember that Caminito is famous for the tango, which was born in the little tin houses that line the block. In the spring and summer there are tango festivals organized by the municipality. They are particularly interesting because of the unusual backdrops that enhance the dancing.

Calle Necochea, which meets Avenida Pedro de Mendoza at Vuelta de Rocha, is the street of Italian *cantinas* and late night entertainment. It is also the street where Aristotle Onassis lived in the days before he became a billionaire ship-builder and the husband of Jackie Kennedy. It is one of La Boca's best loved yarns.

When Onassis was still in his teens he immigrated to Argentina from the ravaged city of Smyrna in Turkey. He thought opportunity awaited him and he was right. He started as a boatman, ferrying people back and forth on the muddy Riachuelo under the Black Bridge.

Later he started a cigarette manufacturing business (he rolled each cigarette by hand at the beginning). This enabled him to buy his first broken-down old boat. The boat was restored, sold at a good profit and proved to be more lucrative than cigarettes or telephones (he was also working nights in central Buenos Aires as foreman in charge of the telephone systems that were being installed during his tenure there). The rest, as they say, is history. Ask any local about the man and they'll point out the café he frequented and the room he rented in those days of great expectations. Budding shipping magnates and others all have a great time in the *cantinas* of Necochea Street.

You may also want to visit the **Santuario de Nuestra Señora Madre de los Immigrantes** at Necochea 3112. The church was consecrated in 1967 and has a special significance for the people of La Boca, who identify strongly with feelings of rootlessness or transience. The Virgin honored by this church watches over people who have left their comfortable roots and had the courage to start a new life, as many residents of La Boca have.

Calle Olavarría is one of La Boca's most interesting streets. Look for the lovely **St. John the Evangelist Church**, which is a rebuilt version of the original church that stood on this site in 1855. This is really a neighborhood church, shown in the art work brought from Turin to grace the inner chapel. It is typical of a turn-of-the-century church in the north of Italy, the ancestral home of many La Boca residents.

Nearby you'll see **Plaza Solís** (at Suarez), a small square lined by naval supply houses and sailor cafés. Here you'll glimpse the underside of La Boca, away from the relative glitz of the *cantinas*. A notable sculpture called *Sailor's Mother* depicts a woman whose expression betrays the anxiety of waiting for a child to return from the sea.

La Boca Fútbol (Soccer) Stadium

While the Italians have given La Boca its most distinctive touches, the British too have left their mark. They introduced soccer to the Argentineans and two of the country's finest teams started in La Boca. The La Boca Club was formed in 1905 by a group of men who played together in nearby Solís Square. The stadium at Calle Brandsen 805 is called the **Bombonera** (Candy Box) by locals. Inaugurated in 1940, the cement structure has a capacity of 70,000 persons.

Members of the La Boca Athletic Club participate in sports other than soccer. Basketball, cycling and *bochas*, an Argentinean version of bowling, are pursued with energy, but never with the zeal or passion attached to *fútbol*. The *fútbol* rivalry between La Boca and River Plate (the other team that started here) is legendary and their matches are always exciting to watch. As one Buenos Aires resident told me "Para nosotros fútbol es como comer (For us, fútbol is as important as eating)." When the La Boca Juniors win their weekly encounters with other First Division clubs, you'll surely spot the blue and gold colors of the Junior flag waving above the stadium. This is a great place to watch a game. Check schedules with your concierge or in the sporting event listings in the *Buenos Aires Herald*..

Lunch in La Boca

Have a slice of pizza or more likely a whole individual pie in a pan on Almirante Brown. This road parallel to Necochea is La Boca's main shopping area and is well known for its pizza parlors. Men selling pizza on the streets of La Boca were a common sight even at the turn of the century. Hence the area considers itself the prime purveyor of this snack.

La Boca After Dark

The *cantinas* of Necochea are informal and lusty. If you are an extrovert and enjoy singing and dancing for your supper, by all means spend a night here. For specifics check "Dining in La Boca."

Palermo

Palermo, north of Recoleta and Palermo Chico, resembles many of Buenos Aires' middle class neighborhoods. What makes Palermo special is that it is home to a wonderful park, the city's zoo, planetarium, exposition hall, botanical garden, its loveliest race track and the polo fields. There is a used book fair along Avenida Libertador on weekends as well. Quiet on weekdays, Palermo is crowded on weekends year-round.

Getting There

It's easy to get to Palermo. The best way is to hop Subte Line D (Catedral -Pacífico) to the final stop, where you'll find yourself at Plaza Italia in the heart of Palermo. The ride takes 20 minutes. Buses 10, 152 and 60 leave from downtown as well.

Palermo Park

Head to the park during the week to avoid the crowds.

Inaugurated in 1875, this has been a favorite weekend getaway ever since. The land was once uninhabited marshland. Fortunately for *porteños*, the dictator Juan Manuel de Rosas (who ruled for 30 years) decided to drain the area and build a palatial home on it. He had orange and magnolia trees planted along with various exotic plants. After Rosas was overthrown in 1852, the property lay idle until President Sarmiento decided to turn it into a public park. The area was redesigned, filled with beautiful monuments and sculpted figures (most are gifts to the Argentine people from foreign countries) and opened by President Avellaneda.

The grounds are large, with five lakes and grassy fields for sunning, picnicking and soccer games. There are jogging and bicycling paths. You can rent bicycles near the park entrance and small rowboats or pedal crafts for a tour of the lakes.

Some spots within the park are particularly lovely. Look for the **Patio Andaluz**, also called the Garden of Carnations. It is a small courtyard lit by colonial lamps and a central fountain surrounded by benches decorated with Spanish tiles. The court was a gift from the city of Seville, Spain.

The **Rosaleda** (Rosedale) is an elegant rose garden in the center of the park. The entire area is filled with beautiful sculpture and there are small, romantic tea rooms.

El Puente Blanco (The White Bridge) spans a portion of the lake near the Rosaleda and is marked by an enormous cage filled with colorful birds. Local lore has dubbed this "Lovers' Bridge." It seems that if you walk back and forth across it twice with the same person, that person will become your lover.

If you cross the bridge and follow the red brick road, you'll soon find yourself in the **Jardín de los Poetas** (Poet's Garden), marked by a bust of the Italian poet Dante Alighieri.

Before you leave the park, pay a visit to the **Japanese Garden** on Calle Casares and its authentic tea house. Within the garden there is a pond with five small islands joined by bridges. The charming rock-garden pagoda creates a

The Tea House is open from 10 a.m.-8 p.m. every day except Monday.

lovely setting for the Tea House, where the atmosphere couldn't be more idyllic. In the evenings the Tea House gets rather crowded and it pays to call ahead (tel. 785-7049 for reservations). Really lovely!

Touring the Park

An inexpensive way to get an overview of the park is to hire a *mateo*, a horse-drawn carriage, for a 20-minute tour of the highlights. You can then head back to your favorite spots on foot. *Mateos* are hired at Plaza Italia or Avenida Sarmiento near the entrance to the zoo.

Look for the "Spaniards' Monument" at the entrance on Avenida Libertador. It was a gift from Spain on Argentina's centennial.

The **Jardín Zoológico** (Palermo Zoo) is a great stop if you are traveling with kids or even if you aren't. Just over 100 years old, it specializes in South American wildlife, although it has species from all over the globe. The original animals were bought in Germany but over the years the zoo has grown to house more than 100 species, plus birds and reptiles. It's hard to see lions and panthers in cages, but the architects have attempted to house the animals in a setting as close to their natural habitat as possible. The llamas live in an Inca temple and the Asian elephants inhabit a Hindu temple.

Don't miss the majestic condors, native birds of the Cordilleras, which are difficult to raise in captivity.

In addition to the animals, the **Sarmiento Theater** stages plays for kids and games and events that they will enjoy. If walking is too much, hop on the mini-train that leaves continuously from the gate on Avenida Las Heras. The entrance to the zoo is at Avenida Las Heras and Sarmiento.

The **Jardín Botánico** (Botanical Garden) is across from the zoo on Avenida Las Heras. This 150-acre retreat is a frequent destination for *porteños* seeking a restful spot to read a book or take a nap in the sun. You can wander through the grounds, home to over 6,000 different species of plants, and sit and relax throughout. There are lovely sculptures, fountains and greenhouses. One personal favorite is the Pond of the Water Lilies near the entrance.

Open Daily: 8 a.m.-8 p.m. summer and 8 a.m.-6 p.m. winter.

A small museum, **Museo Botánico**, houses plants and trees native to Argentina as well as exhibits explaining the uses of sugar cane, jute and cocoa.

Entrance is free. Open 8 a.m.-12 noon and 2 p.m. - 6 p.m. Closed Wednesdays.

The **Galileo Galilei Planetarium** at Avenidas Figueroa Alacorte and Sarmiento in Palermo Woods is well worth a visit if only to see the sky of the southern hemisphere, which is very different from that of the north. Look for the Southern Cross. No children under 7 are allowed. Outside, stop for a look at the sundial, which was a gift from Japan.

Shows on Saturday and Sunday. Check schedules.

The **Predio Ferial de Palermo** (Palermo Fairgrounds), across from the zoo, is the site of expositions year-round. While attending a car or toy show may not be exciting, if you are in Buenos Aires in July or August when *La Rural* is underway, you should consider attending. It is an agricultural exposition with exhibits from all over the world. Most interesting are the riding shows, featuring *gauchos*. It's not something urban North American's get to see often.

The **Argentine Racetrack** and **National Polo Fields** are also in Palermo, a few blocks north of the park on Avenida Libertador.

The Parks of Buenos Aires

Buenos Aires is a city of plazas and parks, filled with striking monuments, cool fountains and winding flower-bedecked paths. Many of the parks have sporting facilities such as golf courses, tennis courts, and bike paths. Others host art and book fairs on weekends.

Parque Tres de Febrero, Avenida Presidente Pedro Montt at Avenida Infanta Isabel, is not far from the Rosaleda in Los Bosques de Palermo. Aquatic cycles and canoes used by dreamy lovers and families at leisure join swans as the primary attractions.

Parque Jorge Newbury, Avenida Figueroa Alcorta 3585. This large municipal park, not far from the Aeroparque Jorge Newbury, has bicycle paths and outdoor tennis courts.

Street Fairs

The following are flea markets that go on regularly for the locals. The merchandise runs the gamut in cost and quality, but the atmosphere is always 100% *porteño*.

The Caminito Street Art Fair, La Boca, every day from 11 a.m.-7 p.m. One of the best street fairs in the city, the colorful tin houses are the inspiration for many of the small oils and watercolors on sale here. Prices range from a few dollars to sky high.

The Plaza Dorrego Fair, Defensa and Humbert I in San Telmo. 10 a.m.-5 p.m., Saturday and Sunday. This is the foremost place for antique hunting. Street performers will entertain you as you browse.

The Parque Lezama Artisan's Fair, Martín Garcia and Paseo Colón, Weekends 11 a.m.-6 p.m. This is a weekend ritual for the avant-garde. Another artisan's fair is also held weekends on the **Plaza Alvear,** Avenidas Pueyrredón and Libertador.

The Plaza Manuel Belgrano, Avenida Juramento and Obligado in Belgrano. Weekends 11 a.m.-6 p.m. This is another lively art fair with a bohemian flavor.

The Plazoleta Santa Fe, Avenida Santa Fe at Urriarte in Palermo. Weekends, 11 a.m.-6 p.m. Another fair worth a visit.

The Plaza Houssay, Avenida Córdoba and Junín, Weekdays 11 a.m.-6 p.m. This is a popular midweek place to visit.

Book Fairs

Most books are second-hand and in Spanish. If you read Spanish, you might find a few gems. You may run across a few books in English, as well as some eye-catching prints and posters. Fairs are held Monday through Friday from 10 a.m. to 6 p.m. on the **Plaza Lavalle** between

We picked up a first edition of an early Borges book. A real gem.

Lavalle and Libertad; on the **Plaza Almagro** at Presidente J.D. Perón and Salguero; and on the **Plazoleta del Tango** at Avenida Corrientes and Bouchard, not far from Luna Park.

Spectator Sports

Soccer (Fútbol)

As is true throughout South America and Europe, soccer is a national passion in Argentina. They have won two World Cups, and barely lost in the 1990 Championship game (though the Argentinean team did not fare so well in the 1994 World Cup). Diego Maradona, the Argentine star, ranks among the finest players of recent times. Children learn to play soccer as soon as they can walk and clubs function in much the same way as U.S. Little Leagues. There are many local teams in Buenos Aires, but the most intense rivalry is between the La Boca and River Plate teams. Matches are held from September to June on Sunday afternoons at the **River Plate Stadium**. Tickets should be purchased in advance (your concierge may be able to help you here). The stadium seats 38,000 and has standing room for an equal number of fans.

The stadium is located 10 minutes away by cab.

Polo

The British influence is huge in Argentina and polo has been played here since 1875. The nation's top stars rank among the world's finest players. **The National Polo Fields** on Avenida Libertador in Palermo are the site of exciting matches. There are two playing fields and a grandstand for spectators. Championship games are played in November and December.

Check listings in the Buenos Aires Herald.

You will be surprised at how exciting a match can be and by the amazing skill of the players. Before you know it, you'll be rooting for one of the teams just as you would back home.

Pato

Pato (duck), a sport native to Argentina, is also played on horseback. It originated in the early 17th century with the *gauchos* and *criollos* who lived on the pampas. At that time, a duck was placed into a leather bag and tossed from team-mate to teammate until a goal was scored. The game was so rough that players were trampled to death and it had to be banned. Aficionados revised the rules to create a gentler version and the sport was revived in the 1940's. Though just as fast-paced as before, pato is now played by four-man teams and the duck has been replaced by a leather ball with handles. The object is to score by throwing the ball through a net hung from a field post – much like a basketball net.

Matches are held at *estancias* near the city and occasionally at the Palermo Polo Fields. Check listings in the *Buenos Aires Herald* or with your concierge or the tourist office.

Horseracing

The **Hipódromo Argentino** in Palermo is the scene of big money races and assorted championships. It has dirt tracks and seating for 70,000. Admission runs between $12 and $24 for seats. The minimum bet is $2. Check the *Buenos Aires Herald* for schedules or call the racetrack at 774-6807. Good luck.

Weekly handicap magazines are ubiquitous at kiosks.

The suburb of San Isidro is easily reachable by cab or the Bartolome Mitre commuter railroad that heads to Tigre.

The **Jockey Track** in San Isidro is another popular track. Races are run on grass and are generally held on Wednesdays and during the weekend. Check the *Buenos Aires Herald* for schedules or call the track at 743-4011.

Boxing

Boxing matches are held at the **Luna Park Stadium**, located downtown at the corner of Corrientes and Bouchard. Fights are usually held on Wednesday and Saturday evenings. Tickets run between $6 and $15 for ordinary bouts. Major events will cost significantly more.

Other spectator sports taking place in or near the city include tennis, rugby, cricket and auto racing. Check the *Buenos Aires Herald* for listings.

Participant Sports

If walking through Buenos Aires does not satisfy your need for physical activity, you'll find plenty of more active alternatives, including biking or jogging through Palermo and Costanera Norte.

Tennis

Clay courts are the norm here. Call in advance to reserve a court and to confirm fees.

Buenos Aires Lawn & Tennis Club, Olleros 1510, tel 772-9227.
San Remo Tennis Club, Chacabuco 1260, tel 362-5399.
La Mirage Tennis Club, Salta 1275, tel 23-9332.

Solís Tennis Courts, Calle Solís 1252, tel 27-5400.

Squash

Tribunales Club de Squash, Montevideo 556, tel 49-8358.
Hipo's Tennis Squash, Avenida Libertador 6301. Tel 781-8910.

Golf

Golf courses are located at private clubs near the city. You may be able to play at some of them during the week. For general information on golf in Argentina, contact the **Argentine Golf Association** at Avenida Corrientes 538, tel 394-3743.

Boulogne Golf Club, Boulogne, tel 765-7525.
San Isidro Golf Club, San Isidro, tel 766-6625.
Campo Municipal de Golf, Bosques de Palermo, tel 772-7576.
Driving Range, Costanera Norte.

Horseback Riding

Centro de Actividades Hípicas, Avenida Figueroa Alcorta, tel 772-3826.

Ice Skating

Frappe, Avenida Sarmiento 1662. Open 10 a.m.-1 a.m.
Madison Rink, Avenida Las Heras 3060. Open 9 a.m.-midnight.

Swimming Pools Plus

Pools (indoor, outdoor, heated, etc.) are located at sports centers in different parts of the city, as well as in many hotels. Besides swimming pools, they have many other sports facilities. **Windsurfers** can get in some practice at the **Parque Norte** at the intersection of Calles Cantilo and Güiraldes in Costanera Norte. **Parque Jorge Newbery** is at Avenida Figueroa Alcorta 3,800 in Palermo. **Parque Presidente Sarmiento**, Avenida Del Tejar, 4,600, has several swimming pools and tennis, basketball and handball courts. **KDT Sports Park**, Avenida Figueroa Alcorta, has a running track, an indoor pool and several tennis courts.

Two Special Attractions Outside the City

La Reserva Ecológica de la Costanera Sur

This ecological reserve is a wetlands park located on the waterfront south of the city. It is a five-minute taxi ride from Plaza de Mayo but you can walk there in under 30 minutes. Stretching for over two miles, this network of lagoons and marshes was created in the 1970's, as the beaches that once lined the southern shore became polluted. Dikes were built of landfill refuse; then the river's silt and mother nature took over. There are trails along the dikes and the area is filled with flowers. Birds roam freely, unafraid of human visitors. Cranes, swans and colorful birds we'd never seen before soar through the air over the tall grasses. Open daily from 7 a.m. to 7 p.m. Closed major holidays.

Daytrip to Tigre

Tigre, a suburb of Buenos Aires, is a popular getaway from the city, particularly on warm spring and summer weekends. Located on the delta formed as the Paraná River joins the River Plate, the town is crowded with fabulous homes, rowing, boating and yacht clubs, as well as small eateries. These are the vacation homes and private clubs of wealthy *porteños,* who spend long weekends and school holidays here. Less affluent homes are here as well, and *porteños* flock to the area on weekends because it is very green and has many recreational areas. Tigre is easily reached by commuter rail from Retiro Station in under 45 minutes and for less than $2 roundtrip.

Pack a picnic lunch to eat along the grassy areas that line the river (these stretch for miles) or on one of the catamarans or speedboats that tour the area. The waterfront promenade is easily walked and there is a small natural museum.

There are 16 stops from Retiro Station to Tigre. Some are important bedroom communities you might like to explore. Many Buenos Aires professionals live in Olivos, Martínez and Belgrano. You can get off at any of these stops. Trains run frequently. Tigre is a relaxing way to spend a summer afternoon.

Buenos Aires Museums

Buenos Aires is a museum buff's delight. The city boasts dozens of museums with collections dedicated to art, both classical and pop, sculpture, history, weapons, coins, science and theater, to name but a few. While the city proudly upholds its reputation for classical art, Buenos Aires was also the first city in Latin America to host an exhibition of pop art by Andy Warhol.

Just as Paris was a center for scores of expatriate artists, Buenos Aires could boast of its own Delacroix – **Prilidiano Pueyrredón** – a major figure whose vast historical tableaus tell the colonial history of Argentina and resurrect from the ashes the visages of the haughty and handsome nobility of its early years.

Although we discuss many museums in detail, we have by no means covered all. Hours and phone numbers were accurate at press time. But double-check them before setting out since they do have a tendency to change.

In recent years art in Argentina has taken on a more embattered sensibility. This feeling is most evident in the art of **Urruchua**, a member of the old school of moderns who paints with his Basque patriotism on the tip of his brush. In a great number of Argentinean artists, this embattlement has its source in the nation's troubled history. The influx of immigrant artists, including a large number of Asians, has added a new dimension to the cultural scene.

Buenos Aires has a wonderful collection of sculpture, both small and monumental in size, including an impressive collection of pieces by Rodin. Religious art is another genre where superb examples of native talent are to be seen. Much of this art comes from Peru and is of the Cuzco school. A great deal of religious art was brought to Argentina from Spain and Portugal as well.

Since the museums are scattered throughout the downtown area and in the *barrios*, you can combine your neighborhood tours with museum visits.

EL MUSEO NACIONAL DE BELLAS ARTES
Avenida Libertador 1437, Recoleta.
Tel 803-4062.
Open: Tuesday-Sunday 9 a.m.-12:45 p.m.; 3 p.m.-7 p.m.
The National Fine Arts Museum is one of the finest in South America. If you have time to visit just one museum, this should be it. Be sure to allow yourself plenty of time. Comparable to the best museums in Europe and North America, its collections can't be seen in a single day, making a bit of pre-planning necessary.

The museum was founded in 1895 by a group of intellectuals who decided that the city desperately needed a space to house its growing collection of art treasures. The original museum was on Calle Florida, but it quickly outgrew that space. Its collections were later installed in the large Belle Epoque building which you see today.

The museum's 34 halls are overflowing with masterpieces from every epoch and culture. Most outstanding among them are the Rodin sculptures. His *Hand of God* and the *Head of Balzac* are as dramatic as the *Danaides* are sinuous and beautiful. The French Impressionism collection is also quite noteworthy and includes works by Degas, Corot, Courbet, Manet, Sisley and Van Gogh. The five rooms devoted to Degas are a wonderful surprise and include several of his *Ballerina* studies. Leger, Modigliani, Bourdin, Daumier, and Pissaro round out the collection.

The museum also has an admirable collection of 16th and 17th century art that includes works by Rembrandt and Rubens as well as Gobelins tapestries. Spanish paintings includes El Greco's *Jesus on the Mount of Olives* and an entire room devoted to Goya.

Nor has contemporary art been overlooked. Paintings by Othon Friesz, Giorgio Morandi, Kandinski and Klee, as well as some lesser known pieces by De Chirico, Nevelson, Picasso and Franz Kline make this a notable collection. Located in another wing of the museum is a stupendous collection of Argentinean art, which is not unlike French Impressionism, although the subject matter might be the *pampas*, or the privileged ladies of early Buenos Aires society. The historical painters and portraitists were instrumental in creating the true Argentinean style. Key artists to look for are Emilio Pettorutti, Ernesto de la Cárcova, Pueyrrdón, Morel, Pellegrini, Butler and Panozzi.

EL MUSEO HISTÓRICO NACIONAL
Defensa 1600, San Telmo.
Tel 27-4767
Guided tours in English can be arranged.
Open: Thursday-Sunday, 2 p.m.-6 p.m.
Housed in the Italianate Villa Lezama built in 1857, the National History Museum traces the history of Argentina in a series of displays, each devoted to a stage of the nation's development

– the Discovery, the Conquest, the Viceroyship and Jesuit Missionaries, the English Invasions, and the Wars of Independence. Highlights include bolts from Christopher Columbus' ship, the *Santa María*, an original map of Buenos Aires drawn by Juan de Garay, a fascinating Indian sundial from the 16th century, and the emblem of Potosí, a shield worked in silver and gold depicting South America that was presented to General Belgrano by the citizens of Potosí, Bolivia.

EL MUSEO DE MOTIVOS ARGENTINOS JOSÉ HERNÁNDEZ
Avenida del Libertador 2373, Recoleta.
Tel 802-7294.
Open: Tuesday-Friday 1 p.m.-7 p.m.; weekends 3 p.m.-7 p.m. Admission free on Wednesdays.

The José Hernández Museum of Argentine Folklore was donated to the city in 1984 by Don Felix Bunge, a conscientious statesman, to ensure the preservation of the folklore and legends of the Argentine countryside and native population. Marvelous displays of engraved *mates* and *bombillas*, cowboy belts and spurs highlight the great artistry of the silversmiths of the *pampas*. Other *gaucho* paraphernalia include ponchos, rawhide traveling trunks, saddles from Brazil and Uruguay, and handmade *boleadores*, which are lariats with hard leather balls attached to the ends.

Among the most interesting pieces on display are pottery, textiles, wool and leather ornaments. There is also a fine exhibit dedicated to typical musical instruments such as the Criollo Harp; small guitars known as Charangos which are played in the northwest as well as other Andean countries; and drums, music boxes, Indian harps and flutes from Corrientes and Santiago del Estero.

MUSEO HISTÓRICO DEL CABILDO Y LA REVOLUCIÓN DE MAYO
Calle Bolívar 65.
Tel 30-1782.
Open: Thursday-Sunday 2 p.m.-6 p.m.

This white-washed colonial building, easily the quaintest in Buenos Aires, was built in 1725 and was the site of the original junta. Its clock tower and arched porticos have become symbols of the city. Occupied by the British in the 1800's, it underwent many architectural changes until it was declared a national museum in 1960. Today it houses a fine collection of artifacts from Argentina's colonial period including military weapons, flags, treaties, and religious art from the Jesuit Missions.

Most impressive is the Sala Capítular where the meetings leading to Argentina's independence were held. It has been faithfully restored to recreate the spirit of that period.

EL MUSEO DE LA CASA DEL GOBIERNO
H. Yrigoyen 219, entrance at Calle Balcarce 24.
Tel 30-1774.
Hours: The museum was under renovation at press time and was open by appointment only.

Located not far from the Cabildo across from the Plaza de Mayo, the Government House Museum is housed in what was originally a fort and later became the Customs House. It is a fascinating building with subterranean passageways and cavernous chambers. Sections of the original walls are still standing. There are 19 underground galleries dating from the early part of the 17th century which were discovered in 1942. The museum features memorabilia from the different administrations throughout Argentina's history starting with the founding of Buenos Aires in 1580 by Juan de Garay.

EL MUSEO MITRE
Avenida San Martín 336.
Tel 394-8670.
Open: Tuesday-Friday, 1 p.m.-6 p.m.
This is the former home of the much celebrated general who went on to found the intellectual daily newspaper *La Nacion*, in addition to serving as President of the Republic. The museum, much of which is just as it was when the general was living there, is best known for its library, coin and map collection, and its collection of historic documents.

EL MUSEO DE LA CIUDAD
DE BUENOS AIRES
Alsina 412, San Telmo.
Tel 313-2123.
Open: Monday-Friday, 11 a.m.-7 p.m.; Sunday 3 p.m.-7 p.m. Free admission on Wednesday.
The residence of an upper class family at the turn of the century has been recreated. A rotating display of vintage photographs features scenes representative of the period, including *bandonéon* players who live on "amor perdido" (lost love) and the centavos in their cigar boxes, tango dancers and throngs of youth spilling out of late-night cafés.

Located in the lovely Palermo Chico barrio. San Martín is the Argentinean hero.

EL INSTITUTO NACIONAL SANMARTINIANO
Calle Mariscal Ramón Castilla at Aguado (Palermo Chico).
Open: Monday-Friday 9 a.m.-12 noon; 2 p.m.-5 p.m. Weekends, 2 p.m.-5 p.m.
General San Martín's home in Boulogne Sur Mer, France, where he lived in exile from 1834 to 1848, has been faithfully reproduced in this two-story museum founded in 1946. The San Martín Academy and Library are on the ground floor, while documents, writings and other of the General's personal effects are on display upstairs.

MUSEO DE ARTE HISPANOAMÉRICANO ISAAC FERNÁNDEZ BLANCO
Suipacha 1422.
Tel 327-0272.
Open: Tuesday-Sunday, 3 p.m.-8 p.m.
Set in a Spanish-Baroque Villa complete with courtyard and colorful Talavera tiles, the Museum of Hispanic American Art is home to an extensive collection of colonial art from throughout South America. Among its collections are religious art from the Cuzco School as well as Misiones, traditional Jacaranda furniture from Brazil, beautifully ornate *peinetones* – the tortoise shell hairpieces favored by wealthy señoras, and *mates* and *bombillas* in all sorts of fanciful shapes.

EL MUSEO DE TEATRO COLÓN
Tucumán 1161.
Tel 35-5414.
Open Monday-Friday, 10 a.m.-6 p.m. Guided tours ($4) every hour on the hour, 9 a.m.-4 p.m., Monday-Friday; Saturdays, 9 a.m.-12 noon.

This small museum within Buenos Aires' world famous Colón Opera House features a collection of original scripts, photographs, instruments, costumes and documents associated with the artists who have performed here since 1908. We urge you to take advantage of the guided tours offered every hour.

You will enjoy this tour even if you're not an opera buff.

EL MUSEO ETNOGRÁFICO JUAN B. AMBROSETTI
Moreno 350, San Telmo.
Tel 34-4970.
Open: Tuesday-Friday, 2 p.m.-6 p.m., weekends until 7 p.m.

The Juan B. Ambrosetti Ethnographic Museum boasts one of the most important anthropological/ethnographic collections in the world, with over 35,000 pieces, all of which have been classified into groups such as anthropology, archaeology, craftsmanship and folklore. Artifacts from early South American cultures, especially those of Peru and Patagonia include interesting ceramics from the Andes. Also of interest are urns from as far away as Micronesia, Melanesia and Polynesia, and a Buddhist altar over 1,000 years old from the Shin-su sect in Japan.

EL MUSEO DE BELLAS ARTES DE LA BOCA
Avenida Pedro de Mendoza 1935.
Tel 21-1080.
Open: Wednesday-Friday, 8 a.m. to 6 p.m.; Saturday, 8 a.m. to 12 noon, 2 p.m. to 6 p.m.; Sunday, 10 a.m. to 6 p.m.

Contemporary Argentine artists including Pío Collivadino, Eduardo Sivori, and sculptors Yrutia and Rocha are well represented at La Boca's Museum of Fine Arts. The museum is housed in the former residence of the artist Benito Quinquela Martín, who bequeathed the building to the city in his will. The painter's series of 11 paintings, *Cemetery of Ships*, is featured, as well as a collection of wooden mastheads salvaged from Italian ships during the last century.

EL MUSEO NACIONAL DE ARTE ORIENTAL Y DECORATIVO
Avenida Libertador 1902, Recoleta.
Tel 802-0914 or 801-5988.
Open: Wednesday-Monday, 3 p.m. -7 p.m.

The National Museum of Oriental and Decorative Art is located in the Errazuriz Palace, which was the residence of Chilean Diplomat Matos Errazuriz and his wife until 1937 when it was purchased by the Argentine government.

It is actually two museums in one. The Museum of Oriental Art is on the top floor and features splendid examples of Chinese, Hindu, Tibetan, Japanese and Islamic art. Collections include silver, copper and bronze coins from the Han Dynasty circa 200 B.C.; ceramic dogs from the Ching Dynasty; Samurai weapons and Katana sabres of the Shoguns; Turkish swords and scimitars; Nepalese and Tibetan religious artifacts; and a collection of fifth-century Buddhas from India.

The Museum of Decorative Art is on the ground floor and features dozens of Argentine family portraits, immense gold and silver collections, and fabulous art and furniture from around the world.

**EL MUSEO HISTÓRICO Y NUMISMÁTICO
DE LA BANCO DE LA NACIÓN
ARGENTINA
Bartolomé Mitre 326.
Tel 342-4041.
Request a private tour on extension 607. Open
Monday-Friday 10 a.m.-4 p.m.**

The Museum of History and Numismatics of
the Argentine National Bank is located in the
huge marble and stone edifice built by architect
Alejandro Bustillo on the site of the original
Colón Theater. On display are the earliest Argentine currency and documents relating to numismatics. The fountain in the main room of the
first floor was a gift from the Bank of Uruguay.

Art Galleries

In addition to scores of museums, Buenos Aires
is also home to some fine private galleries. Here
are just a few of our favorites. Check a recent
issue of *Where* for a more complete listing.

**ZURBARÁN GALLERY
Cerrito 1522.
Tel 22-1566.
Open: Monday-Friday, 10:30 a.m.-9 p.m., Saturday 10:30 a.m.-1 p.m.**
The best of Argentina's creative talent is featured at the Zurbarán. Exhibits favor the more
traditional contemporary artists who find their
inspiration in the *pampas* and daily life of the
gauchos as well as the Spanish masters Goya and
Velasquez.

COLECCIÓN ALVEAR DE ZURBARÁN
Avenida Alvear 1658.
Tel 41-3004.
Open: Monday-Friday 10:30 a.m.-9 p.m.; Saturday, 10:30 a.m.-1 p.m.
Sister to the Zurbarán, the Colección Alvear features works by well-known Argentinean and European artists. Among the artists represented here is Fernando Fader (1882-1935). Considered by many to be Argentina's premiere artist, he is best known for his scenes of early Argentina.

PRAXIS
Arenales 1311.
Tel 812-6254.
Open: Monday-Friday 10 a.m.-8 p.m.; Saturday, 10 a.m.-2 p.m.
A leader in avant-garde Latin American art, Praxis has branches in São Paulo, Santiago, Lima and Mexico City and has earned an international reputation for the fine artists it represents, including the South American painters Botero, Tamayo, Matta and Rivera. Original works as well as outstanding lithographs and screenprints are featured here.

WILDENSTEIN
Córdoba 618
A member of a group of galleries frequented by sophisticated patrons of the arts the world over, this is one of the most revered names in the world of art. Highly professional; all sales are accompanied by a certificate of authenticity.

Buenos Aires After Dark

Every time we visit Buenos Aires we are amazed at what a late night city it is. After midnight, as we're starting to wilt, the *porteños* are still going strong, crowding the clubs, discos, theaters, and coffee houses night after night. This is true year-round, even on weekday nights, and we have concluded that *porteños* function on very little sleep. Since you are on vacation, you can reset your inner clock by taking a late afternoon nap. That way you'll still be wide awake by the time the dinner hour comes along.

Your evening options are many. The city offers fine opera and classical ballet, sultry tango shows, discos, and over 1,000 cinemas showing first-run films, undubbed. You can spend an evening dancing on the tables in a La Boca *cantina* or on the dance floor of a swank Recoleta nightclub, browsing in a late night bookstore, or people watching at a sidewalk café. Sporting events are held in the evenings too.

Entertainment Information

The concierge at your hotel should be able to provide you with information about opera, ballet and theater performances as well as reserve tickets. The same holds true for major sporting events. There are several publications that list events and performances throughout the city. You can pick these up at virtually any kiosk.

The Buenos Aires Herald, founded in 1876, is an informative English language daily and your best choice for finding out what's going on. The entertainment section provides a complete up-to-date listing of what's playing in the cinemas, theaters and clubs throughout town. It costs 80¢ and is available at newsstands.

Where, an English language booklet issued monthly includes information on theater, music, sports and special events as well as a dining and nightlife guide. It's free.

Theaters & Concert Halls

The concierge may be able to get you better seats than if you handle it yourself. If you prefer to do it on your own, check the diagram in the box office for seat availabilities.

Buenos Aires is an important stop for international artists. Of course, the chance of your getting last minute tickets will depend on who is performing. If you're considering a trip to the theater, remember that most performances are in Spanish, though there are also some English-speaking theater troupes who perform in the city. Check listings in *The Buenos Aires Herald*.

TEATRO COLÓN (Colón Opera House)
Plaza Lavalle
Tel 382-0554.
Box Office: 10 a.m.-8 p.m., Tuesday-Sunday.
The Teatro Colón, on the Plaza Lavalle, is an opera house on a grand scale and the most opulent in the country, if not in South America as a whole. Often compared to La Scala in Milan, the

acoustics in its seven-tier auditorium are next to perfection. Arturo Toscanini, María Callas, Enrico Caruso, Luciano Pavarotti, Zubin Mehta, Leontyne Price, and Leona Mitchell are among the international masters who have performed here since the theater opened its doors on May 25, 1908. The Buenos Aires Philharmonic performs here regularly, as do touring opera companies and orchestras from around the world. Leona Mitchell, performing in Verdi's *The Masked Ball*, opened the 1994 season.

Be sure to take a guided tour of the Opera House, offered several times daily, and visit the Colón Museum. See the sightseeing section for details.

The theater is closed throughout most of January and February and reopens in March with a limited summer schedule. The season is in full-swing during the winter (June-August). Call the box office. Ticket prices usually range from $40 to $50 for an orchestra seat to $16 for *a paraíso* or balcony seat. Standing room tickets are $5.

TEATRO NACIONAL CERVANTES
(Cervantes National Theater)
Libertad 815
Tel 815-8883
Since it first opened its doors in 1921, the Cervantes has consistently brought fine theater to the forefront of the city's cultural life. One of the most important theaters in Argentina, it is home to the National Theater Company, distinguished for the quality of its productions.

EL CENTRO CULTURAL SAN MARTIN
(The San Martín Cultural Center)
Corrientes 1536
Tel 46-8611
Several theaters, including the Teatro Municipal General San Martín, and concert halls are housed in this large complex. Often featured

here are classics such as *King Lear* and *Antigone* as well as works by contemporary Argentine playwrights and composers. Concerts and plays are occasionally performed for free.

EL TEATRO COLISEO (Coliseum Theater)
Calle M.T. de Alvear
Tel 393-7115
This is another great forum for world class events and a particularly wonderful place to see the ballet – Natalia Makorova and Julio Bocca were recently guest performers here.

THE LUNA PARK STADIUM
Corrientes and Bouchard
For information call the Colón Theater Box Office.
Luna Park is the setting of a great many special events. The Colón Theater is responsible for most of the programs here; the stadium serves as its annex. When Luciano Pavarotti appeared here, the need for a stadium of its size was obvious.

THE RIVER PLATE STADIUM
Avenida F. Alcorte 7597
More than just the home of Argentina's favorite soccer team, the La Boca Juniors, the River Plate has hosted international rock stars, including Bruce Springsteen. Consult *The Buenos Aires Herald* or *Where* for current performances.

BELGRANO AUDITORIUM
Virrey Loreto 2348
Located in the charming suburb of Belgrano, this is one of the city's finest concert halls. Musical fare runs the gamut from chamber music to symphonies.

The Cinema

Going to the movies is a real treat in Buenos Aires. There are hundreds of movie theaters, with *multi-cines* becoming just as popular here as they are in the U.S. Much more formal than back home, many have bars and the ushers actually show you to your seat. Movies are not dubbed and new releases make it here quite quickly. Cinemas are concentrated along Lavalle, Corrientes and Callao. Check *The Buenos Aires Herald* for current listings.

Tango

More than anything else, Argentina is known for the tango, that hauntingly seductive dance in which the partners seem to stalk each other, alternating in the roles of hunter and willing partner. Its origins can be traced back to the African slaves who lived in Buenos Aires 200 years ago. Developed over decades, this tantalizing dance was brought to the limelight by famed dancer Carlos Gardel, who ignited the salons of Paris and Europe in the early part of this century. By the late 1930's the tango was immortalized by Hollywood in a number of films.

Tangos are nearly always narratives set to music – invariably melancholy, bittersweet songs of love and passion. These tales are conveyed by the long gliding steps and closely entwined bodies of the dancers. The tango is a ritual dance. At times the man assumes the part of *guapo* (dandy) who seduces innocent maidens. At other times the primly dressed young ladies do a "church social" version of the dance which is quite tame in comparison.

An evening spent at any of the *tanguerías* or folkloric clubs in Buenos Aires guarantees a glittering show, with the performers taking the audience through a century of tango styles. Well-regarded musicians often accompany the dancers. The accordion-like *bandoneón* is the most typical of the instruments in a tango ensemble. At the finale, most clubs encourage the audience to join the dancers onstage for a simple tango. However, there is really no such thing. The tango is a difficult dance to learn well, but you will have a great deal of fun trying.

Most *tanguerías* are in San Telmo around Calles Balcarce and Chile. The following is an overview of some of our favorites. Call ahead for show times, as schedules often vary from night to night. All of these clubs accept major credit cards. Cover charges are sometimes pretty substantial.

Keep your eyes open for tango composer and musician Astor Piazzola – he is the most acclaimed tango artist in the world today. You would be lucky indeed to catch one of his performances.

CASABLANCA
Balcarce 668, San Telmo
Tel 331-4621 (reservations requested)
Show Times: Monday-Friday, 10 p.m.;Saturday, 9 p.m. & 11 p.m.
Casablanca is the finest *tanguería* in Buenos Aires. A frequent guest is President Carlos Saul Menem, who often brings foreign heads of state

here for a taste of Argentine culture. Apart from foreign dignitaries, Eric Clapton, Oliver Stone, David Rockefeller and Robert Duvall figure among the many who have enjoyed the evening show featuring over 40 musicians and dancers performing a series of tangos, as well as folkloric dances and music of the Andes and Pampas. The $35 admission includes open bar and appetizers. Seating is arranged theater style, with an orchestra level and mezzanine.

MICHELANGELO
Balcarce 433, San Telmo
Tel 343-6542 (reservations requested)
This club was once a smuggler's den before Buenos Aires formally existed. The cavern-like interior is the perfect setting for the stunning tango performers and the international music shows that make this one of the city's most popular spots year after year. Call ahead to check on the constantly changing program. Admission is $35 with drinks or $60 for dinner and the show.

LA VENTANA
Balcarce 425, San Telmo
Tel 334-1315 (reservations requested)
Show time: 10:30 p.m.
La Ventana features an impressive roster of visiting singers and dancers from the South American circuit. Its wide repertoire of European and popular as well as folkloric music has an international appeal. Admission is $40 per person.

CAFE HOMERO
J.A. Cabrera 4946, Palermo
Tel 773-1979

The elegant Café Homero features a show and dancing. It attracts a well-to-do local crowd. Remember, you'll probably need to take a cab back to your hotel. However, we have heard that Café Homero is planning to move to the more conveniently located Plaza Mall.

BAR SUR
Estados Unidos 299, San Telmo
Tel 362-6086

Local tango aficionados claim that Bar Sur is one of the few spots where you can see pure tango rather than a show geared for tourists. This is the best recommendation a place can have. Drinks and a cold buffet are available.

CALLE DE LOS ANGELES
Calle Chile 318
Tel 361-3633

Located in a lovely courtyard, Calle de Los Angeles is a fine low key spot for dinner. There is usually a tango show here, although not as flashy as those at the *tanguerías* listed above.

Pubs & Cafes with Live Music

Make this a must when planning your evenings.

On a smaller scale than nightclubs, these nightspots feature bands and orchestras, which add atmosphere and a special touch to a simple night out.

CAFE VIENES MOZART
Esmeralda 754 (at Córdoba)
Tel 322-3273
Open: 5:30 p.m.
Located in a traditional part of the city, this beautiful café features fine Viennese pastries and live music, vocal and instrumental, ranging from zarzuela, to tango, to classical, including chamber music. Stand-up comedians perform here as well. Performers are first-rate. Check listings in *The Buenos Aires Herald*. A terrific place, it is especially popular on the weekends. Occasionally it is necessary to buy tickets in advance, depending on the performer. Call ahead to find out. Located on the second floor.

CAFE TORTONI
Avenida de Mayo 825
One of Buenos Aires' most traditional cafés, the huge Tortoni was founded in 1858 and is still going strong. There are jazz shows here on the weekends featuring talented up-and-coming artists. There is often a cover charge.

BAR BARO
Tres Sargentos 415.
Tel 311-6856.
This loud, brassy and wildly painted bi-level pub is a favorite among journalists and artists, There is always a lively crowd at the bar, drinking and eating peanuts, dropping the shells on the floor seemingly without a care in the world. Especially popular with regular patrons are the cold cut and cheese platters, along with a draught beer. Follow their example and you won't go wrong. Live jazz and blues is featured on Thursday through Saturday evenings. Inci-

Look for the red door with brass knockers.

dentally, Bar Baro is Buenos Aires slang for fantastic or really terrific.

EL VERDE
Reconquista 878
Tel 315-3693.

Reconquista is a dark street just one block from the River Plate.

If you want to mingle with the locals, El Verde is a great place for you. It's always crowded, upstairs and down, with singles and couples alike. Boar heads dominate the decor of this friendly pub. The music kicks off at 11:30 p.m.

SATCHMO
Agüero 2279

This is one of Buenos Aires' busiest jazz clubs – the drinks are long and potent, the crowd sharp and urban, and the musical fare ranges from one-man shows to bands and jazz improv. The atmosphere is casual and friendly.

SHAMS
Federico Lacroze 2121, Belgrano
Tel 773-0721.

The country's best pop and rock performers are often found at Shams. The lovely area attracts equally lovely people, so look chic when you head for this one. Weekends are rambunctious and crowded at this large pub.

THE BAUEN HOTEL PIANO BAR
Callao 360

The Bauen provides the perfect atmosphere for a quiet *tête-à-tête*. The mood is romantic and semi-formal, and the music is always soothing. This could be just what you need after a day of sightseeing or a few hours at one of Buenos Aires' high-powered nightspots.

Discos

Discos are definitely alive and well in Buenos
Aires. Drinking and dancing go on until 5 a.m.
and somehow the *porteños* still make it to the
office in the morning. Some discos have cover
charges.

NEWPORT
Junín 1715/19, Recoleta
Tel 803-3332
One of the newest and hottest nightspots in
Recoleta. A hip young crowd gathers here most
evenings. Nautical flags hang behind the busy
bar. Live music is often featured and you'll find
MTV-style videos playing on monitors
throughout. There are even a few on the ceiling.

Crowded.

SHAMPOO
Quintana 362, Recoleta
Tel 42-4427
Open: 11 p.m.-5:30 a.m.
Though the doors open at 11 p.m., things really
don't get started at this elegant nightspot until
around midnight when the beautiful people
start pouring in. Mirrors and plants comple-
ment the large video dance floor and the
couchettes and tables scattered throughout.
There are international shows nearly every
night. Prices are steep, making it pretty easy to
meet the $30 minimum.

TRUMPS
Bulnes 2772, Palermo
Tel 801-9866
Open: Midnight-6 a.m., every day.

Ivana, Gabriela Sabatini, Jack Palance and Maradona have signed the guest register at this exclusive nightspot in Palermo Chico. It is as informal as only the very rich can afford to be. Understatement is key to the decor, with its small black lacquer tables topped by dim lamps.

AFRIKA
Hotel Alvear Palace, Avenida Alvear 1885
Tel 804-4031
Afrika ranks among the city's most popular nightspots. On the formal side, guests tend to be in their 30's and up. You'll find plenty of intimate nooks to relax in while listening to the live music, or you can join the crowd on the dance floor. It is best to arrive after midnight. The $25 cover includes a drink.

MAU MAU
Arroyo 866
Tel 393-6131
Unusual for a disco, Mau Mau has been a favorite for over two decades. More formal than most of the newcomers, the crowd here also tends to be older than the usual disco crowd and the drinks are expensive by Buenos Aires standards. Nevertheless, Mau Mau has managed to become something of a legend.

HIPPOPOTAMUS
Junín 1787, Recoleta
Tel 804-8310
This is a "traditional" disco in Recoleta – a huge dance floor, strobe lights, pounding recorded music and mirrors, both on the ceiling and underfoot. This smartly designed, somewhat formal club has several levels and thus never feels as crowded as it inevitably is. Dancing contin-

ues until the crack of dawn. There is a popular restaurant here as well.

PALADIUM
Reconquista 945
Tel 312-9819
Paladium is worth a visit just to see the outrageous building it occupies – it was once the substation of the Buenos Aires Power Company. Inside is some of the best dancing around to the hottest tunes. The liveliest young people in the city congregate here and it is invariably packed.

Weekends only.

TEQUILA
Costanera Norte y La Pampa
Tel 788-0438
More a bar than a disco, Tequila is still a great place to go when the sun goes down. It does sport a small dance floor and a few video monitors. Because it is small, it is fairly easy to mingle here.

A Gay Club

CONTRAMANO
Rodríguez Peña 1082
Contramano is Buenos Aires' hottest gay club and one of the few in town. You'll recognize it by the canopy outside. The dance floor is always packed and so is the bar.

The Cantinas of La Boca

Cantinas are traditional, informal places where the waiters love to sing and the owner does his best to get the newcomers involved. "Cantina" once referred to a sailors' mess hall which explains the rowdy, carefree atmosphere you'll enjoy in La Boca's modern day cantinas. Some are simple Italian cafés, while others are more like informal nightclubs.

A note to the uninitiated: if the owner thrusts a microphone at you be prepared to sing a song from your national repertoire. *New York, New York* and *Somewhere Over the Rainbow* are two well-recognized North American favorites. Necochea, formerly called *Camino Viejo* (Old Road) jumps until the wee hours on weekends. The following is a brief listing of cafés and cantinas in La Boca.

Curtains are painted on the glass windowpanes and the tables are lined up cafeteria-style in **Los Tres Amigos**. Kids run among the aisles and through the tables as if it were a playground and the paper maché decor is appropriately tacky and fun. Pizza and vermicelli are heaped high on the plate here and you'll be considered a wet noodle if you don't accept the invitation to dance a tarentella or improvise a ditty in front of the boisterous crowd.

Just as boisterous are **Il Piccolo Vapore, La Fragata, Gennarino** at Necochea 1210, **La Gaviota** at 1254, and **Spadavecchia** at Necochea 1180, although tour bus crowds can become a bit of a nuisance here.

The Carritos of Costanera Norte

Costanera Norte is a waterfront promenade that runs along the River Plate. One inlet of the promenade, Avenida Rafael Obligado, about 10 minutes from downtown by cab, is lined with popular restaurants serving Italian and grilled beef specialties. These eateries stay open until the wee hours and it is easy to move from one restaurant to another. Spending an evening here is a lot of fun. For more specifics about *carrito* dining, turn to the restaurant section.

LA PLAZA
Avenida Corrientes, 1400 Block

Like a chameleon, La Plaza is constantly changing. Much depends on the weather, but also on what's playing. Open for only a short time, this cobblestone alley that links Calles Montevideo and Paraná is designed on multiple levels reached by steps and ramps. There are several theaters and their shows change, but one usually has dramas and the other music. The center of La Plaza is an open-air amphitheater where concerts are held. Seating is on concrete benches. There is a branch of Café Homero there for tango lovers, along with many inexpensive restaurants and gift shops. For the price of a beer or *pancho* you can enjoy a jazz combo or a juggler. It's a landmark in the making.

Open all day and into the early morning hours.

For Quieter Types . . .

CLASICO Y MODERNO LIBROS
Avenida Callao 892

A wonderful bookstore/café, this is a quiet hideaway for those who enjoy steaming capuccino or herbal teas while engrossed in a thriller or Garcia Marquez classic. The bookstore in the rear has some pricey English titles and opens at 10 a.m. The café, which is Bohemian in decor, is open seven days a week, 24 hours a day. There is music around 11 p.m. on Friday and Saturday nights. Book signings and readings are held (for those who speak Spanish).

Cabarets

The following clubs fall into the special category of cabarets – offering typically elaborate shows with a Vegas-like format. Some include regional entertainment like the tango, but most are international in flavor. Expect to pay a cover charge at the door.

KARIM
Carlos Pellegrini 1143
Tel 393-1884
Show Times: 11:30 p.m. & 2:30 a.m.

Karim is still going strong after decades of strip tease shows and variety entertainment. As one would expect, the crowd here is not wet behind the ears – 30-plus seems to be the average age. The young ladies will also dance with patrons following the shows. It is all rather above board and patrons do not seem to mind paying a lot for a drink.

KARINA
Avenida Corrientes 636
Tel 40-1708
Open: 10 p.m. on, with two shows nightly.
Music and striptease always play a major role in
the shows at Karina. Single men congregate
here because of the attractive female performers
who are available for dancing. Single women do
not enter this or any similar club unless they are
"in the business." Couples are welcome.

For Men Only

Men on the prowl looking for someone to share
a drink or evening with should step into one of
these fairly upscale pubs on Calle Reconquista.
Success is 100% guaranteed provided you have
some money in your pocket. **Cutty Sark** is the
most exclusive of the locales. **Captain Morgan**,
a few doors down, is just a step below. **Black**, a
piano bar with a large dance floor at Ayacucho
1981 (second floor) across from the Alvear Palace Hotel, is another fine place to meet a beautiful *porteña*. It's even nice enough to come to with
a date. Head up one flight of stairs.

Shopping

Buenos Aires is a delightful place to shop. Whether you are an indefatigable shopper or a casual one, you'll be pleased by the diversity both in goods and in ambience. A shopping foray here can mean a visit to an elegant fur salon where a nutria jacket will be made to order, or to a chic boutique for buttery soft leathers fashioned into stunning coats, handbags, belts and luggage. Twenty-four-karat gold jewelry set with South America's colorful gemstones, patterned knits and funky antiques are also great buys. Argentina's handicrafts make lovely and often inexpensive gifts for friends back home. You never know where you'll find the perfect item – at a boutique on a pedestrian-only street, in a *galería* (mini-arcade), a lovely shopping center or noisy outdoor flea market.

Prices will depend on the strength of the peso against the dollar, but will generally be less than in New York or Paris for items of similar quality. Most shops accept U.S. currency on a par with the Argentine peso.

If you are just looking for some small gifts for friends back home or an unusual accessory for your home, you will enjoy the shops selling Argentine handicrafts and even bargain hunters will like the challenge of haggling in one of the lively flea markets in all parts of the city.

Best Shopping Areas

Calle Florida - A shop-lined pedestrian promenade that runs for 11 blocks from Avenida Rivadavia to the Plaza San Martín. The better boutiques are on the higher numbered blocks near the Plaza. Florida has many *galerías,* which are bi-level arcades built into office buildings. They sell all kinds of items from leathers to knitwear. **Galerías Pacífico**, the city's poshest shopping center, and **Harrod's**, the city's only department store, are also on Calle Florida. Some of the upscale boutiques that were formerly on Calle Florida have moved into Galerías Pacífico and other shopping centers.

Avenida Santa Fe - A long street with stately buildings, Avenida Santa Fe is best known for its designer clothing shops for both men and women, and for its art galleries. Santa Fe, which branches from Plaza San Martín, has a small cluster of shops there, but the finer stores and scores of *galerías* are near Avenida Callao.

Recoleta - Twenty-four-carat gold jewelry with fabulous colored stones, European designer imports for men's and women's apparel and lots of gift items are sold in the boutiques and arcades on Avenidas Alvear and Quintana. There are many art galleries in the area as well, particularly along Calle Arroyo. One of the few downtown streets that winds, Arroyo is a J-shaped street that connects Calle Esmeralda with Avenida Alvear.

San Telmo - If you know what to look for, the quality and broad variety of the antiques in San

Telmo can be impressive. Many shops are located on Calle Defensa, both north and south of the Plaza Dorrego, and there are also *galerías* specializing in antiques. The Sunday flea market (9 a.m.-5 p.m.) has over 100 stalls and specialties include antique jewelry, rare books and ancient typewriters.

Shopping Centers

Several upscale shopping malls have opened in Buenos Aires in recent years. First on the scene was the **Patio Bullrich** at Avenida Libertador 750. When it first opened its doors in 1867, the Patio Bullrich was a gathering place for wealthy livestock breeders and cattle were sold at auctions here. Later, the auction trade switched to antiques, fine furniture and works of art. Recently converted to a modern shopping center, its three levels are subdued and elegant. With all the storefronts identical and with a glass covered roof allowing natural light to filter in, the effect is one of relaxed comfort. There are restaurants, coffee bars and cinemas. Shops open at 10 a.m. and stay open to 9 p.m. daily. Restaurants and cinemas stay open late.

The city's most lavish shopping center, **Galerías Pacífico**, at the corner of Calles Florida and Córdoba downtown, was voted the Best Shopping Center of 1992 by an international shopping center organization. The building's history dates back to the 1890's when a group of French businessmen tried to open a branch of the French department store *Bon Marché* in Buenos Aires. An economic crisis thwarted their plans and construction was halted with only one wing of the store complete. That wing would operate as a center for the arts under various guises, including a stint as the original site of Buenos Aires Fine Arts Museum, until it was acquired by the Railway of the Pacific. The railway renamed the building *Edificio del Pacífico* and installed its administrative offices there.

In 1945 the railway decided to install a shopping arcade on the ground floor. To attract merchants and shoppers, the building was renovated, a result of which was its signature cupola. Argentine artists Berni, Castagnino, Spilimbergo and Urruchia were commissioned to paint the murals, which are still admired by shoppers today.

Not successful, the building stood abandoned from 1961 to 1989, although the stores continued to operate on Calle Florida. Slated for demolition in 1989, it was rescued by a group of investors who restored the landmark building and opened the center in 1992. Today its three levels house fine leather shops, apparel for both men and women, handicraft stores and small eateries. Every store has a unique front, which makes each level distinctive.

The ultra-modern **Alto Palermo** shopping center on the corner of Coronel Diaz and Beruti is home to 180 shops spread out over three levels and in two connected buildings. Alto Palermo most resembles a U.S. shopping mall: a mix of upscale shops such as **Calvin Klein**, **Yves St. Laurent** and **Cacharel** with those selling stereo equipment and local clones of the Gap and Banana Republic. An interesting design with an atrium and glass elevators, the $45 million

Alto Palermo opened in 1990. It is crowded on weekends, so shop here on weekdays if you want the personal service you can expect in Patio Bullrich and Galerías Pacífico.

To get to Alto Palermo, take the D line on the *Subte* to Palermo's Bulnes Station. Shops are open 10 a.m. to 10 p.m. daily, while restaurants and cinemas are open much later.

Unicentro, the city's largest shopping center (it could easily enclose the former three), is located in the suburb of Martínez. It is not distinctive enough to merit a specific visit but Martínez is on the way to Tigre.

Once

This is the Orchard Street of Buenos Aires. If you venture along Corrientes past the 2,000 block, you'll start noticing little shops with slightly shabby exteriors and dimly lit interiors. Most of the city's wholesalers are here. Always check quality before purchasing anything and never accept the price as marked; bargaining is three-quarters of the fun. To find what you're looking for, don't hesitate to ask questions of the salespeople and other shoppers. They will direct you to the best bargains, often in factories where terrific prices more than make up for a lack of beautiful displays.

There are so many diverse shops in Once that naming just a few would be a terrible injustice. Most are concentrated within the boundaries of Corrientes above the 2,000 block and between Calles Pasteur and Azucenaga. Be sure to try the ethnic finger foods such as the spicy knishes (there is a sizeable orthodox Jewish population and a smaller Hasidic one) and the hot, crusty pretzels sold in the small coffee shops along the street.

Take the D line on the *Subte* to the Pasteur Station and you'll be in the heart of Once. Several buses travel through here as well.

Hotel Shopping Arcades

Branches of the city's finest emporiums are found in the five-star hotel arcades. All the H. Stern Jewelers shops, an internationally known jeweler, are located in hotel arcades. Prices are on a par with shops in the centers and on the shopping streets. Many designer clothing shops are in hotel arcades.

Shopping Tips

Bargaining

While bargaining is acceptable and even expected in Once and in the flea markets, shoppers do not bargain elsewhere. You can request a *descuento* (discount) if you buy many items or pay in U.S. dollars in the smaller family-run establishments.

Credit Cards

Credit cards are accepted virtually everywhere in Buenos Aires as well as in the larger cities and resorts of Argentina. American Express, Visa,

MasterCard and Diners Club are the most widely known.

Hours

Shops in Buenos Aires are open by 10 a.m. and tend to stay open until rather late in the evening – normally 7 p.m., but often till 9 or 10 p.m. Smaller shops close for siesta (lunch break) at 1 p.m., reopening at 4 p.m. Shops in the shopping centers and larger stores do not close. Most are closed on Sunday but, once again, the shopping centers remain open.

Caveat

The rest of this section will discuss the outstanding buys in Buenos Aires, followed by a listing of those shops we feel offer great selections, have excellent reputations and are well respected by *porteños*. In many cases shops have been suggested by *porteño* friends as places they themselves shop. Listing shops can be risky business in a city that is undergoing such rapid growth as Buenos Aires is. Should you arrive at one of our suggestions and find an empty lot instead, we apologize in advance. In many cases, the shop will have relocated nearby or to one of the shopping centers.

Best Buys

Leathers

Leather is a natural choice in Argentina – this is cattle country after all. Designer coats and jackets, exquisite handbags, stylish shoes and durable luggage are fashioned in cowhide, suede pigskin, exotic alligator and lizard, even ostrich. They are buttery soft and you can choose from a variety of colors. Styles and prices vary from shop to shop.

FRANKEL'S LEATHER WORLD
Florida 1075 & 1085

A Calle Florida favorite, Frankel's has a particularly good selection of coats and jackets for both men and women. They also sell handbags of porcupine and lizard. Its location, between the Plaza and Sheraton Hotels, makes this large attractive shop and its sister handicraft store around the corner popular stops for visitors to the city. Service is helpful and friendly.

CASA LÓPEZ
Plaza San Martín
M.T. de Alvear 640 & 658
Galerías Pacífico and Alto Palermo Shopping Centers

With several shops, Casa López is the largest purveyor of leather accessories in the city. Quality is high and styling is both contemporary and classic. You'll find a tasteful selection of fine clothing, handbags, belts and other accessories in leather and suede. The staff is professional and friendly and speak English.

WELCOME
Marcelo T. de Alvear 500

Slightly off the beaten track, but only two blocks from Calle Florida, Welcome has a large selection of highly styled handbags in both calfskin and suedes. Prices are moderate here.

MICHELS
Calle Florida 600/500 Blocks
The two small Michel shops are crowded with small leather items such as snakeskin billfolds, lizard belts and ostrich leather bags. Friendly staff.

WILLY KENI
Avenida Alvear 1812
Willy Keni is the place to shop for high-fashion leather items for guys and gals. Although prices are on the high side, the one-of-a-kind items you'll find here are worth the extra bucks. Highly recommended.

PETER KENT
Paraguay between Florida and Maipú
Willy Keni has a rival in this shop featuring top one-of-a-kind designs in leather for guys and gals. The service is first-class, and they will alter any item you purchase at no extra charge. Quality and prices are tops.

NAMIR CUEROS
Calle Florida 936 (Galería)
Namir will make a leather jacket or coat to order in 24 hours. You can select from a variety of leathers and colors.

Other Fine Leather Shops:
Pullman in Galerías Pacífico, **Santa Marinella** in the Alvear Palace Arcade, and **Kueros King**, Calle Florida 971.

Leather Shoes & Boots

Argentineans love wearing boots. Perhaps it's a tradition that goes back to their *gaucho* forefathers. Just as practical on city streets as they are on the *pampas*, boots are among the most fashionable buys you can find. They follow European styles, particularly Italian ones.

Our Favorite Shops Around Town:

Boniface, Calle Florida 598 and Parera 145, with great shoes for men and women. **Botticelli**, Calle Paraguay 693, Avenida Quintana 488 and Santa Fe 1756. Also for men and women, **Emilio Bianco**, Calle Florida 660, 755 and 898, and the Alto Palermo Shopping Center. In addition to ready-to-wear, custom made shoes for men and women are featured here. **Hedres**, Avenida Santa Fe 778 (near Plaza San Martín), represents Christian Dior in Buenos Aires and has highly styled footwear.

Fur Salons

Furs are both stunning and excellent buys in Buenos Aires. If you shop in the Austral summer you can even say furs are great bargains here. Native furs include nutria, which is a glossy expensive-looking fur belonging to the otter family that compares favorably with mink. Some nutria items are fashioned using the long outer hairs, which are waterproof and bristly to the touch. They are not as elegant or as soft as the garments made of the shorter furs. Fox is another indigenous animal whose fur is used for garments. Fox from Tierra del Fuego has rust color fur while Patagonian fox is grayish in color. Minks are raised for fur in the country and items can be made to order and shipped to your home.

CHARLES CALFUN
Calle Florida 918
Calfun enjoys a fine reputation for its stunning fur garments. Hard to resist are the suede coats or the silk raincoats lined with fur. Calfun also sells leather items.

FRANCOIS SABER PIELES
Calle Florida 963
Another long-established shop with items that are similar to those at Calfun, this chic shop is fun to browse. Saber is the Fendi representative in Buenos Aires and it sells their leather goods as well as suede and wool sweaters.

R.G. FURS
Avenida Santa Fe 776
Highly styled fur coats and jackets.

DENNIS FURS
Calle Florida 989
This furrier has earned a spotless reputation. Shop carefully and you should be able to get a terrific buy on fox and/or nutria. Dennis Furs is the exclusive representative for Yves St. Laurent Fur Designs.

Jewelry

Brazil and Colombia provide the brilliantly colorful gems and emeralds, but the distinctive designs and flawless workmanship is supplied by European immigrants from Belgium and other parts of Europe. If you're not looking for the real thing, the wholesale district of Once is home to several *bijouterías*, shops which sell faux jewelry. Most of the costume jewelry sold there is imported from Europe, but some is also made locally.

H. STERN JEWELERS
Plaza, Sheraton, Hyatt and Alvear Palace Hotels and at the Ezeiza Airport.

While the name is international, world renowned jeweler Hans Stern has remained faithful to his philosophy that each of his shops features jewelry designed by local artists in order that it reflect its country of origin. Hence, in the Buenos Aires shops you'll find a lovely selection of jewelry featuring rhodochrosite. This delicate rose-colored stone is from the northwest province of Catamarca and is mined and sold only in Argentina. Its export is prohibited by law.

Other items feature the colorful gemstones mined in Brazil such as aquamarines, tourmalines and topazes. These stones, found in a variety of colors, are set in unique pieces of jewelry in contemporary and classic styles. Lovely pieces use the deep blue lapis lazuli stones mined in nearby Chile.

A shopping bonus at H. Stern is the affidavit issued to each customer stating that 35% or more of the metals or gems used at H. Stern are of Argentinean or Brazilian origin. This means you are exempt from customs duty.

REYNALDO MACHADO
Calle Florida 987
This shop has a fine selection of Gucci, Movado and Baume Mercier watches.

RICCIARDI
Plaza Hotel, Calle Florida 1001.
This is one of Argentina's most prestigious jewelers with an impressive clientele, including the late Eva Perón. Ricciardi specializes in antique silver, which is often just as expensive as gold. Ricciardi is also the maker of the presidential baton.

Browsing or Shopping, These Shops Also Merit a Visit:

Antoniazzi-Chiappe, Avenida Alvear 1895, is one of the two stores in the world that offers "blue gold" along with unusual designer jewelry. At **Ile de France**, Calle Florida 860 in the Galería del Sol, you'll find a mixed bag of expensive evening jewelry and fabulous fakes. **Santarelli**, Calle Florida 688 and Calle Florida 860 in the Galería del Sol, features a marvelous selection of antiques and estate jewelry.

Knitwear & Sheepskin

Grazing in grassy fields adjacent to the cattle are well-fed sheep – lots of them. Argentine wool, which is first rate, is exported to all parts of the world. Sweaters, both cashmere and lambswool, are terrific buys, as are knit dresses and suits. Sheepskin jackets have become very popular in the U.S.

JOTA Y CUEROS
Pasaje Tres Sargentos 439
A factory rather than a store, which makes sheepskin jackets to order, this is an excellent stop.

SILVIA Y MARIO
M.T. de Alvear 55
A large selection of cashmere sweaters is featured here.

LOS CUATRO ASES
Calle Florida 519
"The Four Aces" is on the main shopping drag, so you can't miss it. You'll appreciate the bulky ski sweaters here. Some of the best buys are the Alpaca sweaters, usually knitted in loose pull-on styles, in natural cream and brown tones.

Also Worth a Stop:

Buffagni, Calle Montevideo 1183 and Calle M.T. de Alvear (Recoleta), where you'll find fine cashmere sweaters and cardigans for men and women; and **Gian Franco Serachi**, Calle Paraguay 4922, known for its one-of-a-kind wool and cashmere sweaters for all ages.

Antiques (Antiguedades) & Silver

Buenos Aires is overflowing with antiques. Throughout the city you'll find shops filled with period furniture and lovely *objets d'art*. Clocks and silver are plentiful in the antique shops and markets. Auctions are also quite popular and, if you're seriously shopping for antiques, you must arrive early since the best pieces go quickly. The city's antiques center is in San

Telmo and it is centered around Plaza Dorrego. The Sunday flea market, which is open year-round, and its smaller seasonal sister, which operates on Saturdays but not in the winter, are fun to poke around. Serious antique hunters should head to the shops and galleries along Calle Defensa both north and south of the Plaza.

Pasaje de La Defensa at Defensa 1179 is a bi-level *galería* in a historic building. Shops are off a courtyard and feature everything from antique clothing to glassware.

Galería Ponte Vecchio at Defensa 1135 nearby has shops selling antique furniture and lamps.

Galería El Solar de French in Plaza Dorrego, has several antique shops. **Oscar's** at #33 has lovely silver items, as does **Tarquina** at #6.

Other Good Stops Along Calle Defensa:

El Rastro de San Telmo at #1047; **Lo Tenía Mi Abuela** at #995; and **Viejo Bazar** at #945. **Masini** at Estados Unidos 402 (at Defensa) has antique toys.

PALLAROLS
near the Plaza Dorrego in San Telmo.

Now in its sixth generation of providing wealthy *porteños* with the finest silver in the world, this fascinating shop is run by Buenos Aires' most enduring silversmith. This dynasty of silversmiths began in the 18th century in Barcelona, Spain. If you're interested in taking up the craft yourself, Pallarols also holds classes.

GALPÓN DE CAMPO
Maipú 982
Country-style antiques such as hammered copper pieces, ceramics, and rustic-looking furniture are featured here. It's a great place to look if you're shopping for a beach or country house.

Handicrafts - Regional Gift Shops

The arts and crafts of Argentina make wonderful gifts. In *artesanía* shops throughout the city you'll find *facones*, elaborately sheathed daggers used by the *gauchos*, and *rastras*, silver-studded cummerbunds worn in regional fiestas. Alpaca ponchos ward off the cold and woodcarvings from the delta are charming and inexpensive. Typical handicrafts include tooled leather book covers, silver mate sets for making bitter yerba tea and pillboxes decorated with beautiful rhodochrosite inlays.

FRANKEL'S GIFT CENTER
San Martín 1088
A huge bi-level shop with a terrific selection of handicrafts. Best buys include colorful ponchos, "antique" mirrors, ceramic and carved wooden items.

ARTESANÍAS ARGENTINAS
Avenida Córdoba 770
This shop is run by a non-profit organization whose mission is to preserve the native arts and crafts of Argentina. Members travel throughout Argentina to buy ponchos, mates, tapestries, woodcarvings and other items directly from the craftsmen. All purchases are accompanied by a certificate of authenticity.

MARÍA CUMBÉ
Calle Paraguay 445
María Cumbé is one of the finest shops in the city if you're seeking pre-Columbian art and jewelry or typical handicrafts.

Other shops with large selections of handicrafts are **Kelly's** at Paraguay 431 and **El Rodeo** at Paraguay 655.

Argentine Fashions for Women

These boutiques sell the fashions of local designers. Some have an international following, but even the unknowns offer a few surprises.

ADRIANA COSTANTINI
Avenida Alvear 1892, first floor (Recoleta)
This designer has an eye for texture and color in a line of distinctive casual wear and unique evening wear that has earned her a staunch following since her initial appearance on the avenue.

BEATRIZ JORDAN
Avenida Rodriguez Saenz Peña 1047
This is another place for classy designer wear. You can dress yourself from tip to toe with Jordan's ample selection of belts, hats, stockings and other accessories.

ELSA SERRANO
Calle M.T. de Alvear 1602, Patio Bullrich Shopping Center
Elsa Serrano is another of the city's most talented designers.

Equestrian Shops

Even non-riders will enjoy visiting these shops specializing in apparel and gear for the horse and rider. In addition to riding boots, habits and saddles, most sell hand-tooled leather goods and custom-made boots and gloves.

ROSSI Y CARUSO
Avenida Santa Fe 1601,
Patio Bullrich Shopping Center
This is a blue blood establishment in the leather business. Their pedigree is such that the royals of Spain have been shopping here for generations. Riding equipment is the specialty at "R y C," but the suitcases and accessories are the ultimate in craftsmanship and quality.

LA MARTINA
Avenida Paraguay 661
Handbags, leather accessories and fine apparel are featured, along with riding gear.

Bookstores (Librerías)

Buenos Aires bookstores are known for their enormous tables, indoors and out, piled high with books on virtually every topic ranging from European and South American literature, to politics and politicians (especially popular here), to biorhythms and physics. Spanish predominates, but you can usually turn up some titles in French or English. Antique books are for sale throughout the city and book fairs are held all year long.

There are hundreds of bookshops of all shapes and sizes scattered throughout the city. The following are just a few of our favorites.

ABC
Avenida Córdoba 685
One of the city's largest bookshops, ABC has a wide selection of imported books, including a great many in English. Keep in mind that, since they are imported, they will usually be on the expensive side.

EL ATENEO
Calle Florida 340
This is Buenos Aires' most complete bookshop. Most books are in Spanish and cover a wide range of topics.

GOETHE
Calle San Martín 577
Just as the name implies, this small shop specializes in German books and magazines.

KENNEY
Calle Arenales 885
Kenney specializes in children's books as well as English imports.

MILBERG
Lavalle 2223 (Once)
In this Jewish bookstore you'll find a wide range of books on the Jewish experience in South America and throughout the world of the Diaspora. Books are primarily in English, Spanish and Yiddish.

LIBRERÍA HERNÁNDEZ
Corrientes between Paraná and Uruguay
Hernández attracts a university crowd due to its large selection of avant garde literature in English and Spanish.

Antiquarian Bookshops

Buenos Aires is also home to a number of stores and dealers who specialize in antique books.

ALBERTO CASARES
Suipacha 521
Alberto Casares is one of the city's most knowledgeable dealers and has a wonderful collection of antiquarian and contemporary books. The pride of the shop is its collection of the writings of Jorge Luis Borges, probably the most complete in the world. In fact, Borges was present on November 27, 1985 for the inauguration of the shop's exhibit of first editions of his work. It's only fitting that this would be the last afternoon he would spend in Buenos Aires. He left for Geneva the following day where he was to remain until his death seven months later.

Collectors of Antiquarian Books Should Also Visit:

Librería Fernández Blanco, Tucumán 712; **Tomás Pardo**, Calle Maipú 618; **Librería de Antaño**, Calle Sánchez Bustamente 1876.

Bonbons

If packed carefully, candy travels well and is a great gift. *Alfajores*, those irresistible pastries filled with *dulce de leche* and dipped in chocolate or sugar, are among the most common sweets. You'll have no problem finding a *bonbonería* in Buenos Aires.

MINOTTI
Calle Florida 162,
Avenida Santa Fe 1794
Minotti specializes in Havanas, the chocolate-covered *alfajores* from Mar del Plata.

CORCEGA
Calle Florida at Lavalle
This *bonbonería* will prepare special gift boxes – ideal gifts if you are invited to someone's home while in Argentina. They sell Barrancas, another brand of *alfajores* which come attractively wrapped in silver foil.

LOS DOS CHINOS
Avenida Santa Fe 3301,
Libertador 3505,
Brasil 764
A chain with branches throughout the city, most *bonbonerías* like this city favorite sell local gourmet treats such as Gioconda jams and jellies, and Fenoglio, Suchard, Georgalos and Rama chocolates and confections.

Coffee

Argentina rivals Brazil and Colombia as a major grower of the mighty coffee bean. Argentina's coffee is wonderfully rich and a bag of beans makes a terrific gift. You can purchase fresh coffee at **Cafetal**, a retailer located throughout the city specializing in coffee and assorted coffee gadgets.

Wines & Liquors

Argentinean wines and liquors are excellent and have received several well-deserved awards. *Legui,* a cordial named in honor of one of Argentina's best jockeys, makes a terrific gift. Spirits such as *Los Criadores,* the Breeder's Choice Whiskey, and several local rums and beers are as popular as, and less expensive than, imports. Wines from La Rioja and Mendoza are especially good.

Remember that the wineries in the Cuyo region of western Argentina and in the provinces of Salta and Catamarca produce the country's finest wines. A great place to purchase them while in Buenos Aires is **Bodegas Trapiche** at Juan de Justo 5751.

Music

A recording or two may be just what you need to fight the blues should you begin to feel nostalgic upon your return home. María Sera Lima, Pimpinela, Marilena Ross and Victor Heredia are among Argentina's best known contemporary vocalists. Mercedes Sosa, Olinda Bozán, and Carlos Gardel, who is said to be "singing better every day" (despite the fact that he's been dead for over 50 years!), are the immortals of traditional and tango music. Jazz stylists Chick Correa and Gato Barbieri are local boys who have hit the big time internationally.

Most music shops in Buenos Aires are huge and are busy from morning to night. They are concentrated in the Florida and Lavalle areas.

SUPERMERCADO DEL DISCO
Carlos Pellegrini 481
This enormous shop features every type of music, including the Andean sounds of Atahualpa Yupanqui.

BROADWAY MICROFONO
Calle Florida 463
This is a great place to familiarize yourself with popular Argentine culture since it caters to the under-35 crowd with a vast selection of recordings, wall-size posters and large t-shirts featuring local and foreign pop artists.

Buenos Aires
A-Z

AIRLINE OFFICES: Aerolíneas Argentinas is at Avenida Peru 2 and throughout the city (tel 343-8551). Other options for flights within Argentina are **Austral** on Avenida Corrientes (tel 325-0777) and **LADE,** which flies to and within Patagonia and Tierra del Fuego, Calle Peru 710 (tel 361-7071). The **American Airlines** office is on Avenida Santa Fe (tel 342-0031) and **United** is at Avenida Alvear 590 (tel 326-8333). **Varig,** the Brazilian carrier, has an office at Calle Florida 630 (tel 382-5431). The **LanChile** office is on Avenida Córdoba (tel 311-5334).

ARGENTINE CONSULATES: Argentine consulates are in major cities across the United States, including New York at 12 West 56th Street (tel 212/397-1400); Miami at 25 SE 2nd Avenue (tel 305/ 373-1889); and Los Angeles, 3550 Wilshire Blvd. (tel 213/739-9977). Consulates are also located in Washington D.C., Chicago, Houston and San Francisco.

ELECTRICITY: The current operates on 220 volts, 50 cycles.

ENGLISH NEWSPAPER: *The Buenos Aires Herald* covers both international events and Argentine news. The Friday paper has a weekend section.

FOREIGN EMBASSIES IN BUENOS AIRES: The **United States Embassy** is at Colombia 4300 (tel 774-7611). The **Canadian Embassy** is at Suipacha 1111 (tel 312-9081) and the **Embassy of the United Kingdom** is at Dr. Luis Agote 2412 (tel 803-7070).

MUNICIPAL TOURIST OFFICE: The Municipal Tourist Office is located in the **Centro Cultural San Martín** at Sarmiento 1551 (closed Sunday). Two kiosks have excellent maps and lists of events. On Calle Florida near Córdoba and Avenida de Mayo. Closed Sunday.

NATIONAL HOLIDAYS: Holidays unique to Argentina include:

May 1	Labor Day
May 25	May Revolution (1810)
June 10	Malvinas War
June 20	Flag Day
July 9	Independence
August 17	Death of San Martín
October 12	Columbus Day

NATIONAL PARK OFFICE: The National Park Office is on Avenida Santa Fe, just a few steps away from the Plaza San Martín (tel 311-8865).

NATIONAL TOURIST OFFICE: The main office is at Avenida Santa Fe 883. Hours are from 9 a.m. to 5 p.m. daily except Sunday.

PROVINCIAL TOURIST OFFICES: Virtually all printed material is in Spanish. Each province has an office in Buenos Aires. Some key offices follow:

Buenos Aires	Avenida Callao 237 (40-3587)
Córdoba	Avenida Callao 332 (372-6566)
Chubut	Calle Paraguay 876 (311-0428)
Mendoza	Avenida Callao 445 (40-6683)
Misiones	Avenida Santa Fe 989 (322-0677)
Neuquen	Calle Perón 687 (476-2569)
Rio Negro	Calle Tucumán (372-9931)
Santa Cruz	Calle 25 de Mayo 277 (343-3755)
Tierra del Fuego	Avenida Santa Fe 919 (322-8855)

Around Argentina

You can spend your entire vacation in Buenos Aires and have a terrific time – most people do. But Buenos Aires is only one face of this vast country. If time permits, you should plan to visit some of the country's other wondrous faces.

In the chapters that follow we will bring those faces alive for you. While the information is not as extensive as that for Buenos Aires, each chapter is a comprehensive mini-guide that gives you a feel for the destination and provides the tools you need to explore it. We have selected them with an eye to a variety of experiences in different parts of the country and have not attempted to cover every Argentine town but rather those we feel are of most interest.

To whet your appetite and to allow you to plan a trip that suits your interests, time frame and pocketbook, we offer a capsule sketch below.

Bariloche - Argentina's world-renowned ski resort and summer playground is at the heart of the country's lake region in northern Patagonia. It is enclosed by the mountains and lakes of

Nahuel Huapi National Park, the country's largest.

Cordoba - A colonial charmer, Argentina's second largest city is the centerpiece of a lovely region of rolling hills, fertile plains, rivers and lakes.

Mendoza - This city of parks and plazas was the starting point for General San Martín and his Army of the Andes in their miraculous march across the Andes into Chile and on to victory against Spain in the Battle for Independence. Today it is the capital city of Argentina's wine country.

Iguazú - Iguazú is the name for the spectacular waterfalls, higher than Victoria and wider than Niagara, that stand at Argentina's northeast border with Brazil. It is also the name of the easily accessible rainforest that encircles the falls. Birds and butterflies are your companions here.

Mar del Plata - Once populated primarily by sea lions, nowadays over four million Argentines flock to this lively city, capital of Argentina's vacation coast. The arts and leisure go hand in hand here. You can fill your days with tennis, golf, hiking, horseback riding and, of course, watersports, as well as museums, art galleries and artisan fairs, followed by first rate theater and concerts in the evenings.

Ushuaia - The capital of Argentine Tierra del Fuego, Ushuaia is arguably the world's southernmost city. Picturesque in its own right, it is the jumping-off point for trips through the Beagle Channel and to the islands nearby.

Outdoor Argentina - Active vacation suggestions for those who want to combine a trip to Buenos Aires with vigorous outdoor activities. Skiing, hiking, trekking, fishing and mountaineering are all readily available and well-organized. Here too we include visits to Argentina's unique *estancias* where you can watch the *gauchos* at work, enjoy a typical *asado* and even learn how to play polo.

Travel Within Argentina

Traveling between Argentina's principal cities and attractions shouldn't be a problem. One option is to take advantage of the **Argentina Pass** offered by **Aerolíneas Argentinas** (described in the Introduction). Aerolíneas has flights to all of the destinations we've covered, as well as additional cities in Argentina and throughout South America.

Argentina is a big country. Be sure to check travel times carefully before finalizing your itinerary.

Land travel is also fairly straightforward. National routes (not to be confused with U.S. Interstates) link major, and not so major, cities. You can get virtually anywhere by bus, or rent a car. Bus travel is via motor coach and very comfortable. Though land travel takes more time than flying, you get to see more of the country. If you do have some time to play with, mixing air and land travel is a great way to go.

With the recent privatization of the railroad, rail travel will eventually be another option. Train service is currently provided from Buenos Aires' Constitución Station to Mar del Plata and Bariloche (tel 304-0021) and to Rosario from the B. Mitre Station (tel 311-5410). However, more trains may be up and running when you visit.

Bariloche

There are other ski facilities in South America. There are even other exciting ski areas in Argentina. But, much like Aspen in the United States and St. Moritz in Europe, San Carlos de Bariloche (but always called Bariloche) is the place to be seen. From June through September it draws skiers and après skiers from all over South America and from Europe. Wearing the latest fashions, they ski hard and party harder. Restaurants, discos, casinos, shops, and streets are crowded day and night.

If skiing and/or the party scene is not your cup of tea, you merely have to wait for a change of season. Bariloche, unlike most ski resorts, draws even more visitors in spring and summer than it does during the winter ski season. The warm weather crowd comes "to do" rather than to be seen. They climb mountains, hike, fish, sail, horseback ride, sunbathe and swim. And they can do all the above easily because Bariloche sits on the southern shore of Lake Nahuel Huapi in the national park of the same name. It is the lake, surrounded by soaring mountains, one snow-capped year-round, that will linger in your imagination. Not just a body of shimmering blue water extending as far as the eye can see, it is studded with fingers of land that create hidden coves and small islands. In the winter, the evergreen trees on these land strips stand out, but in spring and summer deciduous trees with shiny leaves and flowers appear. In the fall,

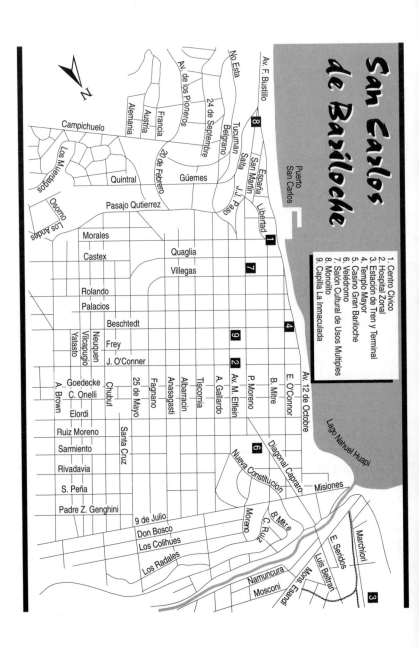

San Carlos de Bariloche

1. Centro Cívico
2. Hospital Zonal
3. Estación de Tren y Terminal
4. Templo Mayor
5. Casino Gran Bariloche
6. Velódromo
7. Salón Cultural de Usos Múltiples
8. Monolito
9. Capilla La Inmaculada

Puerto San Carlos

Lago Nahuel Huapi

there is a burst of reds, yellows and oranges much like that in New England. The town itself moves inland from the lake in a grid pattern, but as the streets move up the mountainside the pattern becomes haphazard. Founded in 1895 by German-Swiss settlers, the commercial center of town, where you will spend much of your time, still retains an Alpine flavor. There are many chalet-style buildings with flower-filled window boxes, chocolate factories, ceramic shops and several restaurants where fondue is as popular as *parrillada*.

Bariloche, capital of the province of Río Negro, is the capital of Argentina's lake district (although geographically it is in Patagonia). This is the perfect base for exploring the lakes and national parks nearby, including those across the Andean range in Chile. For a change of pace from the man-made marvels of Buenos Aires, head to Bariloche and unwind.

Getting There

By Air: Bariloche is 1,200 air miles from Buenos Aires. **Aerolíneas Argentinas** and **Austral** have several flights from Buenos Aires daily. Flight time is two hours and 25 minutes. For the best views, request a seat on the right side of the plane. Flights depart from Buenos Aires domestic airport, Jorge Newbury.

Jorge Newbury is called Aeroparque (Ay-ro-park-eh).

By Bus: **Chevallier** and **La Estrella** bus lines provide daily service to Bariloche from Buenos Aires and other parts of Patagonia. The trip from Buenos Aires takes 22 hours.

Climate

The climate is cool year-round but Lake Nahuel Huapi moderates the temperatures. Summer temperatures average 14°C (60°F), while winters average 2°C (35°F). Snow falls from May through September and there is a lot of rain near the Andean chain. Whatever the season, bring rain gear and layerable clothing.

Arrival

The airport is 10 miles east of Bariloche. It is very small, with only a long runway, wind sock and terminal. Taxis and microbuses meet each flight. There is a Hertz rental car kiosk at the airport.

Orientation

Bariloche is in the province of Rio Negro.

Bariloche, at 2,400 feet above sea level, is the heart of Argentina's Lake Region. The area, dotted with lakes, is nestled at the foot of the Andean mountain range. It is home to 110,000 people, many of whom have moved here from other parts of Argentina and Chile. The commercial center of town, built along the southern shore of Lake Nahuel Huapi, looks like a Swiss mountain village, understandable since Bariloche was founded by German-Swiss immigrants in 1902. This part of town is quite small and, although hilly, can be easily walked. The residential areas are more contemporary in style and rather haphazard due to Bariloche's rapid expansion. Avenues, which run east to west alongside the lake, change names at the Civic Center.

Centro Cívico

The Civic Center is lovely. Several ocher stone buildings enclose a landscaped square over-looking the lake and municipal dock. These buildings were designed by local architect Ezequiel Bustillo, who also laid out the town grid and designed the Llao-Llao resort. The buildings were completed in 1934 and the stone was quarried locally. They house the municipal government offices, the tourist office, police de-partment, the Natural History Museum of Patagonia, and a library. The equestrian statue in the square honors General Roca, who led the Argentine forces against the Mapuche Indians. They fiercely resisted the white settlers who were arriving in the area. A highlight is the clock on the municipal tower which, at the stroke of noon, opens to reveal revolving statues depicting an Indian, a missionary, a Spaniard and a farmer from the time when the area was first being colonized.

Avenida B. Mitre

This busy street starts at the arch leading east from the Centro Cívico. It is crowded with shops, airline offices, hotels and restaurants. West of the Civic Center, it becomes Avenida España. The Bariloche Casino is located here.

Avenida P. Moreno/San Martín

This avenue, one block south of B. Mitre, is another important commercial street. For most of the commercial center of town it is Avenida Moreno, and continues as San Martín west of the Civic Center. Hotels, restaurants, cinemas and shops line the entire length of the avenue.

Calles Morales, Quaglia, Villegas & Rolando

These are the most important north/south streets. Here you will find hotels, restaurants, tour operators and shopping arcades.

Alive Price Scale
Deluxe: $175+
Expensive : $100+
Moderate: $60-100
Inexpensive : $35-60
Budget: under $35

Hotels

Accommodations are plentiful in Bariloche and there is tremendous variety. Choices include out-of-town resorts with spacious grounds and European service and in-town five-star stops with resort amenities and within easy walking distance of restaurants and nightlife. Center city also has scores of small hotels with fewer amenities and lower rates. There are motel-like accommodations all along the road from town to Cerro Catedral ski area, which has its own hotel too. All are completely booked during the ski season (July and August) and you definitely need reservations. Hotel rates vary with the season. High-season rates are in effect in July and August and from mid-December through mid-March. Rates are lower during the spring and fall. All our selections have heated rooms with private baths, TVs (some with CNN, HBO & ESPN) and mini-bars. Many include continental breakfast in the rate. All accept major credit cards.

In-Town Hotels

LAGOS DE PATAGONIA ☆☆☆☆☆
Avenida San Martín 536
8400 Bariloche
Tel/Fax (944) 25846
Expensive

A new member of the Crowne Plaza resort group, Lagos will have been greatly refurbished by the time you read this. Rooms will be re-painted, new furnishings will be installed, and the public areas will have state-of-the art lighting. All these will be pluses for what is already a top notch establishment. Rooms are spacious with sitting areas and a desk. The lobby has a roaring fireplace, which is the center of attention during late afternoon tea and cocktail hour. There is an indoor pool, sauna and solarium. Service is first rate.

HOTEL EDELWEISS ☆☆☆☆☆
Avenida San Martín 202
8400 Bariloche
Tel (944) 26165
Fax (944) 25655
100 rooms
Expensive

Edelweiss is on the main street just one block from the Civic Center and an easy walk to restaurants and shops. Tasteful furnishings, including soft leather sofas and easy chairs with natural color fabrics on the floors and beds, create a relaxing environment. Guests enjoy the health club, sauna, glass-enclosed pool and in-house masseuse and hairdresser. Ask for a room facing the lake.

HOTEL NEVADA ☆☆☆☆
Rolando 250
8400 Bariloche
Tel (944) 22778
Fax (944) 27914
Expensive/moderate

A nondescript exterior opens into a tasteful lobby with plush couches arranged in sitting areas and lively Van Gogh prints on the walls. The interior decor is Swiss, with light woods, carved beams and lots of flowers. The breakfast area is off the lobby and continental breakfast is included in your rate. This area doubles as a tea room in the late afternoon. Rooms are small but well-maintained and extremely functional. The front desk staff is quite helpful.

HOTEL NAHUEL HUAPI ☆☆☆☆
F.P. Moreno 252
8400 Bariloche
Tel/fax (944) 22056
70 rooms
Moderate

Popular with tour groups, the Nahuel Huapi features rooms which, though not large, are comfortable. They are decorated in light woods with matching floral comforters and drapes. Continental breakfast is included in the basic rate or you can opt for the modified American Plan, which includes dinner. Meals are served family-style in the hotel's private dining room. But, since there are plenty of good restaurants in Bariloche, we suggest you forego the American Plan.

HOTEL ROMA ☆☆☆
Avenida San Martìn 102
8400 Bariloche
Tel (944) 22218
Fax (944) 22204
60 rooms
Moderate

Roma's location, right in the heart of town over-looking the Civic Center, makes it an outstand-ing moderate choice. Rooms are spread out over three floors, are carpeted, and have built-in beds with pastel comforters. Breakfast, which is in-cluded in your rate, can be eaten in your room at the picture window overlooking the lake. The Roma has a cafeteria-style Italian restaurant ad-joining its lobby.

Out of Town Hotels

LLAO-LLAO HOTEL AND RESORT
Avenida Ezequiel Bustillo KM. 25
Bariloche
Tel (944) 48065
Fax (944) 48222
U.S. reservations (1-800) 223-5652
164 rooms/suites
Deluxe/expensive

You can look long and hard but you'll never find a hotel with a better location than Llao-Llao (jou-jou). Twenty-five kilometers from Barilo-che in the heart of the national park, it sits on a raised promenade encircled by snow-capped peaks and a kaleidoscope of changing land-scapes. Recently renovated after being closed for many years, the hotel is a world unto itself. With no neighbors, save for the small park ma-rina across the road, Llao-Llao looks like a Swiss monastery outside and an elegant log cabin inside. It has several buildings that are connected by covered walkways. An 18-hole golf course is being constructed, and there are tennis and paddleball courts, a health club with heated pool and whirlpool, plus a large shopping arcade. All the restaurants are enclosed by glass picture windows to take full advantage of the stunning views.

Llao-Llao is a terrific choice for a honeymoon or special anniversary.

EL CASCO ☆☆☆☆☆
Avenida Ezequiel Bustillo, KM. 11
Box 436, Bariloche
Tel (944) 61088
Fax (944)61032
25 rooms
Deluxe/expensive

Hidden from the road by trees, El Casco is a lovely hideaway on the shores of Lake Nahuel Huapi. Its owners and staff provide the attention to detail that makes it the choice of European jet-setters and wealthy Latinos every ski season. Each room is unique, with its own name, individual color scheme and furnishings. All are elegant. Fresh flowers on your night table, chocolates on your pillow each night, and a ready smile from the staff make your stay enjoyable. The public rooms are formal, with paisley high-backed chairs and low wood-beamed ceilings. Service is first-rate.

The dining room, which overlooks the lake and hotel marina, serves continental cuisine featuring local seafood.

LA CASCADA ☆☆☆☆☆
Avenida Ezequiel Bustillo, KM. 6
Bariloche
Tel (944) 41046
Fax (944) 41076
25 rooms
Deluxe

A member of the Relais & Chateaux Association, La Cascada is reserved where Llao-Llao is expansive. Its intimate size allows La Cascada to pamper its guests with serenity and service. All rooms and public areas are decorated in muted tones and face the lake and perfectly manicured grounds. Guests congregate around the umbrella-shaded tables on the outdoor terrace for cocktails and afternoon tea. The chef here is always spectacular and non-guests frequently visit the attractive restaurant. Breakfast, which is included in the rate, is served in a small dining area. A cozy indoor pool and sauna, quiet reading rooms and an open terrace are on the lower level.

Only a five-minute ride from the center, the dining room here is a local favorite.

Restaurants

You will not go hungry in Bariloche. There are scores of restaurants in town, ranging from picturesque Swiss-style eateries featuring fondue, to steakhouses serving thick steaks, sizzling *parrilladas*, and cozy *confiterías*. Many menus feature trout caught locally and prepared in a variety of ways – from smoked to almondine. As is common throughout Argentina, dinner is served late, with the most popular hour being 9 to 10 p.m. in winter and even later during the summer. Restaurants are small and you'll want to reserve for dinner in season. All accept major credit cards.

Alive Price Scale
(per person)
Expensive : $40+
Moderate : $25+
Inexpensive : under $20

**LA MARMIT RESTAURANT
& CONFITERIA**
Avenida Mitre 329
Tel 23685
Moderate

A delightful choice, this stone chalet is tastefully furnished in Swiss style, complete with hanging cowbells and posters. It operates as a *confitería* from 11 a.m. to 8 p.m., serving omelettes, salads, and hearty homemade soups. At 8 p.m. the fare becomes more substantial and fondues with beef or cheese are featured.

LA VIZCACHA
Rolando 279
Tel 22109
Moderate

Watch soccer games here.

You'll have to look for this eaterie, which has windows just at ground level. While the decor is Swiss, with heavy carved tables and chairs and green tablecloths, the food is primarily grilled meats, local trout and pasta.

CASITA SUIZA
Quaglia 342
Tel 23775
Closed for lunch on Wednesday and Thursday
Expensive

A whitewashed chalet-style building with carved wooden balconies and hanging planters, this place looks right at home on hilly Quaglia Street. There are several dining areas, with mauve cloths and fresh flowers on every table. A menu in Spanish, German and English features loin of pork with sauerkraut, gulasch, Hungarian-style chicken, as well as fondues.

RIGOLETTO
Villegas 363
Tel 26672
Lunch: 12 noon-2:30 p.m.
Dinner: 8 p.m.-11 p.m.
Moderate

A favorite of ours, Rigoletto serves Italian specialties in a very attractive setting. Its single dining room has floral wallpaper that matches the curtains and hanging lamps. The menu includes such specialties as pasta with pesto and meat sauces, ravioli and canneloni. Hearty soups and veal dishes are excellent.

CASA MAYOR
Avenida Elflein 190 at Quaglia
Tel 23089
Expensive

An elegant restaurant, Casa Mayor's dark wood walls are set off by red and green tablecloths and hanging plants. Specialties include *ciervo* (venison) and *trucha* (trout), as well as grilled meats. Appetizers and desserts are served from rolling carts.

RESTAURANT EUROPA
Palacios 145 (at Mitre)
Tel 231333
Moderate

Distinctive decor and good food sets Europa apart. There is one dining area and the rear wall is glassed and overlooks a lovely garden. Red lacquered chairs with black leather trim encircle tables with black and white tableclothes. The food includes pastas, grilled meats and chicken, as well as local trout with mushrooms or almonds. Europa serves a three-course lunch and is crowded with local business people.

LOS PIONEROS
Quaglia 259
Tel 23027
Moderate

Probably the largest restaurant in town

One of the larger dining spots in town, there can be quite a buzz when all the tables here are full, which is often. Grilled meats, *empanadas* and fresh salads are specialties. The shop that adjoins the restaurant has chocolates and small gifts.

RESTAURANT 1810
Avenida Elfein 167 (near Quaglia)
Tel 23922

This is another excellent steakhouse. Short on decor, but the steaks, served with two dipping sauces, are superb. Nearby, **Jauja** at Quaglia 366 (tel 22952) is smaller and more attractive. The meats are very good as are the pasta dishes, although service can be slow. The trout platters are considered superb by locals.

Lighter Dining

LA ALPINA
Moreno 98 (at Quaglia)
Inexpensive

Try the hot chocolate near the fireplace on a cold afternoon.

With booths and tables encircling a large wood-burning fireplace, La Alpina resembles a ski lodge. Whitewashed walls and low beamed ceilings add to the warmth, which you'll appreciate when the wind is blowing – as it so often is. Fare here includes burgers, sandwiches, *chorizos* and pastries. Very popular.

QUORUM
B. Mitre 285
Inexpensive

A personal favorite, Quorum is many things in one – a supermarket, a gourmet take-out shop, a bakery, a butcher and fresh fish shop and a cafeteria. Select your foods at the gourmet counter (everything from soups to sliced meats and fish to prepared meat and vegetable salads, pastries and drinks); pay the cashier, and carry your tray up one flight to the dining room. Terrific.

EL VIEJO MUNICH
B. Mitre 102
This German-style *confitería* serves omelettes, sandwiches, grilled meats and sausages. It has heavy carved booths and tables with checkered cloths.

Fast Food

Fast food stops include **Pumpernic** at Mitre 301 for burgers; **El Mundo I and II** at B. Mitre 370 and 759 for pizza; and a foodcourt at **Puerto San Carlos**, the municipal dock.

Sun Up to Sundown

Bariloche is a year-round resort destination, but it is most popular during the Argentine winter (June-September) when it becomes South America's most alluring ski resort, and in the Argentine summer (December-March) when visitors arrive eager to explore Nahuel Huapi National Park and Lake. Outdoor activities in summer (as well as late spring and early fall) include trekking, mountain climbing, bicycling, horseback riding, fishing and all manner of watersports. Winter brings both Alpine and Nordic skiing, snowmobiling and dog sled rides. The area offers towering mountains, lush islands in the lake, condor hideaways and interesting Patagonian towns.

Wa⫶m Weathe⫶ Ba⫶iloche

You can easily walk through Bariloche. There are few don't-miss sights, but one absolute must is the **Museo de la Patagonia** on the Plaza Centro Cívico. Small but informative, the museum has three floors of exhibits. The first floor shows the animals that are indigenous to Patagonia, including the condor. The second floor describes the founding of Bariloche. Look closely at the early photos and you'll see some young men wearing Nazi armbands. (These photos were taken long before Hitler.) The third floor focuses on the Indian tribes that lived in the area. Tools, kayaks and clothing are among the displays. Stop in at the adjoining library.

The Tourist Office is also on the Plaza Centro Cívico.

A stroll along the waterfront heading east (right) is relaxing. You'll soon come to Plaza Italia, marked by a statue of Remus and Romulus. Beyond it there is a huge cathedral. Stunning on the outside, the interior is disappointing and looks unfinished. You can tour the town by mini-bus but it's a lot more fun to take *Pochi*, a small two-car trolley which leaves on the hour from the steps in front of the Civic Center. Tours start at 9 a.m. and the last tour leaves at 6 p.m., with a break or siesta from 1 p.m. to 2 p.m.

Pochi trolley tours last 50 minutes.

Nahuel Huapi National Park & Lake

Nahuel Huapi National Park is comprised of 815,000 acres. Its northern end is in the province of Nequen, while its southern end is in Río Negro. This is where Bariloche is located. The jewel of the park, which is studded with lakes, is Lake Nahuel Huapi. Ninety-six kilometers long and only 12 kilometers wide at its broadest point, it is irregularly shaped with long inlets (*brazos*) that extend into the land. The name means "Tiger Island" in Araucano, the language of the Mapuche Indians that lived here. Although the activities vary, the park is used year round. In warm weather, from October through April, the park is frequently visited by trekkers.

The National Park Office is located at San Martín 24.

Treks are organized by local tour operators and by the Club Andino, which maintains several *refugios* (shelters) in the park. Treks follow clearly marked trails through forested areas, crossing streams on hanging bridges, climbing to waterfalls, circling lagoons, and stopping near icy-blue glaciers. Your fitness level should determine the trek you join. Club Andino groups usually have 20-40 people and treks last anywhere from 1½ hours to several days. The Club Andino office is at Calle 20 de Febrero 30, two blocks north of the Civic Center (tel 26700). Serious mountain climbers can arrange excursions with experienced guides. Arrangements must be made well in advance.

Fishing/hunting enthusiasts should contact the Club Andino de Pesca Y Caza, Avenida 12 de Octubre, tel (944) 22043.

You can explore the park on horseback or on a mountain bike. There are organized tours or you can rent a bike at the shop at Puchi Moreno 1035 and go it alone. Other organized park activities include fishing, hunting, and watersports. The water in Lake Nahuel Huapi is very cold the year round so you'd do better to swim in one of the smaller lakes in the park. Many of them have beach strips.

Isla Victoria & Quetrihue Peninsula

Isla Victoria (Victoria Island), a long narrow island in Lake Nahuel Huapi, is a popular stop. Reached by catamarans, which leave from either the municipal dock or Puerto Pañuelo at Llao-Llao, the island is interesting for the variety of trees growing there. Brought from all over the world, they flourish here. The northern tip of the island has a forest of *arrayanes* (myrtle trees). These rare trees are twisted and have orange trunks with bark that actually seems to be peeling. There are even more *arrayanes* on Quetrihue Peninsula nearby, where a small area has been designated **Los Arrayanes National Park.** You can combine your visit to Isla Victoria with a stop at Quetrihue Peninsula.

Visiting Nearby Mountains

Several of the peaks within the park can be visited. **Cerro Tronador**, an extinct volcano, is the highest peak in this area. It has several glaciers, one of which you can drive to – **Ventisquero Negro** (Black Glacier). Only part of the road is paved and it is so narrow that traffic is regulated, with cars going up in the morning and down in the afternoon. Check this before setting out.

Cerro Otto is the mountain that directly overlooks Bariloche. You can reach the peak by cable car. The car leaves from a terminal six kilometers from town. Buy your ticket at the kiosk on Main Street. It includes a mini-bus to the terminal and back, as well as the cable car. The views are sensational! Bring plenty of film. Stop for lunch at the revolving restaurant on the peak.

Cerro Catedral, a ski resort in winter, is a kick-off point for treks in summer and an excellent scenic overlook. A cable car takes you to the restaurant allowing for beautiful views enroute as well as from the peak.

Sightseeing

There are organized tours to Llao-Llao and the areas nearby, but you can also bicycle the 25 kilometers or take bus #20 which leaves from stops along Avenida Moreno/San Martín. Route 237 heads west from town on its way to Llao-Llao. Enroute it passes scores of small hostelries, restaurants and tiny villages. You can stop along the way at smaller lakes that have beach facilities.

You can hire a remis, car and driver, to take these trips privately.

There are two organized driving trips. The "Short Circuit" follows Route 237 to Llao-Llao, where it stops for a while. It leaves along Route 79, which climbs to magnificent scenic overlooks, particularly the one at Bahia Lopez. The "Big Circuit," which includes the short one, continues east of Bariloche, passing many lakes and visual wonders. This drive covers 150 miles and takes an entire day.

Buses from Bariloche connect to other parts of the lake region and Patagonia. The city does not have a central bus terminal. **Chevallier** at Moreno 107 (tel 23090) has a bus to **San Martín de los Andes** every day but Wednesday. This town, at the northern end of Nahuel Huapi National Park, is four hours away. **Charter Bus Company** at Moreno 126 (tel 28822) has two buses daily to **El Bolsón. El Bolsón** is a laid back town 3½ hours away via a rough road, surrounded by fruit orchards.

Crossing to Chile

The Chilean Lake Region, just over the Andean range, is the mirror image of the Argentine. Several bus companies make the crossing to Osorno and Puerto Montt, the major towns in the Chilean Lake Region. Contact **Tas Choapa** at Moreno 138 (tel 944 26663) or **Cruz del Sur** at San Martín 453 (tel 944 24044). To make an adventure of the crossing you can do it by boat/bus, which takes a lot longer (two days) but is relaxing and scenically stunning. The boat crosses Lake Nahuel Huapi and you overnight in Peulla, Chile. On the second day you cross Lake Todos Los Santos and board buses for the ride to Puerto Montt. Contact **Catedral Turismo** at Mitre 399 (tel 944 25443 or fax 944 26215).

Winter in Bariloche

Cerro Tronador, an extinct volcano with a peak at 11,725 feet above sea level, is snow-capped year round. Although no longer active, it still makes the thundering sound it was named for. It's actually the thunderous noise of ice sliding down the mountain from one of the glaciers on its peak. Ski fanatics do ski on Tronador in August but it has no lifts. I leave the rest to your imagination.

Skiing in Bariloche means **Cerro Catedral**, a mountain 13 miles from town. In operation since the 1950's, Cerro Catedral is a complete ski resort, with hotels, ski schools and rental facilities. It has a large parking lot, and Micro Omnibus 3 de Mayo leaves for the slopes from Avenida Moreno. Check at **Datos**, Missiones 115, for schedules and stops.

A cable car carries you to the restaurant at 3,300 feet. The views are terrific. There are 32 lifts of all types and they carry skiers to various slopes. There are 18 ski runs, ranging from novice to experienced. Some are quite steep while others challenge skiers with trees haphazardly dotting the run. Cross country skiing is also quite popular.

There are several hotels at the slopes. **Club Hotel Catedral** has 76 rooms and 64 apartments for those planning a long stay. It has several restaurants, a nightclub and a sauna.

Local Tour Operators

Sightseeing tours and adventures such as trekking and fishing are all readily available in Bariloche. There are a great many tour operators in town and trips are well organized. **Cumbres Patagonia** at Villegas 222 (tel/fax 944 23831) offers the widest range of adventure trips, including rafting, mountain biking, trekking and fishing. The staff speaks English well. They have a branch office at Llao-Llao. **Karnak Expediciones y Viajes**, Rolando 245, Of. 18 (tel/fax 944 28236) is another reputable organization that leads treks through the forest, operates rafting trips on the Manso River, and runs birdwatching expeditions, among others.

No sneakers allowed.

Bariloche After Dark

Looking for some late night action? You have several options.

The most popular diversion in town, judging by the number of participants, is the **Gran Bariloche Casino** at España 415. In an attractive new building two blocks from the Civic Center, the casino operates daily from 10:30 p.m. to 3:30 a.m. Roulette, black jack, craps and slot machines are all here. There is a $10 admission charge.

The loud music you hear is coming from **Cerebro**, the nicest discotheque in town. In a large private building at Juan Manuel de Rosas 405 (tel 24948), it is actually just behind the casino. Cerebro has all the latest sound and light effects and draws a young crowd. Just up the street, **Rocket**, at 424 (tel 232579), is also popular. Lots of singles here. A third choice, **Moritz** is on Avenida Mitre at 9 de Julio.

For a nightcap and some background music, head to **Pub de la Costa**, Juan Manuel de Rosas 450, or the basement pub at the **Hotel Lagos de Patagonia**, San Martín 536.

The art gallery at San Martín 64 presents a tango show at 10 p.m. on Friday and Saturday evenings, while the Hotel Los Andes, Moreno 594, offers a folkloric dance program at the same hours.

Shopping

We would normally discourage shopping in a resort area where the typical item for sale is a shabby souvenir at an exorbitant price. Not so in Bariloche. There are unusual items for sale here and prices, while not low, are consistent with what you will pay in Buenos Aires.

Hard to resist are the chocolate shops. Made locally, chocolates are sold loose or pre-packaged. There are chocolate chunks and logs along with strips that look like spaghetti. Delicious and terrific gifts! Check out the variety at **Fenoglio**, Mitre 252, **Mamushka** at Mitre 216, or **Abuela Goye** at Villegas 241.

Cerámica Bariloche is a local factory that produces colorful ceramic items. Most have the typical floral pattern that is favored here. The factory, here since the early 1950's, makes wall clocks, vases, serving platters and candlesticks. The shop at Mitre 112 is open from 9:30 a.m. to 9:30 p.m. every day but Sunday.

Gift shops selling unusual items include **Tito Testone**, Mitre 150 where many of the copper and bronze objects were designed by the owner. **Martina Paz**, San Martín 536, is an attractive shop with coffee mugs, condiment trays, knits and ceramics. Next door, **La Talabartería** sells leather and suede items as well as riding clothes and boots. **Viejo Galeón**, Avenida San Martín 64, sells products (only of wood) that are typical of Patagonia. Gaily printed, they are both decorative and useful. The **Feria Artesanal** on Avenida Moreno at Villegas, is a long narrow building with stall after stall of artisans displaying their jewelry, most of which is silver and studded with colorful stones. Both the artists and their wares look like 60's retreads.

Outdoor enthusiasts should stop by **Martín Pescador** on Rolando near Moreno, where ski clothing and equipment, camping gear, bicycles and backpacks are offered.

Bariloche A-Z

AIRLINE OFFICES: **Aerolíneas Argentinas** and **Austral** share an office at Mitre 199. Hours are from 9 a.m. to 7 p.m. weekdays and 9 a.m. to 7 p.m. Saturdays. Closed Sunday.

AUTOMOBILE CLUB: The **Automovil Club Argentino** has an office at Avenida 12 de Octubre 785 (tel 23001).

BEAUTY PARLOR: The salon at locale 14 in the **Galería Via Firenze** on Quaglia keeps both men and women looking their best.

BOOKSTORE: English language books are available at **Mileno** in the Galeria Firenze on Quaglia.

CINEMA: **Cine Arrayanes** at Moreno 39 has first-run films in their original language.

CURRENCY EXCHANGE: You can change money in the **Banco de la Nación Argentina** at Mitre 180.

GOLF: Llao-Llao's new golf course may be in operation as you read this. Until then, try the nine-hole course at **Pinares Golf**, Kilometer 14 on Bustillo.

GOVERNMENT TOURIST OFFICE: The Government Tourist Office is in the Civic Center. The staff speaks little English and virtually all printed material is in Spanish. Hours: 8:30 a.m. to 8 p.m., Monday through Saturday.

HOSPITAL: For medical assistance, head to Moreno 601 (tel 26100).

NATIONAL PARK OFFICE: You can pick up maps and other information at San Martín 24 (tel 23111). Open weekdays from 9 a.m. to 6 p.m.

PHARMACY: There are many pharmacies in the commercial center. Try San Martín 662 or Mitre 102 for essentials and cosmetics.

POST OFFICE: The main branch is in the Civic Center.

PROVINCIAL TOURIST OFFICE: You can pick up a listing of cultural events (Spanish only) at the office on Avenida Moreno at Villegas.

REMISES: Private cars operating as taxis can be booked through **Bariloche** (tel 27396) or **Hiala** (tel 27660).

SUPERMARKETS: **La Anonima,** Quaglia 331, is a large market with household goods as well as food. **Quorum** at Mitre 275 (see Restaurants) has food only and a take-out gourmet food section.

TAXIS: 24-hour service is provided by **Radio Taxi Bariloche** (tel 22103).

TELEPHONES: Direct line calls to the United States can be made from **Bariloche Center** on San Martín at Pagano.

TENNIS: **Bariloche Raquet Club** is at Kilometre 13 on the road to Llao-Llao. You can arrange for a court. There are also paddleball courts.

Córdoba

When the original settlers first came to Córdoba from Peru in the 17th century, they praised the region for its beautiful weather and landscape of endless plains and gentle sierras, much like those of Castille and Andalucia in their native Spain. They were equally impressed by the abundance of fish in its rivers and streams and the great variety of birds and wild animals roaming the *pampas*. The same holds true today. Thousands of visitors are drawn to its quaint villages and riverside resorts for many of the same reasons.

Córdoba is the name of the province and the capital city.

The city of Córdoba is no less lovely. Founded in 1573 by Jerónimo Luis De Cabrera, a Spaniard from the southern city of Seville, it boasts many of the country's finest examples of colonial architecture. As you wander through the historic district, visiting churches from centuries past, and stroll under the leafy canopies of its pedestrian walkways, perhaps stopping for coffee at a sidewalk café, you'll quickly fall into the relaxed pace of Córdoba and forget that you're in one of Argentina's most progressive cities, an industrial center, second only to Buenos Aires.

Córdoba is the second largest city in the country.

History

When Jerónimo Luis de Cabrera founded Córdoba de la Nueva Andalucia on the banks of the Suquía River, he did so in accordance with the Spanish conventions of the period which required both a water provide and the presence of friendly Indians, who would supply the colonists' need for labor. While the Suquía River easily filled the first requirement, the Comechingón Indians fulfilled the second, quickly becoming a labor force for the raising of sheep and mules as well as agriculture. Cabrera belonged to the wave of Spaniards who crossed into Argentina from Peru and Chile via Inca trade routes to establish settlements in the northwestern corner of the country. The most noteworthy, Santiago del Estero, founded by Francisco de Aguirre in 1553, served as the starting point for Cabrera's journey. His intention was to establish a settlement linking the trade routes of Alto Peru, El Cuyo and Buenos Aires. Indeed, by 1650 Córdoba had displaced Santiago del Estero as the nation's major urban center.

Religion and academics figure strongly in Córdoba's history. Shortly after the city's founding, several religious orders established themselves there, earning her the nickname of "the city of churches." (You'll visit many of these as you tour the colonial district.) Chief among them were the Jesuits, the Franciscans and the Carmelite Sisters. In fact, Córdoba was one of the most important Jesuit centers in South America until they were expelled by Spain in 1767. In 1613 Jesuit Bishop Hernando de Trejo y Sanabria founded the nation's first University in

Córdoba, the Universidad Nacional de Córdoba, turning the city into a center of higher learning and earning her a second nickname which is still used today: "La Docta – The Learned."

The church and the university dominated the city's first three centuries which, with the exception of a few tumultuous events, were relatively tranquil. Midway through the 20th century, however, the city began to experience a period of strong economic growth, still visible in the 1990's. Since 1947, with its growth as an agricultural and industrial capital, the city's population has surged from 350,000 to 1,195,000. Fiat and Renault have plants here, as do several other multinational corporations. The city's cultural life has also intensified. Residents and visitors enjoy several annual music and cultural festivals, both national and international. Córdoba is home to numerous small theaters, *cine clubs* (movie clubs), and café shows in addition to the Teatro Libertador General San Martín, a frequent host to great performances on tour from Buenos Aires and other major cities of South America.

All in all, while faithful to its colonial roots and traditions, Córdoba is a vibrant and dynamic city.

Geography/Topography

The province of Córdoba could easily be called the "breadbasket of Argentina." Not only is this province of seemingly endless plains, rolling hills, rivers, lakes and streams a vacation paradise, it is also one of the nation's most important industrial and agricultural regions.

Located in the center of the country, almost equidistant from the Andes in the west and the Atlantic in the east, its 165,321 square kilometers are crossed by three mountain ranges running north to south, and five rivers. The latter, formed by seasonal rains and winter thaws, have been dammed in many places to create both irrigation systems and the region's principal tourist attraction, her many lakes.

Cordoba's northern landscape is characterized by the flat jungle plains of the Gran Chaco, which extends from Mato Grosso in Brazil south to the Río Salado in Argentina, west to the Andes and east to the Paraguay River. Native to the region is the *quebracho*, a tree known for the superb quality of its wood as well as its resin, used in the tanning of leather.

The fertile *pampas*, home of the legendary *gaucho*, dominate the southern portion of the province. Of Quechua origin, the word "pampa" means treeless plain and aptly describes the flat prairie lands or *pampa seca*, west of Córdoba. Moving east, the gentle hills of the Central Sierra lead to the fertile farmlands of the *pampa húmeda*, home of vast *estancias* where you'll pass fields of grazing cattle watched over by *gauchos*, breeding farms for race horses and polo ponies, and endless fields of corn, wheat and barley swaying in the breeze.

The province's varied landscape is home to numerous species of flora and fauna. Woods such as cedar and *quebracho*, along with cotton and other textile-producing plants flourish in the sub-tropical Chaco, while fruits and cereals are cultivated throughout the *pampas*. Pumas and other wild cats are not unknown to the region. Guanacos, vizcachas, peccaries, foxes, and boars are also common, along with small deer, weasels, rabbits and hares. Bird watchers will find herons, ostriches, flamingoes, storks, falcons, partridges and herons, as well as ducks, parrots and sparrows. Several species of reptile and snake also make their home here.

Climate

Córdoba enjoys a temperate climate with sunny skies all year long. Winters are quite mild, with temperatures seldom dipping below 45°F. Days can get quite warm during the summer months (December to February); temperatures occasionally rise as high as 100°F, but nights are generally cool. Summer is the peak season for resorts throughout the province. So if you're planning to visit then, it is a good idea to reserve ahead.

Getting There

The city is easily accessible by bus, car or plane. Given its central location, the city serves as a hub for both air and land transportation. Aerolineas Argentinas offers several flights daily to and from Buenos Aires, while Austral covers cities throughout the rest of the country including Rosario, Mendoza, Tucumán and Santiago del Estero. If you're traveling to Córdoba from outside the country, you will probably have to change planes in Buenos Aires.

Though at present there is no train service linking Córdoba with Buenos Aires and other cities, the recent privatization of the railroad makes the restoration of rail service more likely.

Buses from throughout the country and Chile arrive daily. Both the train and bus stations are conveniently located in city center on Bulevar Presidente J.D. Perón Service between Córdoba and Buenos Aires is provided by the ABLO bus company (313-2835). If you're driving, National Routes 8, 9, 19, 35, and 60 intersect the city. If you're arriving from Mendoza look for Provincial Route 20 to take you into the city.

1. Iglesia Catedral
2. Cabildo Histórico
3. Centro municipal de inf. y exposiciones Obispo Mercadillo
4. Centro de Exposiciones J. Malanca
5. Iglesia de la Teresas
6. Museo de Arte Religioso Juan de Tejeda
7. Museo Relioso Fray J. Antonio de San Alberto
8. Iglesia de la Compañia de Jesús
9. Universidad Nacional de Córdoba
10. Colegio Nacional de Monserrat
11. Academia Nacional de Ciencias
12. Teatro del Libertador Gral. San Martín
13. Museo del Teatro y de la Música Cristóbal de Aguilar
14. Museo Municipal de Bellas Artes Dr. General Pérez
15. Basilica de Santo Domingo
16. Legislatura
17. Iglesia de Santa Catalina de Siena
18. Basilica de la Merced
19. Iglesia del Pilar
20. Museo Histórico Provincial Marqués de Sobremonte
21. Iglesia de San Roque
22. Iglesia de San Francisco
23. Banco Provincia de Córdoba
24. Teatro Real
25. Banco Social de Córdoba
26. Palacio Municipal 6 de Julio
27. Palacio de Justicia
28. Mercado Norte
29. Hospital de Urgencias
30. Asistencia Pública
31. Paseo Sobremonte
32. Cripta
33. Casona Municipal
34. Estación Terminal de Omnibus

Downtown Córdola

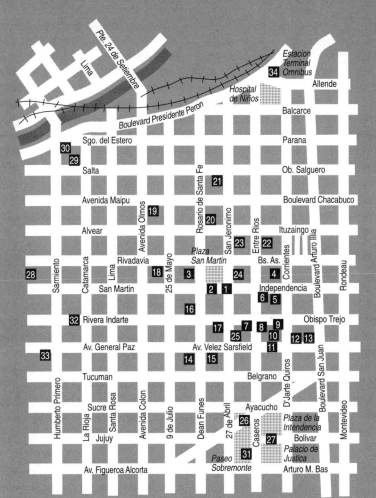

Pte. 24 de Setiembre

Lima

Estacion Terminal Omnibus
34

Allende

Hospital de Niños

Balcarce

Boulevard Presidente Peron

Parana

Sgo. del Estero

Ob. Salguero

30
29

Salta

Avenida Maipu

Boulevard Chacabuco

Rosario de Santa Fe

21

Avenida Olmos

19

20

San Jeronimo

Alvear

Entre Rios

Ituzaingo

Sarmiento

Catamarca

Rivadavia

Plaza San Martin

23

22

Bs. As.

Corrientes

Boulevard Arturo Illia

Rondeau

Lima

25 de Mayo

28

18

3

24

4

San Martin

2   1

Independencia

6   5

16

32

Rivera Indarte

Obispo Trejo

17

7

8   9

33

10

12   13

Av. General Paz

25

11

14   15

Av. Velez Sarsfield

D'Jarte Quiros

Boulevard San Juan

Tucuman

Belgrano

Humberto Primero

Santa Rosa

Avenida Colon

9 de Julio

Dean Funes

27 de Abril

Ayacucho

La Rioja

Sucre

Plaza de la Intendencia

Montevideo

26

Caseros

Jujuy

27

Bolivar

Paseo Sobremonte

31

Palacio de Justica

Av. Figueroa Alcorta

Arturo M. Bas

Arrival

Córdoba's modern Pajas Blancas International Airport is eight kilometers north of the center of the city. Most major car rental agencies have booths here, as does the Tourist Office. Pick up a map of the city before heading out.

A **remis** cab into the city is $11. Airport vans (**combis**) will take you into the center of the city and cost only $2. If you don't have much luggage and are trying to keep expenses down consider a public bus (70¢). Be sure to let the driver know where you want to get off before taking a seat.

Orientation

Typical of cities colonized by the Spanish, Córdoba was designed in a grid-like pattern with the Plaza San Martín at its heart. You'll probably spend most of your time in the colonial district, which is concentrated among the blocks surrounding the plaza. With the help of a map supplied by the tourist office, you should have little or no trouble finding your way around.

As in many South American cities, several streets here change names at the center of the city, which is marked by the Plaza San Martín. Avenidas and bulevares (avenues and boulevards) cross the city north to south and calles (streets), east to west. Hence, **Avenida General Paz**, one of the main thoroughfares of the city, becomes **Avenida Vélez Sarsfield** south of **27 de Abril** (which runs along the south side of the plaza). Similarly, **Avenida San Martín** becomes

Independencia when it meets the Plaza and **Calle 25 de Mayo** becomes **9 de Julio**, a major shopping street.

Córdoba is a real walking city. Several of the streets in the colonial district are *peatonales*, shady pedestrian malls where you'll find outdoor cafés, lovely shops and plenty of street performers. These include **Independencia, 9 de Julio, Dean Funes**, and **Obispo Trejo**, which is also known as the Paseo de las Flores.

The city does not lack for green areas. The largest of these is the **Parque Sarmiento** in the southeast corner of the city. Parks and gardens also line the **Río Suquía**, which runs across the top of the city and then down along its eastern border. **La Cañada**, a brook off the Suquía, bisects the city north to south and borders the western edge of the colonial district. Its promenade is a favorite of strollers, young and old, with its romantic stone bridges and leafy tipa trees. In the northern sector of the city is the **Cerro de las Rosas**, an affluent residential district, once a center for the cultivation of roses. Many fine restaurants and nightclubs are beginning to set up shop there.

Hotels

CORDOBA PARK HOTEL ☆☆☆☆
Bv. San Juan 165
Tel (051) 243-586
Fax: (051) 245-267
112 rooms, 12 suites
Expensive

Alive Price Scale
Deluxe : $175+
Expensive : $100+
Moderate : $60-100
Inexpensive : $35-60
Budget: under $35

Although classified as a four-star hotel, the Córdoba Park Plaza easily merits a fifth. It has an optimal location on the Plaza Vélez Sarsfield, just steps away from La Cañada. There is sightseeing and shopping, along with the full range of business services, including private offices with personal computers and fax machines, and conference facilities. There is also a rooftop pool, sundeck and sauna. And an especially delightful staff make it a perfect choice for those wishing to mix business with pleasure.

A fairly new hotel, its rooms are modern and tastefully furnished. All are equipped with individually controlled air conditioning and heat as well as cable and local television, two private video channels and private CD channels for music. Soundproof windows keep street noises to a minimum. A generous breakfast buffet featuring fresh fruits and juices, *medias lunas*, cereals, eggs and cold cuts as well as champagne on Sunday is included in your room rate. Special weekend and corporate rates are available.

PANORAMA HOTEL ☆☆☆☆
Marcel T. de Alvear 251 (La Cañada)
Tel (051) 245-248
Fax (051) 243-586
146 rooms, 30 suites
Expensive

The Panorama is another four-star hotel that offers everything a five-star does, except a five-star price. Whether you're working out on the treadmill or a stationary bike or unwinding in the jacuzzi, you'll enjoy spectacular views of the city and nearby sierras from the 14th floor **Terraza Club** fitness center. It also features a small swimming pool, tanning bed, and bar. Business facilities include four conference rooms with audio visual equipment, offices with telephones, typewriters and fax machines and banquet services. An elegant lobby, fine restaurant, comfortable guest rooms and privileged location alongside the Cañada round out the list of amenities that make the Panorama a favorite of many regular visitors to Córdoba.

HOTEL DE LA CAÑADA ☆☆☆
Marcelo T. de Alvear 580 (La Cañada)
Tel (051) 231-227
Fax (051) 237-569
50 rooms
Moderate
Located alongside the Cañada, two blocks south of the Plaza Vélez Sarsfield, the Hotel de la Cañada is a fine choice. Though not quite as luxurious, and slightly further from shopping and sightseeing than are our previous selections, these differences are appropriately reflected in the price. The large outdoor terrace overlooking the Cañada is ideal for dining or cocktails. As we found to be true virtually everywhere we went in Córdoba, service here is exceptionally friendly. There is a conference center. Breakfast is offered.

DUCAL SUITES HOTEL ☆☆☆☆
Corrientes 207
Tel (051) 250-010
Fax (051) 250-011
82 suites
Expensive
Situated in the heart of the textile and trading district, the Ducal Suites caters especially to business travelers and frequently hosts trade

shows, conferences and conventions. Although small for suites, rooms are comfortably furnished and come equipped with all the amenities expected of a four-star hotel, including a mini-bar. There is a rooftop pool and sundeck, as well as a small fitness center with sauna and jacuzzi. The dining atrium is especially lovely. There is a breakfast buffet.

GRAN HOTEL DORA ☆☆☆
Calle Entre Ríos 70
Tel (051) 212-030
Fax (051) 212-031
126 rooms
Moderate

If you enjoy staying in the midst of the action, then the Gran Hotel Dora, just a block away from Independencia and two blocks from the Plaza San Martín, is well worth your consideration. Although it does not offer the extras of our previous selections, rooms here are far more than adequate. The Dora has sister hotels in Buenos Aires and Mar del Plata. Breakfast is included.

WINDSOR HOTEL ☆☆☆
Buenos Aires 214
Tel (051) 224-012
Fax (051) 243-864
60 rooms
Moderate

Not luxurious, yet comfortable.

Although furnishings appear to date back to when the hotel first opened in 1956, the Windsor continues to represent a solid value. Around the corner from the Gran Hotel Dora, it is another fine choice for those who like to be in the center of the action. Breakfast is included.

HOTEL FELIPE II ☆☆☆
San Jerónimo 279
Tel (051) 214-752
Fax (051) 226-185
Moderate
For overall value, the Felipe II ranks among the best hotels in the city and is a favorite of thrifty business travelers. 24-hour room service, conference facilities and laundry service are among the perks here. Breakfast is included.

HOTEL CESAR CARMEN
Avenida Amadeo Sabattini 459
at Bajada Pucará
Tel (051) 229-100
Fax (051) 223-470
60 rooms
Moderate
Those who enjoy visiting the city, but prefer to stay in a more suburban setting, should consider the Cesar Carmen Hotel, a three-minute cab ride from the center of town. The quiet, friendly atmosphere is characteristic of the hotel Its spacious wood-hued lobby, replete with potted plants and leather couches, is a popular gathering place, as is the outdoor pool and adjacent snack bar. Most rooms have balconies. The hotel tour service offers escorted trips with bilingual guides to places of interest throughout the province. The hotel is run by the Automobile Club of Argentina. (Members enjoy a discounted rate.) Breakfast is included.

Restaurants

Second to Buenos Aires in number of restaurants, there is no shortage of dining options in

Alive Price Scale
(per person)
Expensive : $40+
Moderate : $25+
Inexpensive : under $20

Córdoba. Meals here are on the same schedule as Buenos Aires, so don't expect to be served in a restaurant anywhere before 9 p.m. Beef, of course, is the mainstay of most menus. Regional specialties include dishes such as *carbonada* and *locro*, both stews. *Carbonada* is made with beef and peaches, while the especially filling *locro* is made with several different types of meat and sausage along with corn or wheat. Pizza could also be considered a regional specialty since, given the city's large Italian population, pizzerias abound.

Córdoba's temperate climate is especially conducive to a late afternoon coffee at a sidewalk café. Pastries are especially good and are often filled with *dulce de leche, dulce de batata* (sweet potato jam) and any of the jams and jellies made from the native fruits and sugar cane. Be prepared to indulge.

GUCCIO RESTAURANT
Avenida Hipolito Yrigoyen 81
Tel 225-135
Continental
Reservations requested
Expensive
Major credit cards
If we were asked to compile a list of Argentina's most elegant restaurants, Guccio would easily be one of our top selections. Richly hued wooden walls, a mosaic ceiling, varnished parquet floors and candles quietly flickering on the tables create an ambience of old world refinement. The menu is just as refined, with appetizers such as *pâté Guccio en salsa naranja* (pâté in an orange sauce) and *crêpes de mariscos* (shellfish crêpes). Entrées include *lomo Guccio* (sirloin),

milanesitos de pollo en crema de choclo (chicken filets served in a creamed corn sauce) and *trucha al chablis* (trout in chablis). There is little doubt why residents choose Guccio for special occasions.

LA COCINA DE OSES
Independencia 512
Tel 230-508
French & international
12 p.m.-3 p.m.; 8 p.m.-midnight
Major credit cards accepted
Moderate
Although this bi-level restaurant may not be as elegant as Guccio, its menu is just as impressive. Selections include *salmón poche con salsa tartara* (poached salmon with tartar sauce), *lomo pimienta con papas a la crema* (pepper steak with creamed potatoes), *pollo de la nueva Córdoba con crema a la cereza con cognac* (new Cordoba-style chicken with a cream of cherry cognac sauce) and the *grand bistek* (steak served with tomato glacé, pâté de foie-gras, noisette potatoes and bordelaise sauce).

VERA CRUZ
Avenida Vélez Sarsfield 214
Tel 234-835 (reservations requested)
Spanish
Lunch & dinner
Expensive
It seems that Vera Cruz attracts Córdoba's best dressed and best looking residents. If you decide to dine here, be sure to dress the part and be prepared for some great people-watching. Head to the bar in the rear for the latter. Very Spanish, both in decor and in menu, the dining room is spread out over several levels, with

stone walls giving it a very majestic air. If you're dining with a friend, the *paella Valenciana* for two is a terrific choice. Our other favorite entrées include the *cazuela de mariscos, congrio salsa verde* (eel in a green sauce) and the *bife chorizo*.

BETOS LOMITOS-PARRILLA
Bv. San Juan 454
Tel 246-225
Steakhouse
Lunch & dinner
Inexpensive
Betos is the epitome of the Argentine *parrilla* where a fantastic steak typically runs under $10. Designed to resemble an *estancia*, the brick walls are decorated with wagon wheels and leather wall hangings and there are several fire places throughout the large dining room. Steaks average $7 to $9.50, while grilled chicken is slightly less. It is very popular, so plan on getting here before 10:30 p.m. if you don't want to wait for a table. A small branch of Betos is located in the Nuevocentro Shopping Center.

LA OBRA: CASA DE CARNES
La Cañada
Tel 228-330
Steakhouse
Open late
Across from La Mama, this bi-level steakhouse is in a lovely setting overlooking La Cañada.

Italian Restaurants

Since Córdoba has the highest concentration of Italians of any city in Argentina, it is no surprise that there are a great many Italian restaurants.

Pizza places abound. **Pizzas Bocatto**, a chain with branches all over the country, are located in the shopping centers as well on 9 de Julio, and they serve pasta as well. If, like most of us, you especially enjoy Italian food, you'll be very happy in Córdoba.

IL GATTO
Avenida Colón 628
Tel 230-334
Italian
Lunch & dinner daily
Inexpensive to moderate
Don't expect to spend a quiet evening here. A lively crowd frequents this very popular Italian trattoria, which sports red checkered tablecloths and cat motifs on the dishes. Typical Italian food is served in generous portions. This is the nicest of four Il Gatto restaurants in Córdoba; the others are at General Paz 120 and Rafael Núñez 3856. There is another Il Gatto in Carlos Paz on Libertad at the corner of Belgrano, as well as in Buenos Aires.

LA MAMA
Santa Rosa 574 on La Cañada
Tel 22-8330
Italian
Lunch and dinner
Moderate
Given the homey atmosphere, La Mama is a very fitting name for this Italian trattoria in a red brick house alongside La Cañada. This is the perfect place to share a bottle of wine with one of their many antipastos or fresh fruit and cheese platters.

Confiterías

If you've already been to Buenos Aires, you undoubtedly discovered that cafés are an integral and quite pleasant part of the Argentine lifestyle. Córdoba's temperate climate and lovely plazas and pedestrian malls create a perfect setting for outdoor cafés.

CONFITERIA DE LA PLAZA
Avenida Buenos Aires on Plaza San Martìn
Next door to the Austral Airlines Office
Located across the plaza from the Cathedral and the Cabildo, the Confitería de la Plaza seems to have been an institution in Córdoba for years, and so will it continue to be. It reminded us of the very traditional St. James in Buenos Aires, with its antique organs, dark paneled walls, and antique cash registers and typewriters all about. The upstairs tables offer a fine vantage point for watching the "goings-on" in the plaza, or sit at one of the many outdoor tables.

CAFE SOROCABANA
Calle San Jerónimo on Plaza San Martín
Umbrellas top the tables at the equally popular Café Sorocabana. In addition to pastries and finger sandwiches, the Sorocabana features pizza, just right for lunch.

HAMILTON
9 De Julio 60
Tel 223-420
International/confitería
8 a.m.-12:30 a.m. Closed Sunday
Moderate

You've got to make a point of coming to this lovely *confitería*/restaurant on the pedestrian-only 9 de Julio. Come early and join rushing executives as they stop in for a quick coffee and a *media luna* on their way to work. Later on they'll mingle at a more leisurely pace over lunch and dinner or tea. An especially fine choice for breakfast or tea in the afternoon, the plant-filled decor – exposed brick, wooden ceilings, comfortable leather couches – is especially conducive to lingering.

Also a retail shop featuring a fine selection of típicos.

ROBERTINO
Avenida Castro Barros 299
Tel 729-946
Confitería
Open 24 hours
If you're out late (and when won't you be in Argentina) and looking for a place for coffee and conversation, this lovely café will be perfect. Friends meet here at all hours, day or night, indoors or out. If you're alone, don't be shy. Join the conversation.

EL RUEDO
Corner of Obispo Tejo and 27 de Abril
The seemingly hundreds of tables lining Obispo Trejo not far from the Santa Catalina Convent belong to this fine *confitería* at the corner of 27 de Abril.

Sunup To Sundown

Colonial charm and lovely scenery makes Córdoba a delightful place to unwind. Whether you're a city dweller or country type, you'll feel quite at home here.Why not spend a day or two in the city and then venture out into the country-side?

Walking Tour

The best way to get the feel for any new city is by walking. Córdoba is no exception. In fact, the city made for strolling, either under a leafy canopy on one of its many pedestrian shopping streets, along the banks of the Cañada or the Suquía or through the colonial district. Since you will easily find your way along the Cañada and the shopping streets, we've designed this walk to help you get the most out of the colonial section of the city, which is clustered in the blocks surrounding the Plaza San Martín. Take the time to read the plaques mounted outside many of the historic buildings, just in case we've missed a fact or two. Peek into the interior courtyards of the colonial homes. Let your imagination run free, and you'll easily find yourself transported back to the colonial period.

We'll start our walk outside the Córdoba Park Hotel on the **Plaza Vélez Sarsfield** and work our way to the **Plaza San Martín.** Typical of the cities settled by the Spanish, Córdoba was designed in a rectangular grid pattern with the Plaza San Martín as its heart. The majority of the city's most historic buildings are within a few blocks of the plaza.

Heading north on Avenida Vélez Sarsfield, our first stop will be the **Teatro del Libertador General San Martín** (General San Martín Theater) at 365. Inaugurated in 1891, it is older than the Teatro Colón of Buenos Aires, which was inaugurated in 1908. Its French Nouveau style is typical of the buildings constructed in the latter part of the 19th century. The lovely interior is highlighted by four tiers of seats and boxes. Well known Argentine and international artists perform frequently. Check the listings in *Pagina 12* for performances during your stay. (The box office is open from 9 a.m. to 1 p.m. and from 3 p.m. to 7 p.m.). The theater's history is documented in the **Museo del Teatro y de la Música Cristóbal de Aguilar** (tel 32128). A little further up the block at 249 Velez Sarsfield is the **Academia Nacional de Ciencias**, which dates back to 1899. The academy itself was founded by President Sarmiento in 1869. Today it is home to the **Dr. Alfredo Stelzner Minerology and Geology Museum** as well as a **Botany Museum**.

Turn right onto Calle Duarte Quirós. You're now in the midst of Córdoba's Jesuit history. This block is known as the **Manzana de las Luces**, a reference to the Enlightenment, or **Siglo de las Luces**, as it is known in Spanish, when this area was really the focal point of the religious and cultural life of the city.

Walking here is a pleasure. Streets are numbered, making it easy to find your way.

First on the block is the **Colegio Nacional de Montserrat**, which was founded in April of 1695. The exterior of the building was redone in 1928 in a Spanish Renaissance style. Take note of the school's unique clock tower before moving on to the interior patio. Be sure to visit the library for a look at the school's gallery, which includes a portrait of Duarte Quirós dating back to around 1750, as well as a 1763 painting by Luis Gonzaga Coni.

After leaving the school, stroll along the **Peatonal Obispo Trejo**, also known as the Paseo de Las Flores, to the city's original university (**La Universidad**). The first in the Río de la Plata, it was founded by the Jesuit Bishop Hernando de Trejo y Sanabria in 1613 and served as a center of higher learning throughout the colonial period, thus earning Córdoba the nickname "La Docta - The Learned." The university was administered by the Jesuit Fathers until they were expelled from South America by the Spanish Crown in 1767. It was recently restored under the direction of the Argentine Architect Kronfus. The two-story building, a colonial-style cloister by design, surrounds a lovely patio in its interior, which has at its center a bronze statue of Fray Trejo y Sanabria. In the library is a small altar dedicated to Dr. Dalmacio Vélez Sarsfield, author of Argentina's Civil Code.

Next door to the university is the Jesuit Church, **La Iglesia de la Compañía de Jesús**, the city's only church whose structure dates back to the 17th century. Constructed between 1644 and 1674, the stern austerity of its facade makes the opulence of the interior all the more surprising. Many of the baroque altars were installed during the 18th century while the Carrara marble work on the walls is more recent, from the 19th century. The portraits of the Apostles in the main nave are by the Córdobes painter Genaro Pérez. Most striking, however, is the church's ceiling, especially given the way in which its design came about. Midway through construction, the builders ran out of the funds needed to finish it using the large stones customary during that period. The walls would not have been able to support such weight in any case.

Jesuit brother Phillipe Lemer offered an ingenious solution. Cedar was brought from the Jesuit *reducciones* in Misiones Province. Using wooden pegs, the builders crafted the frame of an inverted hull of a ship to form the roof. The ribs were coated with gold and the spaces in between were filled with tiles adorned by colorful arabesques and branches of leaves. Construction took nearly 12 years to complete. Amazingly, the roof has remained watertight after 300 years and the original pegs are still in place. Incidentally, the church's sacristy and *retablo* were also made from cedar. These, however, were moved to the cathedral upon the expulsion of the Jesuits and later to the Church of Tulumba.

A similar system was used to form the roof of the **Capilla Doméstica** (Domestic Chapel) next door, which was completed three years earlier. In its case, the roof was constructed using the same inverted hull as a frame. Between the beams were placed *tacuaro* canes (a native wood) that had been bound together with leather straps and then plastered over and covered with painted cloth. The chapel's baroque alter is also made of cedar from Misiones.

After leaving the chapel, turn right on Caseros and head towards Independencia, the street where you'll make a left. Your tour of the Manzana de las Luces continues with the **Monasterio de Carmelitas Descalzas de San José** (the Church and Convent of Carmelite Nuns). Also known as **Las Teresas**, the complex consists of the convents of San José and Santa Catalina (located behind the cathedral on Obispo Trejo), as well as the Carmelite convent and chapel.

The birthplace of Córdoba's first local poet, Fray Luis de Tejada (1604-1680), it has been home to the cloistered nuns of the Carmelite order since its founding in 1628 by the poet's father Don Juan de Tejada, who donated the property to the order. Fifteen years earlier Fray Fernando de Trejo y Sanabria had founded the Santa Catalina Monastery, located behind the Cathedral one block up on Obispo Trejo, with money donated by Don Juan's wife, Doña Leonor de Tejada.

Take note of the baroque entrance to the convent. The ornate frieze above the gateway is reminiscent of the elaborate *peinetones* (combs) which were much in favor among the aristocratic women of the period. Although the chapel dates back to the 17th century, most of the construction is from the 18th, when it was substantially renovated. The woodwork is especially noteworthy. Be sure to take a close look at the choir, a superb tribute to the skill of the colonial (18th-century) artisan. A life-size statue of Santa Teresa de Jesús graces the altar.

Most of the convent is, of course, closed to the public. However, visitors can get an insight into cloistered life at the **Juan de Tejeda Religious Arts Museum** which is located in the pink-colored main cloister. Several rooms have been decorated to recreate cloistered life. Also on display are the Treasures of the Cathedral along with ceremonial objects, including vestments, valuable religious images, linens, tapestries and relics. The museum is open Wednesday through Saturday from 9:30 a.m. to 12:30 p.m.

Leaving Las Teresas, continue along Independencia to the **Plaza San Martín**, the heart of Colonial Córdoba.

The plaza's importance has not diminished in the 20th century. Always a beehive of activity, most of the pedestrian shopping streets such as **Independencia, Obispo Trejo, and Dean Fulnes** start at the Plaza. Just as in Buenos Aires, an equestrian statue of San Martín presides over the activity, and the **Madres de la Plaza de Mayo** congregate here every Thursday as they have done since the 1970's in their vigil to the memory of their sons and daughters who disappeared under the repressive regime of President Videla. Flowers and palm trees grace the plaza, while the omnipresent pigeons wait to be fed. Friends, old and new, gather here daily, often becoming temporary adversaries as they dispute the key issues of the day. Shoe shine boys and street performers alike ply their trade. Day and night, crowds gather around street performers and will often join in without the slightest hesitation. If you can find a spot, sit on one of the plaza's many benches and take it all in. Or better yet, why not pause at one of the sidewalk tables under the awnings of the **Confitería Sorocabana** before continuing. This is Argentina, and indeed Latin America, at its best.

The Aerolíneas Argentinas and Austral Offices are alongside the Plaza.

Traced in mosaics among the cobblestones of the plaza are the outlines of the Cabildo and the Cathedral. Take a few minutes to study the exterior of the cathedral, the climax of colonial architecture in Córdoba and one of the most important vestiges of Colonial architecture in the country. Since its construction spanned a period of over two centuries, it represents a blending of several different periods, styles and trends. As is typical of churches throughout Latin America, much of its rich ornamentation is the fruit of indigenous labor. Upon careful study, you'll find indigenous images and motifs skillfully blended with Christian ones.

Although the site for the **Cathedral** was selected in 1577, construction did not begin until 1683. It was not consecrated until 1784 and not finally completed until 1914. Construction involved a seemingly endless series of delays, including interruptions and collapses, which gave rise to its unique blend of both neoclassic and baroque styles. The massive austerity of the neoclassic portico is juxtaposed by the indigenous influences in the baroque dome and steeple. The neobaroque ornamentation of the interior and the exterior gates is as recent as the 19th century. The richness of the exterior decoration is a blend of indigenous artistry and creole/baroque designs.

Three main naves separated by massive columns comprise the interior. Several small chapels are scattered along the sides. Many of the murals were sketched by Emilio Caraffa, who then directed Manuel Cardenosa and Augusto Orlandi in enlarging them. The original baroque altar was moved to the Iglesia de Tulumba in the 19th century and replaced by the silver altar in place today. Take some time to wander through the cathedral before moving on to our next stop, the **Cabildo**.

The main tourist office is in the Cabildo.

Presently undergoing restoration, the simple classic lines of the Cabildo contrast sharply with the rich ornamentation of the cathedral. One of the few remaining *cabildos* in the country, it was the center of all civil activity during the colonial period. From its balconies authorities presided over bullfights, executions, public meetings and other events. Its 15 archways, graced by lovely colonial lanterns, once served as a provincial market place. Construction of the imposing, yet simple, geometric structure began in 1607 and completed in 1785 by the engineer Juan Manuel López under the government of the Marquis of Sobremonte. A clock tower was added towards the end of that century. There is a small museum inside the Cabildo, which is open from 9:30 a.m. to 12 noon and from 4 p.m. to 8 p.m. The provincial tourist office is located here, along with the headquarters of the provincial police.

Walk across the plaza to the northeastern corner. At Rosario Santa Fe 39 you'll find the **Capilla y Oratorio del Obispo Mercadillo**. Especially noteworthy is its elegant facade and the singular design of the wrought iron balcony, both of which contrast sharply with the imposing size of the cathedral across the plaza. This former chapel is all that remains of the large 18th-century home that was once the residence of the Bishop Mercadillo. The seat of the Bishop of Tucumán was transferred here in 1698. Today it is home to the municipal tourist and information office. Stop in for a current listing of exhibitions and performances.

Continue east on Rosario de Santa Fe. At the corner of Alvear you'll come upon one of the most beautiful colonial homes in the city, the **Casa del Virrey Sobremonte**. Built during the mid-18th century, it was the home of the Marquis of Sobremonte, Viceroy of the Río de La Plata during the period of English invasions at the beginning of the 19th century. Today it serves as the **Museo Histórico Provincial**, the Provincial History Museum and contains a fine collection of important documents, historical artifacts including tools used by the Indians and the *gauchos*, musical instruments and ceramics from throughout the history of the province of Córdoba. Well worth a visit, the museum is open Tuesday through Friday from 9 a.m. to 1 p.m. and from 3 p.m. to 8 p.m. Tuesday through Sunday.

North one block on Alvear you'll come to 25 de Mayo, a lovely pedestrian promenade. Another of the city's most captivating colonial churches, **La Merced Basílica** was built between Alvear and Rivadavia in 1826 on the ruins of a church from 1600. The history of Córdoba is related in a series of ceramics designed by Armando Cica on the wall bordering Rivadavia. Especially noteworthy is the polychrome gold pulpit with its intricate carvings.

Adopt the leisurely pace of the Córdobeses as you stroll under the leafy canopy on 25 de Mayo, which becomes Avenida 9 de Julio. That official-looking building one block off the promenade on Dean Fulnes and Riviera Indarte is the **Legislatura**, the Legislative Palace. It was built in two phases, in 1885 and 1918, and was recently remodeled by Juan Kronfus, the architect responsible for much of the restorative effort currently underway in the city. Its most striking feature is the clock tower. During colonial times this location served as the seat of the municipal government until it was taken over by the province for the legislature. The provincial congress meets here regularly. If you have the time and it's in session, you can request permission at the entrance to sit in.

Turn down Avenida General Paz, the extension of Sarsfield. The elegant French Art Nouveau home at 33 is the **Museo Municipal de Bellas Artes General Paz**. It was built in 1910 to serve as the seat of city government and became the city's Museum of Fine Arts in 1943. Works by local artists, primarily contemporary, are exhibited there as well as at the Emilio Caraffa Museum of Fine Arts in Sarmiento Park. The museum is open Monday through Saturday from 9:30 a.m. to 1:30 p.m. and from 4:30 p.m. to 8:30 p.m.

Head west on Dean Funes to the **Basílica de Santo Domingo**, home of the venerated image of *Nuestra Señora del Rosario* (Virgin of Rosario), who was canonized in 1592 along with *Nuestro Señor de Milagro*s (Our Lord of Miracles), kept in Salta. Alongside the altar in the Virgin's chambers are a pair of English flags captured during the invasions of 1806, along with General Linier's staff. In front of the altar is a beautiful silver *frontal* from the colonial period.

Turn south onto Jujuy to the **Paseo Sobremonte**, one of the city's most traditional plazas. During the late 18th century this was designated as the site of the city's water supply. A large reservoir was constructed and surrounded by orchards. As the city grew during the 20th century, the reservoir became insufficent to meet its needs and was replaced during the 1960's by the fountain that you see today.

Many of the original trees remain. The Palace of Justice and Municipal Palace are located here along with a monument dedicated in 1983 to those fallen in the Falklands War. Try to stroll through the plaza one evening. The lighting creates a singular effect. From here follow La Cañada back to the Plaza Velez Sarsfield where we started the walk.

Other Sights

Parque Sarmiento (Sarmiento Park). Recognizing that its residents lacked wide-open spaces for fresh air and recreation, in 1911 the city fathers commissioned architect Carlos Thays to design this large park in the southeast corner of the city. Today, residents enjoy a wide range of activities here, including boating at the **Isla Crisol**, tennis, skating, horseback riding, working out at the cardiovascular circuit in the **Parque de la Salud**, and outdoor performances at the **Teatro Griego**. The park also boasts an amusement park and a small zoo, inaugurated in 1914, which has a special section just for snakes and a research center devoted to the study of venom for medical purposes. For a spectacular view of the city, climb to the top of the **Coniferal**, a lookout tower within the park.

Not far from the park at the intersection of Paraná and San Lorenzo is the **Casa Giratoria**, the Rotating House. Completed in 1951, it was designed by Abdón Sahade, a Syrian immigrant, who built it from common materials. It is supported by pillars and propelled by two electric motors. A grandson of the designer lives there now and will often open his door to visitors.

Banco Social de Córdoba, 27 de Abril and Avenida Vélez Sarsfield. The Banco Social Building is one of the city's most noteworthy examples of early 20th-century French Art Nouveau architecture. Designed by the architect Jaime Rocca, it was completed in 1929. Enter the building through a majestic arched entranceway on the corner which, like the cupola, is decorated in silver relief.

Banco Provincial de la Provincia de Córdoba, Calle San Jerónimo at the corner of Ituzaingó. Seventeen years after the Banco Provincial was opened in response to the great prosperity enjoyed by the province during the second half of the 19th century, this majestic neoclassic-style edifice was built. Its grandeur is a clear reflection of the prosperity of the period. The bank's interior is richly decorated in wood, bronze and marble. Exhibits are occasionally held in the foyer.

La Casa Ordoñez, 27 de Abril, 375. This is one of the city's few remaining colonial houses with a central patio. Built between 1884 and 1889, the balanced design offers an interesting contrast to the ornate rococo interior. Currently being remodeled to serve as a library, the building formerly served as the seat of the Court as well as the House of Government.

Museo de Bellas Artes Emilio Caraffa (Provincial Fine Arts Museum), Plaza España at the entrance to Sarmiento Park. Since first opening its doors on December 5, 1914, the Emilio

Caraffa Museum has valiantly supported Argentine artists. Indeed, it is home to a fine collection of works from the second half of the last century which had been collected by the provincial government. It has since added a collection of engravings by Pablo Picasso and works by modern Argentine artists in several different media, and it actively supports the arts with a strong educational program as well as film screenings and receptions.

An Excursion: Camino De La Punilla

The provincial tourist office suggests several different circuits to acquaint you with the landscape and history of the province of Córdoba. Because it offers the best tourist facilities and is the most accesible from Córdoba, we've selected the Camino de la Punilla. This route will take you north of Córdoba through several small resort villages and towns in the valley known as La Punilla because its landscape closely resembles the windswept prairies of the tablelands and plateaus of the upper Andes, known as "puna." La Punilla is a lovely region of brooks, streams, rivers and lakes that offers visitors a myriad of watersports and hiking opportunities. Try to set aside a few days for this tour and take advantage of them. If you're traveling during the summer months, keep your bathing suits ever at the ready as there will be plenty of opportunities for a quick dip along the way. There are several small resorts throughout the region that offer swimming in natural pools. Another good idea is to pack a lunch and other refreshments for impromptu picnics enroute. You will be gradually climbing higher into the mountains throughout the trip. Be sure to bring plenty of sun protection; the sun can be quite strong at these altitudes.

Since you will be returning via the same route, you should plan on making some of the stops as you head north and save others for the return trip. By keeping stops short, you can complete this circuit in a day, but it will be much more enjoyable if you stretch it out over several days to get a real feel for the province. We've included several hotels along the way. Although reservations may not always be necessary, you should book ahead during the summer months, December through March and Easter week.

Although a car is best, you can also travel this route by train. At 8:30 a.m., seven days a week, the **Tren de Las Sierras** departs from Córdoba's **Rodriguez del Busto** station (tel 822-256), located not far from the airport at the corner of Rodriguez del Busto and Manuel Cardeñoza. It heads north to **Cruz del Eje**, stopping at all destinations described below. The cost of a one-way ticket for the five-hour trip is approximately $11. Boarding time is 7:45 a.m. The return train to Córdoba departs Cruz del Eje at 2:40 p.m. and Capilla del Monte at 3:58, arriving in Córdoba at 8:15 p.m.

Carlos Paz & El Lago San Roque

Following Route 20 out of Córdoba, your first stop will be Carlos Paz on the banks of Lago San Roque. You may already be familiar with this popular resort town 35 kilometers outside the city, since several of our recommended night-spots and restaurants are located here. This is one of Argentina's favorite resort cities. During the summer months its population swells from 35,000 to nearly 400,000. In addition to its fine hotels and resort, the city boasts lovely summer homes and chalets. One of the most interesting is the **Casa de Casper**, perched on a ravine at the intersection of Miguel Cane and El Redentor.

The lake, of course, is the primary attraction. Visitors enjoy a multitude of watersports, including sailing, motor boating, water skiing, and windsurfing, as well as fishing. The concierge at your hotel should be able to help you participate through one of the local nautical clubs, **Club 400** or the **Jockey Club**. Horseback riding and hiking are also popular.

Surprisingly, San Roque is an artificial lake which came into being with the completion of the San Roque Dam across the Rio Suquía in 1890. At that time it was the largest dam of its kind in the world. A modern dam was built in 1944, but much of the original dam still remains.

For a fantastic view of the area, take the chairlift, **Teléferico Autosilla**, from **Avenidas San Martín**, **General Paz**, **Cárcano** or **Estrada** to the top of the hill opposite **Cerro La Cruz**. There are telescopes at the top for an even better view. The chairlift operates from 9:30 a.m. to 12:30 p.m. and from 2:30 p.m. to 7:30 in the evening. A round-trip ticket is $8. As an alternative, those who are athletically inclined may opt to hike the 2,200 meters to the top of Cerro La Cruz, so named for the 15-meter-high cross at its peak.

Other attractions in Carlos Paz include **Golden City**, a reproduction of a town in the old west complete with bank robberies, duels, and drinking at the local saloon (swinging doors and all) at the intersection of Route 20 with Gobernador Alvárez; and **Magic Mountain**, an amusement park featuring a rollercoaster.

Since it is one of Argentina's most popular vacation destinations, Carlos Paz boasts some really fine hotels. The four-star **Portal Del Lago Hotel** (Tel/Fax: 0541-24-931 or in Buenos Aires, Florida 520, local 48, Tel/Fax: 327-0693) on the shores of Lago San Roque is the most luxurious and also the most expensive.

Facilities include tennis and paddleball courts, outdoor and indoor swimming pools, a spacious sun deck, sauna, art gallery, restaurant and *confitería*. Similar accommodations can be had at the **Hotel Libertador** (tel 0541/23-330) which is also a four-star. The three-star **Las Lajas** (tel/fax 0541-22-339). is especially popular with families. Extras include both indoor and outdoor pools, a small playground for the kids and a game room with pool tables.

Restaurants are plentiful and most are on Avenida San Martín. Of course, *parrillas* and Italian restaurants are among the most popular. For a typical *parrillada*, two fine choices are **Parrilla Tauro** and **El Rancho Pora**. **La Mama**, next door to the casino, and **La Casona** both specialize in pasta. For a more varied menu, try **Restaurant Barras**, where you'll have your choice of indoor or outdoor dining, or **La Posta** for fresh seafood.

La Calera

Rather than take Route 20, you may want to pass through the suburb of La Calera, 18 kilometers outside Córdoba enroute to Carlos Paz. Highlights include the **Capilla Vieja**, an 18th-century Jesuit Chapel whose most noteworthy feature is its delicately carved altar, and the **Molino Viejo**, a water-driven mill from the same time period, used by the Jesuits to grind grain. You can reach La Calera via Avenida Colón, which later becomes Avenida Ejército Argentino. After stopping in La Calera, continue along this road until you reach the San Roque Dam and then drive south along the shore of the lake until you reach Carlos Paz.

Tanti

Time permitting, you may want to take a slight detour to the summer village of Tanti, 15 kilometers northwest of Carlos Paz on Route 20. The Comechigon Indians were the original inhabitants of Tanti which, in their language, means "stone site." Indeed, one of the attractions here is a series of unusual rock formations called the **Cueva de los Pajaritos**, which is just eight kilometers away. The Yuspe River, the Los Chorrillos Brook and the Tanti Stream all run through Tanti and the **Los Chorrillos Waterfall** is seven kilometers away. There is a campground at the falls. In-town sights include the **Cueva de la Virgen de la Medalla Milagrosa** and the Parish Church **Nuestra Señora del Rosario.**

Bialet Masse

From Carlos Paz, take Route 38 north to the village of Bialet Masse, located just beyond the north shore of the lake. This village was named for Juan Bialet Masse who, in 1884, built **El Horno de "La Primera Argentina"** – the furnace which was used to fire the limestone used in the construction of the original dam on Lago San Roque. In addition, you can visit the **Iglesia de San Plácido**. Fruit of a concerted effort by Argentine, Brazilian and Italian architects, this lovely church is set in a beautiful hillside in the **El Balcón** district. River resorts dot the area.

Cosquín

From Bialet Masse continue on to the quaint village of Cosquín which served as a post on the road to Peru during colonial times and today hosts Latin America's largest folk festival for two weeks every January, earning it the title of Folklore Capital of Argentina. The festival takes place in the **Plaza Próspero Molina,** the main square also known as the Plaza Nacional del Folclor. Shaded by willows, the village is nestled between the **Cosquín River** and **Cerro (Hill) Pan de Azúcar**. The scenery here is especially lovely and is best viewed by taking the chairlift 1,260 meters to the top of Pan de Azúcar, which was originally called *Supag Ñuñu* (Virgin's Bosom) by the Indians who inhabited the region. For the intrepid, paragliding is offered at the top of the hill. Other attractions include the **Iglesia Nuestra Señora del Rosario,** a church dating back to the last century with a baptism pillar built by the local Indians and an 18th-century altarpiece; the **Artisan's Museum** at 1031 Tucumán; **the Camin Cosquín Culture and Recreation Center**, which includes an archaeology museum, waterslide and mountain bike track; and the **Quebrada Los Leones**, a gorge accented by lush forests, centuries-old ferns and rushing springs. For an overnight stay, consider the three-star **Hotel La Puerta del Sol** (tel/fax: 0541/51-626).

Valle Hermoso & La Falda

Your next major stop is the lovely village of La Falda. At the beginning of the century, this was a favorite retreat of Buenos Aires' and Córdoba's most wealthy residents. Its popularity has not diminished in the least. You'll find a wide range of accommodations, including camping. The **Tomaso Di Savoia** (tel 0548/23-013) and the **Gran Hotel Nor Tomarza** (tel 0548/22-004), both on Avenida Eden (the principal throughfare), are two very lovely four-star hotels. Among La Falda's outstanding features are the eucalyptus trees, brought here from Australia over a century ago by then-President Domingo Faustino Sarmiento. A festival celebrating the folk music of Argentina's many immigrants and the tango is held in the municipal amphitheater here every February.

There is plenty to do in La Falda, including golfing, swimming, hiking, horseback riding, fishing, sailing and sightseeing. Attractions are the **Capilla Santa Bárbara**, a 1747 chapel noteworthy for its image of Santa Bárbara, dagger in hand; the **La Falda Dam and Lake**; panoramic views from **La Banderita** and **El Cuadrado** hills; the **Gruta** (grotto) **San Antonio**, rumored to contain hidden Jesuit treasures; and **Olsen**, formerly a Comechingon and Sanaviron Indian settlement, today the site of lime and marble quarries and of **La Cascada**, a natural resort.

Before reaching **La Falda**, you'll pass the village of **Valle Hermoso**. Its **San Antonio Chapel** was built between 1714 and 1735 and restored quite recently. The statue of Christ in the interior is from the Cuzco School. Seven kilometers outside Valle Hermoso is **Cascada los Helechos**, site of a lively waterfall and a popular starting point for mountaineering trips.

La Cumbre

Continuing north on Route 38 towards La Cumbre, you'll pass through **Huerta Grande** and **Villa Giardino.** Huerta Grande is remarkable for the numerous brooks and streams running through its center. Popular with tourists and vacationers, it has fine beaches, campsites, hotels and attractive summer homes. Villa Giardino, three kilometers north, is equally lovely. Just as both names suggest, the landscape here is green and lush with plenty of pine trees, flowers, cows and horses grazing in open fields.

At 1,142 meters (3,768 feet) above sea level, **La Cumbre**, is another very popular mountain retreat, a home to writers and artists. Its 18-hole golf course, set against a backdrop of rolling green mountains covered with pine trees, is the finest in the country. Trout fishing from November through April in the **Tiu Mayu River**, 11 kilometers outside town, and paragliding off the **Cuchi Corral Watchtower** into the 400-meter-deep **Valle de los Pintos** are popular pastimes, as are tennis and swimming. A statue of Christ the Redeemer (**Cristo Redentor**) atop the highest hill of the region watches over the town, which is a favorite destination of Holy Week Pilgrimages. If you'd like to spend a night or two here, consider renting a cabin (complete with wood-burning fireplace) at **Cabañas del Golf** (tel/fax: 0548/52008), just 100 meters from the golf course. The chalet-style **Gran Hotel La Cumbre** (tel 0548/51550) is also a lovely choice.

Los Cocos

At 1,220 meters above sea level, Los Cocos is one of the highest points in the region and boasts a near perfect climate. Unlike the rest of the region, however, very few rivers or streams run through the area. Not to worry, most homes and hotels do have swimming pools. A breathtaking view of the region can be had nearly 365 days a year from atop the **Cerro El Camello** (Camel Hill).

Capilla del Monte

Our final destination is Capilla del Monte, 66 miles from Córdoba and the northernmost city in the Punilla Valley. While the area is dotted with palm trees, it is interesting to note that the peak of **Cerro Uritorco**, which towers over the city and is the highest in the Sierra Chica (1,950 meters), is occasionally covered with snow during the winter months. However, Capilla del Monte enjoys an ideal climate, with one of the highest percentages of sunny days in all of Argentina.

Nature enthusiasts will want to explore the surrounding countryside. Three kilometers outside town is **Los Mogotes**, an area of small waterfalls formed by a tributary of the Dolores River as it passes through a narrow ravine. **The Paso del Indio**, a narrow path, winds its way through the area and is great for hiking. Equally lovely is **Huertas Malas**, an area whose only sounds are running water and birds singing. It is reached via a footpath running alongside a creek. Interesting masses of volcanic stone can be studied at **Los Terrones**, located beyond the Uritorco Valley 14 kilometers from town. Botanists will find **Los Paredones**, eight kilometers from Capilla del Monte, especially interesting. Ferns dominate the flora here, along with the *clavel del aire*, an unusual carnation-like plant that is actually a species of aerial plant. And finally there is the **La Toma River Resort**, an area of cristaline ponds and waterfalls four kilometers from town. **Aguas Blancas** nearby features mineral springs and campsites.

Córdoba After Dark

Córdoba has a very active cultural life, with frequent performances by national and internationally acclaimed artists, dance troops and theater groups at the Teatro San Martín and the many small theaters and cultural centers in town. For listings of these and to find out what's playing at one of Córdoba's many movie theaters, check the *Cartelera* in *Pagina 12*, the daily paper.

Apart from cafés, hotel lounges and a few scattered bars, downtown Córdoba does not offer much in the way of nightlife. But this is rapidly changing, as many new pubs and restaurants are beginning to open along Bulevar Chacabuco and the Plaza Vélez Sarsfield. For discos, night-clubs and casinos (there's one in Carlos Paz), you'll have to grab a cab or hop in your car and head to **Cerro de las Rosas**, an affluent residential zone with lots of fine restaurants and bistros by the Chateau Carreras stadium, or to **Carlos Paz**. Remember, most discos don't open until 10 or 11 p.m.

Discos

FLY CITY
Hipolito Irigoyen 282
(corner of Independencia)
Tel 210-107
One of the few clubs downtown, Fly City can get crowded, especially during the weekend. Inside it is quite pretty, with large white columns and a black and white motif. There's a sunken dance floor in the center with plenty of couches and secluded nooks, and a large bar for socializing.

SWEPT
Hipolito Irigoyen 419
Formerly called Swept Away, Swept is another popular in-town choice. It's fairly large and usually doesn't really get going until after 1 a.m.

FACTORY
Avenida Rafael Nuñez 3960
Cerro de las Rosas
Tel 816-301
Open 12:30 a.m.-5 a.m.

Currently one of the city's most popular night spots, this large disco is housed, obviously, in what was once a factory. For a complete evening, have a late dinner or cocktails next door at **Navajo**. Also in a former factory, this lovely *parrilla* features North American Indian decor in a theater-type setting.

Ten minutes by cab.

DISCO MOLINO ROJO
Carlos Paz
Given the way discos and nightclubs in general come and go, El Molino Rojo is definitely an anomaly. It's been open for over 30 years. Although the music has changed over the years, little else has. You'll recognize it by the large red mill in front.

30 minutes by cab.

A Casino

The finest casino in the area is the **Casino Carlos Paz** on Avenida San Martín in Carlos Paz. It is open from 2 p.m. to 5 a.m. seven days a week and there is a $4 admission charge. Tables include roulette, black jack, *punta y banco,* seven fax, monte and Hazzard. The average minimum bet is $10 and the maximum is $100. The casino also has a bingo salon.

Shopping

Window shoppers will find Córdoba close to heaven on earth as they stroll along **9 de Julio**, **Independencia**, **Riviera Indarte** and other pedestrian-only streets and arcades, past the beautifully dressed windows of the city's finest shops. **9 de Julio** reminds us very much of Calle Florida in Buenos Aires, except that it is far prettier, with shade provided by a leafy canopy as you cross Independencia.

Artecasa, located just off the Plaza San Martín on Independencia, features works by soon-to-be discovered and fairly well known Cordobes artists. They will gladly design a custom frame for anything you select. **Grimoldi Shoes** and **Angelo Paolo Leather** have shops on 9 de Julio, as does **Ted Lapidus**. You'll recognize these names from Buenos Aires. **Christian Dior** has a shop on Riviera Indarte. You'll find many other fine shops in the area, several of which are located in the **Via Nueva** arcade which stretches between Tucumán and 9 de Julio.

Of course, the shopping mall is not unknown here. **Garden Shopping**, centrally located at the corner of Ituzaingo and Corrientes, and **Nuevo Centro Shopping**, slightly further out at Avenida Duarte Quiros 1400, house a wide range of fine shops, including designer boutiques (both clothing and housewares), record shops, book stores and cafés. They're open until at least 9 p.m. during the week (restaurants stay open until midnight) and later during the weekend.

Your best option for **handicrafts** and *típicos* such as *mates and bombillas* (the gourds and silver straws used to drink *mate*), ponchos, silver and leather items is the large artisan fair which is held every day until 8 p.m. on the Plaza Italia. Also known as the **Paseo de las Artes**, it is on the Cañada, south of the Plaza Vélez Sarsfield, at the intersection of Marcelo T. de Alvear and Achaval Rodriguez. Shops selling regional crafts are located throughout the colonial section. Be sure to shop around as prices and quality vary.

Córdoba A-Z

AIRLINE OFFICES: The **Aerolíneas Argentinas** Office is at Colón 520. For information call 450-003 or 46-045 for reservations. **Austral** is on the Plaza San Martín at Buenos Aires 59 (tel 228-008).

BOOKSTORE: Bibliophiles should stop in at **El Mundo del Libro** at the corner of Dean Funes and Obispo Trejo.

BUS STATION: The bus station is on Bulevar Presidente J.D. Perón, 300. For information, call 42-073.

CAR RENTAL: Avis has an office at Corrientes 452 (tel 227-384) as well as a booth in the airport (tel 816-473). **Dollar** is on Avenida Chacabuco at 163/185 (tel 244-923).

DAILY NEWSPAPER: *Pagina 12* is Córdoba's daily newspaper. Check the *Cartelera* on the last page for up-to-date entertainment listings and flight information

FUTBOL: Córdoba was one of the host cities to the 1978 World Cup and built the **Chateau Carreras Stadium** especially for the occasion. With a capacity of 45,000, concerts and music festivals are held here as well as soccer matches. The stadium is 10 kilometers outside the city on the banks of the Suquía River.

MEDICAL EMERGENCY: In case of a medical emergency, call the **Centro de Especialidades Médicas o Asistencia Pública**, Sarmiento 450 (tel 46-110 or 226-880).

TOURIST OFFICE: A branch of the Tourist Office is located in the Cabildo. The main office is at Avenida Tucumán 25. For information call 44-027.

TAXI SERVICE: To call for a cab, try **Tele Taxis** at 713-333 or 716-666. For a cab to the airport, contact **Remis** at 816-244 or 808-865.

TRAIN STATION: The **Bartolomé Mitre** Train Station is at Bulevar J.D. Perón 101. For information call 224-168.

TRAVEL AGENT: If you need to make travel arrangements or to modify your plans, the agents at **Passerini Viajes S.R.L** at Obispo Trejo 357 (tel 243-118 or 226-269) are very helpful.

Mendoza

If we were asked to name the city best described by the word "resilient," Mendoza would have to be it. Devastated by a major earthquake in 1861, the city was reincarnated as a verdant garden in the midst of a desert plain. If you were dropped in the middle of this city of nearly 125,000 residents, surrounded by orchards and vineyards and lush with parks and plazas, you would never imagine that you were in the most arid region of Argentina – the Cuyo.

Following the example set by their Indian predecessors, Mendoza's residents know how to make the most of their limited water supply. Just as dams have been built across many of the rivers outside the city to provide water for the orchard and vineyards, irrigation channels or *acequias,* often shaded by groves of sycamores, run alongside the streets of the city. Mingling what little rainfall there is with water running down from the Andes, they provide the city with most of its water. Despite the scarcity of water, or perhaps because of it, Mendoza is also an exceptionally clean city. Electric trolley buses replace much of the exhaust fumes and noise common to other South American cities, making it all the more delightful.

Just like the wines the province is famous for, Mendoza is a city to be savored. It is not monumental in proportion, nor overwhelmingly historic, but you can use Mendoza as home base for trips into the countryside and to nearby ski resorts. Or simply enjoy the city on its own terms.

History

As part of a campaign to create a line of settlements linking Buenos Aires on the Atlantic with Santiago de Chile on the Pacific, Don Pedro del Castillo crossed into Argentina from Chile and founded the city of Mendoza on March 2, 1561, naming it for the then-governor of Chile, Don Garcia Hurtado de Mendoza. For reasons unknown, shortly thereafter the city was moved to another location, only to be refounded in 1562 by Don Juan Jufré, who would christen it "La Resurrección." Chile would rule the region until the formation of the Viceroyalty of the Rio de la Plata in 1776.

The first 250 years of Mendoza's history were fairly uneventful. Most settlers were from Chile and trade with that country was key to the region's economic development. Mendoza's location just west of the **Uspallata Pass** (or the **Camino de los Andes** as it is more commonly called), through which all trade with Chile passed, made the city a natural link for commerce between the neighboring countries. Modifying and improving the irrigation methods developed by the Huarpe Indians, they planted grain, vineyards and orchards to give rise to Mendoza's agricultural economy. Silver, copper and lead mining was also pursued, although not with any great success.

Despite its great promise, Mendoza's, and indeed the entire Cuyo region's, economy went into decline during the first half of the 19th century. Once Argentina declared independence, trade with Chile weakened. Formerly allies, the two countries became competitors. Buenos Aires became Argentina's administrative and commercial center. Unfortunately, the high cost and high risks associated with ox cart freight, the only means of transportation available at the time, limited the potential for trade between Mendoza and Buenos Aires. The wine industry suffered with the introduction of lower-priced imports from France, Spain and Italy. Wealth expected from mining never came into being. But Mendoza's economy would spring back to life in 1884 with the introduction of the railroad.

The crowning event in Mendoza's history came during the War of Independence from Spain, the event commemorated by the Cerro de la Gloria in the Parque San Martín. In 1816 General José de San Martín, who at that time was also the Governor of the Cuyo, based his army, the Ejército de los Andes, in Mendoza. He had formed the army the year before as part of the war effort. The infantry was comprised primarily of blacks, whose liberty had been purchased by the provincial government. The cavalry was predominantly *mestizo* (of mixed Spanish/Indian descent), while officers were Spanish and *criollos* (native-born Spanish). They were joined by exiled Chileans under General Bernardo O'Higgins, who had been defeated by the Spanish in 1814 at the Battle of Rancagua.

In September, 1816 San Martín met with the Pehuenche Indians at a camp 30 leagues south of Mendoza to request permission to lead his army across their territory and attack the Spanish from the south. But this was far from his real intention. In one of the most daring and best orchestrated feats in military history, San Martín led his troops (which numbered well over 4,000), heavy artillery and all, across some of the highest peaks in the Andes into Chile. Tahere, taking the Spanish by surprise, he defeated them in the Battle of Chacabuco in February of 1817. This smashing victory marked a change in the balance of power in the war which would culminate with the surrender of the Spanish forces in April, 1818 at the Battle of Maipú and the creation of the independent nation of Chile. San Martín would use Chile as his base of operations until 1821 when, in the last phase of the War of Independence, he drove the Spanish from Peru.

Unfortunately, even San Martín's military prowess could not safeguard the city of Mendoza against a natural disaster. At dusk on March 20, 1861, Holy Thursday, a major earthquake shook the city, devastating it. Of Mendoza's 12,000 residents, 4,000 perished. The rest of Argentina was joined by Brazil, Chile, Paraguay, Peru, Uruguay, England and France in an international effort to aid the city. To prevent the recurrence of a similar tragedy, the city was rebuilt as we know it today, with broad avenues, low buildings and plenty of parks and plazas that can serve as refuges in the event of a future quake. Another one struck the city in 1985. Yet, apart from structural damage, no fatalities were reported.

Geography/Topography

The city of Mendoza is capital of the province of the same name, which joins the provinces of San Juan and San Luis in the central region of the Argentine Andes to form the Cuyo. Cuyo, which means "land of stone" in the language of the Huarpe Indians and "land of sand" in Mapuche, is the driest region of Argentina. First discovered in 1551 by Francisco de Villagra, who came to the region from Peru, the area was actually settled by colonists from the Central Valley of Chile in the late 16th century. The Cuyo was one of the first areas of the River Plate region to be settled.

With the Andes marking its western border with Chile, the province of Mendoza is bordered by the provinces of San Juan to the north, San Luis to the east, and La Pampa and Neuquen to the south. Mountains cover one-third of its area, with arid plains in the east and piedmont in the center comprising the remainder. Volcanoes, active and extinct, dominate much of the southern landscape. Like their counterparts, the Andes to the west, whose peaks are covered by eternal snow and ice, these mountains extend to heights of over 6,000 meters. The most important peaks of the Argentine Andes are in Mendoza. These include Nevado de Juncal at 6,110 meters, Pollera at 6,235, Iglesia at 6,300, Tupungato at 6,800 and, the mightiest of all, Aconcagua at 6,959 meters.

Surprisingly, the barren and desolate Andean landscape provides the mineral-rich waters that make agriculture the primary industry in Mendoza. In late spring, the waters from melting glaciers and snows rush down shallow rock-strewn channels cut into the Andes to the Desaguadero, the region's principal river. It, in turn, feeds many tributaries, one of which is the Mendoza, the main river in the province, until the mountain waters eventually reach the irrigation channels. These serve the 2.5% of the province that is cultivated. Of Mendoza's cultivated area, 63% is dedicated to vineyards, while fruit trees – peaches, apples, plums, pears, and almonds – cover much of the rest.

Climate

Mendoza is crowned by a cloudless azure sky nearly 360 days a year. Summers are hot and dry with daytime temperatures reaching well into the 90's. But you may need a sweater for the early morning hours and evenings when temperatures are sharply cooler. Winters are mild with temperatures normally in the 40's. Cold snowy days, though rare, are not entirely unheard of. Rainstorms are few and far between, although thunder and hail storms are common during the summer. The little rain that does fall is collected in the irrigation channels which run throughout the city. The climate is decidedly cooler in the higher elevations, with frequent winter snows. The Zonda Wind, common to areas of high temperatures and scarce humidity, frequently blows across Mendoza.

Getting There

By Plane

Aerolíneas Argentinas and **Austral** offer several flights daily to Mendoza from Buenos Aires and other cities across the country. If you're arriving from outside Argentina, you will probably have to catch a connecting flight in Buenos Aires.

By Car

National Route 40, which bisects Argentina from north to south, passes through Mendoza. National Route 7, which starts in Buenos Aires and finishes at the Cristo Redentor Tunnel at the border with Chile, also passes through Mendoza.

By Bus

The **Chevallier** (tel 313-3264, in Buenos Aires) and **Jocoli** (tel 313-2085, in Buenos Aires) offer service between Buenos Aires and Mendoza.

Arrival

El Plumerillo International Airport is located six miles east of the city. A **remis** cab into Mendoza will cost around $9. The Tourist Office (**Subsecretario de Turismo**) has a kiosk in the airport where you can pick up maps and tourist information. There is a branch of Avis Rent-A-Car in the airport as well. The train station is just a few blocks from the Plaza Chile at the intersection of Avenida Las Heras and Belgrano. The bus station, Terminal del Sol, is at the intersection of

TAXI

Avenida Acceso Este y Costanera, 6 blocks east of the Plaza de España.

Orientation

You should be able to walk virtually anywhere within the city. Four blocks in size, the **Plaza Independencia** is the heart of Mendoza. It is surrounded by four plazas, each two blocks away: **Plaza Chile** at the northwest corner; **Plaza San Martín** at the northeast; **Plaza España** at the southeast; and **Plaza Italia** at the southwest corner. **Avenida Sarmiento,** a major thoroughfare, runs through the center of the Plaza, east to west, and is a pedestrian mall, **Paseo Sarmiento**, east of the plaza until it intersects Avenida San Martín. West of the Plaza, Sarmiento becomes **Emilio Civit** until it reaches the entrance of the **Parque San Martín**, where it undergoes another name change to become Avenida Libertador.

Three blocks east of the Plaza Independencia, **Avenida San Martín**, also known as La Alameda, runs north to south and is one of the city's major commercial streets and home to many fine restaurants. The principal market place, **El Mercado Central,** and many large handicraft shops are on **Avenida Las Heras,** which runs east to west and is one block north of the Plazas Chile and San Martìn. **Avenida Mitre**, another important street, bisects the Plaza Independencia north to south.

Hotels

You should have no problem finding a fine hotel at a reasonable price in Mendoza. Though there are no five-star hotels, there is no shortage of comfort and attentive service at the city's three- and four-star hostelries. Often all that is missing is the high price. Because of the city's small size, most hotels are centrally located.

Alive Price Scale
Deluxe: $175+
Expensive: $100+
Moderate: $60-100
Inexpensive: $ 35-60
Budget: under $35

HOTEL ACONCAGUA ✫✫✫✫
San Lorenzo 545
Tel 242-450
Fax 311-085
160 rooms
Moderate

Best location.

The modern Hotel Aconcagua stands out among the buildings surrounding the Plaza Italia. Rooms here are fairly standard, yet comfortable. Be sure to request one with a view of the Andes. If you're in your room in the late afternoon you should be able to watch the sunset over the mountains. There is an outdoor terrace and pool on the second floor as well as a sauna. The Aconcagua also has a fine international restaurant.

PLAZA HOTEL ✫✫✫✫
Chile 1124
Tel 23-3248
Fax 23-3000
80 rooms
Expensive

"Majestic" best describes the neoclassic facade of the very regal Plaza Hotel, located in the heart of the city on the Plaza Independencia. You'll find old world style and comfort

Next to the Teatro
Independencia.

throughout, from the subdued elegance of the spacious lobby sitting area and formal dining room to the comfortable furnishings of the guest rooms and suites. A beautifully landscaped lawn and terrace surround the outdoor pool. The Plaza also has a small beauty salon, a game roomand a VIP lounge.

GRAN HOTEL HUENTALA ✩✩✩✩
P. de la Reta
Tel 240-766
Fax 240-664
76 rooms
Moderate
The centrally located Gran Hotel Huentala is another fine four-star choice with facilities almost comparable to those at the Aconcagua.

HOTEL CRILLON ✩✩✩
Calle Peru 1065
Tel /Fax 248-079
80 rooms
Moderate
The only real differences between the Crillon and our four-star selections is its slightly lower price and lack of a pool. Otherwise, it matches them in service and comfort. Rooms are tastefully furnished and carpeted. The Crillon is located on Peru, just a block away from the Casino between Calles Sarmiento and Rivadavia.

GRAN RITZ HOTEL ✩✩✩
Peru 1008
Tel 248-506
Fax 340-064
38 rooms
Moderate

Not far from the Crillon, the Gran Ritz offers guests the familiar service that is best enjoyed at a small hotel. Especially lovely is the TV/sitting room with comfortable couches and plants all around.

GRAND HOTEL BALBI ☆☆☆
Avenida Las Heras 340
Tel 233-500
Fax 380-626
108 rooms
Moderate
Located on one of the city's busiest streets, the Grand Hotel Balbi sports an enclosed parking area as well as a pool, bar and restaurant.

GRAN HOTEL PRINCESS ☆☆☆
25 de Mayo 1168
Tel/Fax (061) 234-537
36 rooms
Moderate
This fine three-star is well cared for and very popular. An outdoor pool and lovely garden are among the perks enjoyed by guests. The Princess also has its own bar, restaurant and parking lot. Given its small size, you may have to reserve ahead for a room here. Breakfast is included.

GRAN ARIOSTO HOTEL
Infanta Mercedes de San Martin 48
Tel 293-051
Fax 340-064
40 rooms
Moderate
Under the same management as the Gran Ritz, the Gran Ariosto is in a quiet residential part of town. It has a large lobby and rooms are car-

peted and very comfortable. Breakfast is included.

Alive Price Scale
(per person)
Expensive: $40+
Moderate: $25+
Inexpensive: under $20

Restaurants

Italian *trattorias* and *parrilladas* are among the most prevalant and finest of Mendoza's restaurants. Regional specialties include *asado criollo* (barbecued goat and veal), *humitas* (sweet tamales), *patitas aliñadas* (spiced legs of beef or veal), *ternera con cuero* (veal cooked in its skin), and *tomatican* (stewed tomatoes). Of course, it would be almost unconscionable not to accompany one of these regional specialties with one of Mendoza's fine wines. Interestingly enough, Mendoza also supplies the country with mineral water. The country's most popular, Villavicencio, comes from a spring 1,750 meters above sea level.

BRASERIAS
Las Heras 510 (corner of Chile)
Tel 25-4482
Parrilla
Lunch & dinner
Moderate
The menu stretches nearly as far as the expansive indoor/outdoor dining room at the ultramodern Braserias. You can choose from among the different cuts of meat and chicken grilling on the circular *parrilla/asador* , or try any of the numerous pasta or international dishes featured on the menu. Whether or not you're in the mood for cocktails, be sure to take a look at the special drink (*agasajos*) menu. You're likely to discover something new. Ceiling fans keep

things cool inside while you'll be at the mercy of the weather outside.

RESTAURANT TREVI
Palace Hotel
Las Heras 70
Tel 23-3195
Italian/international
Lunch & dinner
Moderate
This is another of the city's many Italian restaurants.

LA PLAZA
Espejo, corner with 25 de Mayo
Tel 233-394
International
Lunch & dinner
Moderate
Large stained glass windows and wine bottles decorate this otherwise unpretentious bistro. Crêpes, fish, salads, meat and chicken are featured on the fairly simple menu.

TRATTORIA AVENI
25 de Mayo 1154 (across from the Casino)
Tel 380342
Italian
Lunch & dinner
Moderate
Given its location, you can wisely assume that the Trattoria Aveni is a favorite among high rollers. As a matter of fact, it was recommended to us by a local VIP.

LA MARCHIGIANA
Patrias Mendocinas 1550
Tel 23-0751
Italian/Argentine
Lunch & dinner
Moderate

A large adobe house with a thatched roof and garden in front is home to this fine, always-crowded Italo-Argentine restaurant. Patrons are drawn to the lovely *estancia*-like setting and good food. Pastas and typical Argentine dishes, *parrillada* of course, dominate the menu.

TRATTORIA VECCHIA ROMA
Avenida España 1619
Tel 251-491
Italian
Moderate

You may have to wait for a table. This very popular *trattoria* is always busy. Reminiscent of a cellar, the decor is fairly simple and so is the menu, uncomplicated yet very good.

IL TUCCO
Paseo Sarmiento 42
Tel 292-265
Between 9 de Julio & San Martín

Yet another simple and extremely popular *trattoria*. Be prepared to wait for a table at dinner time.

LOS LAGARES
Avenida Aristides Villanueva 650
Tel 290-554
Argentine Parrilla

The dining room is spread throughout several rooms of this brick house, where you'll feel less like a restaurant patron and more like a guest.

Grilled meats are the specialty but the international menu does offer some other options.

BOCCADORO
Mitre 1976
Parrilla
Tel 255-056
Lunch & dinner
Very similar to Los Lagares, Boccadoro is another *parrilla* in a former residence. Try to get a table in one of the rear rooms for some real ambience.

Sunup To Sundown

Once in Mendoza, you'll find yourself naturally falling in step with its unhurried pace. A morning or afternoon can be delightfully spent strolling through the city's many parks and plazas, alongside the *acequias* (irrigation ditches) flowing through the city. Mendoza's nearly ideal climate makes trips to the surrounding countryside all the more inviting. Pack a picnic lunch and head out to the nearby wineries. Finally, to experience Argentina's changing landscape, head west towards Chile on Route 7, through the fertile vineyards and orchards just outside the city to the rugged steppes of the Andes in the Parque Provincial Aconcagua, home of the highest peak in the southern and western hemispheres, Mount Aconcagua.

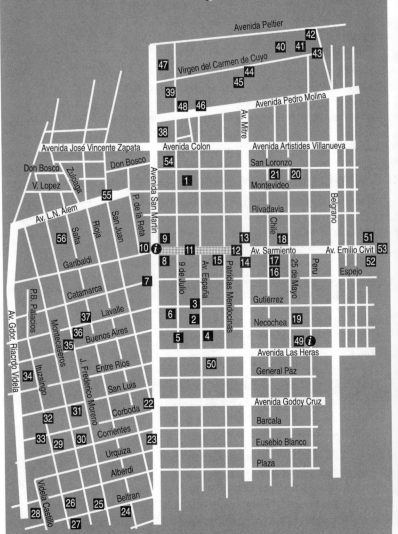

Mendoza

Microcentro
1. Plaza España
2. Plaza San Martín
3. Banco Hipotecario Nacional
4. Basilica de San Francisco
5. Banco de Mendoza
7. Subsecretaría de Turismo
8. Pasaje San Martín
9. Edificio Gómez
10. Diario Los Andes
11. Paseo Peatonal Sarmiento

Ciudad Nueva
12. Plaza Independencia
13. Museo Municipal de Arte Moderno
14. Teatro Municipal Julio Quintanilla
15. Legislatura Provincial
16. Teatro Independencia
17 Plaza Hotel
18. Colegio Nacional Agustín Alvarez
19. Plaza Chile
20. Plaza Italia
21. Museo del Pasada Cuyano

Ciudad Vieja
22. Alameda
23. Biblioteca y Museo Sanmartiniano
24. Iglesia de Santo Domingo
25. Monumento a Anibal Troilo
26. Plaza Pedro del Castillo
27. Ruinas de San Francisco
28. Museo del Area Fundacional
29. Solar de la Maestranza del Ejército
30. Solar de la Casa de San Martín
31. Iglesia de la Merced
32. Parque O'Higgins
33. Teatro Municipal Gabriela Mistral
34. Acuario Municipal
35. Plaza Sarmiento
36.. Catedral de Mendoza
37. Escuela de Música

Barrio Civico
38. Edificio de Correos
39. Municipalidad de Mendoza
40. Aduana de Mendoza
41. Centro de Congresos y Exposiciones
42. Antigua Bodega
43. Palacio Policial Museo Agualcil Mayor Capitan D Ruiz de Rojas
44. Casa de Gobierno - Sala de la Bandera
45. Poder Judicial
46. Tribunales Federales
47. Instituto Nacional de Vitivinicultura
48. Comando VIII Brigada de Infantería de Montaña
49. Museo Popular Callajero
50. Mercado Central
51. Casa Lópee Frugoni
52. Casa Arenas
53. Portones Parque Gral. San Martín
54. Iglesia de la Compañia de Jesus
55. Plazoleta Pellegrini
56. Hospital Central

Walking Tour

We'll start our walk at the intersection of calles
Alberdi and Ituzaingó on the **Plaza Pedro del
Castillo**. Named for the original founder of
Mendoza and two of the most important events
in the city's history, this is Mendoza's most historic square. The original Plaza Independencia,
it was here that the city was founded in 1562
and that General San Martín and his *Ejército de
los Andes* (Army of the Andes) swore allegiance
to the Argentine Flag and named the Virgin of
Carmen of the Cuyo their patron and protector.
The city's first *cabildo* or town hall was on the
east block of the plaza. Also here are the only
remains of the original city following the devastating earthquake of 1861, the **San Francisco
Ruins**. Built by the Jesuits in 1638, the church
and its adjacent school were later ceded to the
Franciscan Fathers following the expulsion of
the Jesuits in 1767. The church was seriously
damaged in 1782 by the first earthquake, which
destroyed the city. The plaza was declared a
national landmark in 1967. Also on the plaza is
the **Museo del Area Fundacional** (tel 256-927).

Walking south on Ituzaingó, you'll be alongside
the **Parque Bernardo O'Higgins** with its gardens, numerous species of trees and open
meadows. Also here is the outdoor **Teatro
Gabriela Mistral**, which hosts cultural activities all summer long.

Turn right onto Calle Corrientes and continue
west. The modern home on the corner of Corrientes and Calle José Federico Moreno occupies
the site where General San Martín and his wife,
Remedios de Escaleda, lived while he was gov-

ernor of Mendoza from 1814 to 1816. It was the birthplace of their daughter, Merceditas. The flag of the *Ejército de los Andes* was embroidered there.

Four blocks later you'll come to **Avenida San Martín**, one of the principal thoroughfares of the city. The park-like promenade running alongside it is known as **La Alameda**. Typical of many Spanish cities, it dates back to the days of San Martín. All that remains from that period is the **Balcón Colonial**. Also on the Alameda is the **Centro Comercial y Turístico**, where you can watch traditional weavers plying their craft and enjoy performances of traditional and not-so-traditional dances. The **Museo Histórico General San Martín**, which features memorabilia and documents from the War of Independence, is nearby at Remedios de Escaleda 1843 (tel 257-947).

Continue south along Avenida San Martín to Calle Buenos Aires. Like many of the streets which intersect San Martín, Buenos Aires undergoes a name change, becoming Necochea on the west side of the Avenue. Turn onto Necochea and a block later you'll be on the northside of the **Plaza San Martín** with the ever-present statue of the General, majestically atop a galloping steed, at its center. Step inside the **Basílica de San Francisco**, final resting place of General San Martín's daughter Merceditas, her husband Mariano Balcarce, and one of their children, and home of Our Lady of Carmen of the Cuyo, patron saint of the *Ejército de los Andes*. The baton the Virgin is holding was gallantly awarded to her by General San Martín following his victo-

ries against the Spanish in Chacabuco and
Maipú during the War of Independence.

This area is also the heart of the city's banking
district. Clustered around the plaza are the
Banco de la Nación Argentina, the **Banco de
Mendoza**, and the **Banco Hipotecario Nacional**, a fine example of the "neoplateresque"
architecture of the 1920's.

After spending some time in the Plaza, head
back to Avenida San Martín and continue south
to the **Paseo Sarmiento**. Outdoor tables line this
garden-like pedestrian promenade, dotted with
fountains and pergolas, and with plenty of
shade provided by a leafy canopy overhead.
Many of the airlines have offices along this wide
promenade and there are several fine shops
here as well. The Paseo's many *confiterías* and
bars make it a popular meeting place, both day
and night. Why not stop here for a coffee or a
refreshing drink before continuing your walk.

The Paseo Sarmiento runs into the verdant
Plaza Independencia. The heart of new Mendoza, it was founded when the city was rebuilt
following the earthquake of 1861. Little wonder
that this enormous plaza, which covers an area
of four blocks and is filled with a wide variety
of plants and trees, was originally called Parque
Independencia. The **Museo Municipal de Arte
Moderno** (tel 257-279) and the **Teatro Municipal Julio Quintanilla** are both in the center. A
hippie fair is held here on the weekends.

*Notice the
acequias (irriga-
tion ditches).*

Just a few steps away from the plaza is the
Legislatura Provincial, which had been built at
the end of the last century to serve as a social

club, only to be acquired by the provincial government who designated it the seat of its Legislature. Also nearby, at the corner of Calles Chile and Peru, is the **Teatro Independencia**, the city's primary center for the performing arts.

A few blocks south of the Plaza Independencia are the **Plaza Italia** and the **Plaza España**. Especially lovely is the Plaza España, east of the Plaza Independencia at the intersection of Avenida España and Montevideo. The history of the city's founding is colorfully told in Majolica tiles imported from Spain. The fountain at the plaza's center, also decorated with Spanish tiles, is reminiscent of those in Seville and other Andalusian towns. The **Plaza Italia**, dedicated to the many Italian immigrants who started anew in Mendoza, is west of the Plaza Independencia at the intersection of Montevideo and 25 de Mayo. Just off the plaza at Montevideo 544 is the **Museo del Pasado Cuyano** (tel 241-092). Once the home of Don Francisco Civit, one of the first governors of Mendoza, and seat of the Junta of Historic Studies, this fine museum contains an extensive collection of memorabilia and documents from throughout the history of the Cuyo region, including arms, flags and batons from the War of Independence.

Other Sights

Barrio Cívico

Following Avenida Mitre south from the Plaza Independencia, you'll find yourself in the administrative heart of Mendoza, the **Barrio Cívico** or **Parque Cívico** (Civic Park) as it is also called. Provincial as well as city government buildings are set amid expansive green lawns, fountains and groves of pine, olive, linden and cedar trees. For a fantastic view of the city and the surrounding area, climb to the **Terraza Jardín Mirador** (Watchtower Terrace) on the seventh floor of the **Municipalidad de Mendoza** (the Municipal Palace). Next door at Calle Peltier 611, in what was the first teaching *bodega* in the province, is the **Museo del Vino Enoteca Giol** (The Giol Wine School Museum). Original oak casks, ancient machinery, and international and national prizes are displayed here. The authentic flag of the *Ejército de los Andes*, which was embroidered by the women of Mendoza, is displayed in the **Sala de la Bandera** (Flag Hall) in the **Casa de Gobierno** (Government Building). The **Aduana de Mendoza** (Customs House), **Centro de Congresos y Exposiciones Emilio Civit** (Emilio Civit Exposition Center), the **Palacio Policial** (Police Headquarters) and the **Poder Judicial and Tribunales Federales** (Provincial and Supreme Court House) are also in the park.

Parque San Martín

A magnificent wrought iron gate across Avenida Emilio Civit where it intersects with Avenida Boulogne Sur Mer marks the entrance to the Parque San Martín. (Note: Emilio Civit becomes Avenida del Libertador in the park.) This ranks with New York's Central Park as one of the largest and most beautiful municipal parks we've ever visited. Its 1,035-acres extend from Avenida Boulogne Sur Mer on the western side of the city all the way to the beginning of the Andes foothills. Virtually a world unto itself, it is home to 10 private clubs, including several tennis clubs, a golf club complete with an 18-hole course, and the Mendoza Regata Club. The park also boasts a large artificial lake which you can tour aboard a Mississippi Riverboat, with departures every half-hour. For the do-it-yourselfer, you can rent a rowboat and explore the lake on your own. There is also a cardiovascular exercise circuit, *the Pista de Salud*, and plenty of paths for biking or roller blading.

Nature buffs will have a field day here. Not only is the park home to nearly 50,000 trees (count them if you can) and 700 species of plants, within the **Parque Aborigin** on the western side of the park are several species of plants indigenous to South America. The park's zoo, **Jardín Zoológico**, is next to the Parque Aborigin and is considered one of the finest in South America. Here, hundreds of animals native to the wilds of the continent roam in partial freedom.

A source of great pride to the city is its rose garden, or *rosaleda*, which runs along the eastern shore of the lake. Originally established in 1919, it was renovated in 1993 and 4,500 new rosebushes were planted. This is definitely a sight not to be missed, especially when the roses are in bloom.

The park is also home to several science museums, including the **Universidad Nacional del Cuyo Archaeological Museum**; the **Domingo F. Sarmiento Natural Science Museum**; the **J.C. Moyano Natural Science and Anthropology Museum**; the **Provincial Forest and Park Museum**; and the **M. Tellechea Mineralogy Museum**.

Additional sights in the park include the **Frank Romero Day Amphitheater**, in the western sector of the park not far from the base of the Cerro de la Gloria (see below), site of the crowning of the Queen of the Vintage at the annual Wine Festival; and the **Estadio Islas Malvinas**, which was built for the 1978 World Cup. There is also a race track, **Club Hípico**.

El Cerro de la Gloria

The majestic feats of the Andean Army (*Ejército de los Andes*) in their victory against Spain in the War of Independence have been immortalized in bronze by the Uruguayan sculptor Juan Manuel Ferrari in the **Monumento al Ejército de los Andes**. Located at 984 meters above sea level, the view from atop the hill of Mendoza of the surrounding region is well-worth the climb. To get here follow Avenida Libertador through the Parque San Martín.

Avenida Las Heras & El Mercado Central

Two blocks north of Plazas Chile and San Martín, Avenida Las Heras was one of the city's original commercial zones and is home to several handicraft shops, outdoor cafés and **El Mercado Central**. This huge indoor market covers one full city block starting at Patricias Mendocinas and extending north to General Paz. Your senses will go wild as you pass vendor upon vendor selling fresh fruit, meat and fish along with local wines, chocolates, dried fruits, preserves and a host of other specialties. A visit here will give you a glimpse into the everyday life of Mendoza's residents.

Route 7 Westward to Chile & Aconcagua

A highpoint of your visit to Mendoza (no pun intended) is the drive from Mendoza to mighty Mt. Aconcagua, not only the highest peak in the Andes but in all of the western and southern hemispheres. Traveling west along National Route 7, which stretches across Argentina to connect Buenos Aires with Chile at the Paso Internacional de La Cumbre, you'll begin a steady climb into the Andes. Thermal springs and interesting rock formations will dominate the landscape as it changes from the fertile fields and orchards just outside the city to the rugged steppes of the Parque Provincial Aconcagua.

The **Villavicencio Gorge** is an area of springs, pools and cascades 30 miles outside Mendoza. Nowadays it is perhaps best known as the source of Villavicencio Mineral Water which you will undoubtedly have seen, if not sampled, on restaurant menus and in shops throughout the town. Although long since closed, the thermal springs here gave rise to a very popular bathing resort. It is believed that the area was originally a gathering place for the Indians after *guanaco* and *ñandú* (see below) hunts. During the early days of the colonial period, it served as a primary rest stop on the road between Mendoza and Chile.

Villavicencio is as good as any mineral water in the world, comparable to Perrier and San Pellegrino.

In the beginnings of the 18th century, Captain José Villavicencio made his home here, building a ranch and grape press mill and basing his mining operations in the Paramillo de Upsallata mines. Traces of the gold, silver and lead mines can still be found throughout the area.

Nearby, **Los Caracoles** offers a 15-mile climb of panoramic views, accentuated by steep ravines, along a twisting highway (one-way only). You'll pass the **Del Toro Gorge** and **El Balcón**, the 600-meter abyss where Darwin studied the petrified remains of the Araucanian civilization during his journey to Chile. The route leads to a mountain plain populated by *ñandúes*. A member of the rhea family, as is the North American ostrich, these tall flightless birds are found throughout Argentina and are known for their great speed. Your first glimpse of Upsallata, next enroute, will be from **Cruz de Paramillos**. At 3,000 meters above sea level, this is also a fine vantage point from which to admire the striking contrast between the *pre-cordillera*, or foothills, and the Andes.

Lovely **Upsallata** takes its name from the Quechua word *chuspallacta*, which means enclosed town. It is set in a beautiful valley formed by the Cordillera del Tigre to the west and the Santa Elena Gorge and Cordón de Bonilla to the east. Through here the Inca Road is believed to have passed. In fact, Inca artifacts, including arrowheads, painted ceramics, and hieroglyphics, have been found nearby in Ranchillos Fundición, Tamborillos, and Yalguaraz. The area was equally important to General San Martín and his Army of the Andes. Many of the weapons they used in their fight for independence were cast at **Las Bóvedas**, a group of well-preserved buildings five kilometers outside town. **Las Casuchas de Upsallata**, also nearby, which date back to the 18th century, provided shelter to travelers as well as San Martín's troops. The General's first battle in the War of Independence took place at **Puente Co-**

lonial Fortín Pichueta, a fortress just 15 miles outside Upsallata.

A popular destination, Upsallata boasts several restaurants, regional handicraft shops and hotels, including the four-star **Hotel Valle Andino** which is located on Route 7 (fax: 0624/20-003). Skiers often stay in Upsallata rather than at the resorts, which tend to be slightly higher priced.

Continuing on Route 7 you'll pass through the railway town of **Punta de Vacas**, 2,400 meters above sea level and one of the last stops before the tunnel to Chile. The International Customs Office is based here. The main tributaries of the Mendoza River flow through this town. The Las Vacas River is fed by the glaciers of Aconcagua while the Tupungato is fed by the glaciers of the Juncal, Nevado, Plomo and Tupungato Mountains. The south-flowing Las Cuevas River passes through here as well.

Taking its name from the *Cruz de Caña* (Cane Cross) Stream which crosses it and the naturally formed sculpture of a cathedral and praying monks at its base, **Los Penitentes,** at 2,580 meters above sea level, is best known as a winter resort. The **Cerro Las Leñas** (Las Leñas Hill) shelters the slopes from west winds to ensure fine dry powder and average daytime temperatures of 59°F, with plenty of sunshine. Skiers enjoy optimal conditions throughout the season, which usually runs from June to late September or mid-October. Los Penitentes is only 22 miles from its Chilean counterpart, Portillo, making it easy (depending on driving conditions) for avid skiers to combine both resorts in one trip.

Just six miles beyond Los Penitentes is **El Puente del Inca**, a naturally formed sandstone arch spanning the Las Cuevas River. The bridge is 47 meters long and 28 meters wide. There are five thermal springs in the area, each with its own healing qualities based on its distinct temperature and mineral content. While the area can be visited any time of year, winter, when the thermal springs and snows meet to create a singular effect, is especially lovely. Just in sight of the bridge is **Los Puquios**, a cemetery dedicated to those who lost their lives while trying to climb Aconcagua.

The **Parque Provincial Aconcagua** is also on Route 7. It was founded on July 29, 1983 to preserve the flora, fauna and archaeological remains of the area surrounding Mt. Aconcagua and covers an area of 175,440 acres. For the most part, the landscape, beautiful in a rugged way, is barren and threatening, with vegetation concentrated along the river banks. Snowdrifts, glaciers and lakes have formed along the slopes of the mountains, which range from 3,900 to nearly 7,000 meters above sea level. Guanacos and foxes roam the park, while falcons, eagles and condors patrol the skies. A permit is required to visit the park and should be obtained from the subsecretary of tourism in Mendoza before you leave the city. Three- to 15-day permits are issued. Trekking arrangements, including hiring guides and mule teams, can be made in Puente del Inca.

At over 21,000 feet above sea level, the northern peak of Aconcagua is the highest in the southern and western hemispheres and is considered a must among serious mountain climbers. In

1897 Matías Zurbriggen became the first person to climb Aconcagua. Hundreds follow his brave example every summer. Aconcagua's southern peak stretches 5,933 meters. The park is home to the highest permanent mountain refuge in the world, Refugio Independencia, at 6,500 feet above sea level. The highest hotel in the world is also nearby, the Hotel Refugio Plaza de Mulas. In 1985 the mummified remains of a young boy dating to the Inca period were found on the southwestern flank of the mountain.

Las Cuevas, 10 miles beyond Puente del Inca, is the final stop before passing through the tunnels to San Felipe, Chile. Towering over the tunnel marking the border with Chile stands **El Cristo Redentor**, Christ of the Andes. The work of Argentine sculptor Mateo Alonso, who cast the figure from the melted bronze of the guns used by the Army of the Andes, this impressive figure of Christ stands as a symbol of the brotherhood between Argentina and Chile. It was dedicated in 1902 and stands seven meters high on a granite pedestal (which adds another six) and weighs in at four tons. At 650 meters above Las Cuevas, the statue offers an incredible view of the entire Mendoza River Valley, Aconcagua, Tolosa and Chile. Follow the signs indicating **Los Caracoles** to reach the top.

Provided you have your passport with you, you may want to drive through the tunnels to Chile. A series of 19 tunnels stretching just over three kilometers cut through the Andes to connect the two countries. The first tunnel was built in 1910 for the railroad and is currently inoperative. The auto tunnel was finished in 1979. The toll is $1.50 to Chile and $3.50 to return. Flags mark the Chilean/Argentine border. Travellers such as ourselves who are accustomed to the Lincoln and Holland Tunnels in New York find it especially hard to believe that these tunnels are 2½ miles above sea level!

Mendoza After Dark

Mendoza's cultural calendar is relatively full with lectures and performances at the university, performances by nationally as well as internationally acclaimed artists at the Independencia and Quintanilla theaters, and performances by local theater groups at the smaller theaters about town. And of course, there's always the movies. Mendoza has eight cinemas, with most offering fairly recent U.S. and international films. Check the entertainment section of the daily newspaper *Los Andes* for listings.

Most of the *confiterías* and bars along the Paseo Sarmiento and Avenida Las Heras remain open well into the night. Other after dark options include:

Gambling

CASINO PROVINCIAL
25 de Mayo 1123
Tel 234-888
Open: Sunday-Thursday 10 p.m.-3:30 a.m.
Friday and Saturday to 4 a.m.
Slot machines: 11 a.m. to closing.
Admission: $2 (night only)
Mendoza's casino is one of the biggest we've ever visited in our travels through South America. It is in a large white building just one block

from the Plaza Independencia. Tuxedo-clad waiters and high ceilings lend an air of elegance to the game rooms, which feature roulette and black jack along with a separate room for slot machines. The minimum bet is $10 at the tables. One nasty rule you should be aware of requires that you declare the value of an ace before hitting another card at the blackjack table (ugh). There is a nightclub with a show and dancing within the casino. Though there is no dress code, you should dress appropriately.

Blackjack aficionados beware. You must declare the value of an ace before hitting another card.

CHARLES DICKENS PUB
Aristides Villanueva 290
Tel 240-847
Open: Every day 9 p.m.-5 a.m.
Location aside, it will be tough to find a pub which more faithfully reproduces the spirit of Ye Olde Leather Bottle Pub where Charles Dickens met regularly with members of the Pickwick Club. Olde English architecture and decor create an atmosphere of cordiality. The menu features sandwiches and typical pub fare accompanied by national and imported beverages. A fine choice for an evening of darts and conversation.

Discos

Although there are a couple of good discos in town, including **Die for You** at Avenida Arístides Villanueva 256 and **Factory** at Avenida San Martín 300 (a very young crowd gravitates to this one), the best discos are in **Chacras de Coria**. At last count there were around 20 discos in this resort town just 14 kilometers outside Mendoza via national Route

7 or 40. At **Let's Go** you can keep an eye on yourself through the closed circuit TV. Older couples feel most at home at **Viva María** and **Don Mario**, which features tunes from the 1960's. Other popular choices include **Sketch**, **Aloha**, **Lennox**, **Al Diablo Disco Pub** and **Mambo Rock Disco**.

Shopping

Obviously, wine will be at the top of your shopping list while you're visiting Mendoza. The region is also known for its cider, dried fruits and preserves, as well as chocolates. Weaving is the most widely practiced handicraft. Technique, color and design vary with the different Indian influences present throughout the region. While items produced in the northeast bear the signature of the Huarpe Indians, with their bright colors and bold designs, the more somber colors and geometric motifs of the south are typical of the Araucans.

Leather craftsmanship also runs high. Saddles, harnesses, *boleadores,* and other ranching equipment are created using an infinite variety of plaiting techniques, limited only by the imagination and skill of the artisan. Basket weaving is also widely practiced. Using a technique developed by the Huarpe Indians, basketweavers from the Cuanacache region of Lavalle weave reeds into baskets and hampers, and then use dyed wool to create colorful designs.

You'll find woven articles such as ponchos, blankets, rugs, wall hangings and assorted clothing in generous supply, along with baskets and crafted leather items in the many artisan shops along **Avenida Las Heras**. Head to the **Mercado Central** for foodstuffs.

No city should be without a modern shopping mall and Mendoza is no exception. **Mendoza Plaza Shopping** is four miles outside the city on the highway to Buenos Aires and is home to 100 shops and boutiques including a branch of the department store Falabella, a large supermarket, several fast food stops and restaurants, and a modern car wash. There is a covered parking lot as well. Visitors to Mendoza enjoy discounts at many mall shops when they obtain a VIP card at the reception area. There is also a lovely shopping arcade in town. **Galerías Piazza** is located on Avenida San Martín between the Paseo Sarmiento and Rivadavia, next door to the Diario Los Andes building. The main shopping streets are Paseo Sarmiento, Avenidas Mitre, Las Heras and San Martín.

If you prefer less conventional shopping, the city's hippie fair is held every weekend in the Plaza Independencia, from 11 a.m. to 9 p.m. on Saturdays and 4 p.m. to 9 p.m. on Sundays. You'll find the usual leather goods, jewelry, art, copper and brass pieces and other "hippie fare."

EL TURISTA
Avenida Las Heras 351
Tel 234-102
This huge shop houses what appears to be an infinite supply of regional goods ranging from wine and preserves to leather goods, clothing, hats, art, and wall hangings.

LAS VIÑAS: CENTRO ARTESANAL ARGENTINO
Avenida Las Heras 399
(at the corner of Avenida Mitre)
Tel 251-520

After taking part in the wine tasting, we found Las Viñas to be an especially fun place to shop. In addition to wines and regional specialties such as chocolates, dried fruits and preserves, handicrafts from across Argentina are featured here. You can find silver jewelry and flatware handcrafted by *gauchos*, musical instruments, lovely ceramics, lots of leather, blankets, rugs and wall hangings, sweaters, and furs.

PURA CEPA
Avenida Mitre 1827
Open: Monday-Friday, 9 a.m.-1:30 p.m., 5 p.m.-9 p.m., Saturday, 10 a.m.-2 p.m., 6 p.m.-9 p.m.

The wine casks out front are a very fitting landmark for this huge wineshop. Wines from the entire region are featured here along with *artesanías*.

LA CASA DEL VINO
Aristides Villanueva 160
Tel 240690

Also a fine shop, the Casa Del Vino offers not only wine but locally-produced candies, preserves and juices, as well as *artesanías*.

KUEROS
San Martín 1331

You'll find a wide selection of fashionable leather items at this fairly upscale shop. The main shop is in Buenos Aires.

If you're in need of a few assorted sundries try **Tía**, a 5¢-and-10¢ type of shop on Avenida San Martín. **Musimundo**, also on San Martín, is a good choice for records and CDs. **Librería Y** is a large bookstore at Avenida San Martín 1252.

Mendoza A-Z

AIRLINE OFFICES: The **American Airlines Office** is at Espejo 167, fifth floor (tel 25-9078). The **United** office is nearby at Espejo 183 in Suite 13 on the first floor (tel 23-4683). **Aerolíneas Argentinas** has an office at Sarmiento 82 (tel 34-0100). **El Plumerillo International Airport** is six kilometers outside town on National Route 40 (tel 30-7837).

BUS STATION: The **Del Sol Bus Terminal** is at the intersection of Costanera and Avenida Acceso Este (tel 31-1299).

CAR RENTAL: The **Avis** office is at San Lorenzo 248 (tel 29-1867). **Dollar** has an office at P. De la Reta 931 (tel 24-0418) and **Hertz** is at Chile 1124 (tel 23-3000). Local agencies include **Aramendi** at San Lorenzo 248 (tel 29-1857); **AL Rent A Car** at San Juan 1012 (tel 24-2666); and **Sugerencias** at Lavalle 354 (tel 25-3537).

CURRENCY EXCHANGE: There are three foreign exchange offices within a few steps of each other on Avenida San Martín. **Cambio Santiago** is at 1199 (tel 24-8024); the **Exprinter Office** is at 1198 (tel 38-0333); and **Maguitur** is at 1203 (tel 38-0396). You can also change money at the **Banco de Mendoza** on the corner of San Martín and Gutierrez (tel 23-4500).

DAILY NEWSPAPER: *Los Andes*.. Entertainment and cultural events are in section two.

EMERGENCY: In case of an emergency, call the **Servicio Coordinado de Emergencia** (Emergency Service Coordinator) at 24-8000. To call the emergency police directly dial 24-4444.

POST OFFICE: The **Central Post Office** is located on the corner of Avenida San Martín and Colón (tel 24-9777).

PHARMACIES: The **Del Aguila Pharmacy** on the corner of San Martín and Buenos Aires (tel 23-3391) is open from 8 a.m. until midnight every day, as is the **Mitre Pharmacy** at Avenida Colón 361 (tel 25-5763).

TAXI SERVICE: To phone a cab call **Radiotaxi** at 30-3300; **Taxi Service** at 22-2094; or **Radiomovil** at 25-5855.

TOURIST OFFICE: The Municipal Tourist Office, **Centro de Información Turística Municipalidad de Mendoza**, has offices at Avenida San Martín and Garibaldi (tel 24-5333), 9 de Julio 500 on the mezzanine (tel 24-6500), and Avenida Las Heras 670. The Provincial Tourist Office , **Subsecretaria Provincial de Turismo**, is at Avenida San Martín 1143 (tel 24-2800).

TOUR OPERATOR/TRAVEL AGENT: Ski trips, winery tours and excursions to the countryside surrounding Mendoza can be arranged through **Empresa de Viajes y Turismo Herrera** at Avenida Las Heras 558 (tel 061/39-1651) or **Turismo SE PE AN** at San Juan 1070 (tel 061/34-0162).

Iguazú Falls

guazú Falls is the least known of the world's three greatest waterfalls, but this has done nothing to steal its mighty thunder. Iguazú is higher than Victoria, her South African sister, and twice as wide as Niagara. Over 1,700 cubic meters of water per second flow through this series of 275 falls on the Iguazú River, the natural border with Brazil, in Argentina's northeasternmost province, Misiones.

They were officially discovered by the Portuguese explorer Alvaro Núñez Cabeza de Vaca during his arduous journey from the Brazilian province of Santa Catalina to Asunción, Paraguay in 1541. He christened them *Saltos de Santa María* in honor of the patron virgin of his trip, but it is their original Indian name that endures today – *Iguazú*, which means "Mighty Waters" in Guaraní.

As the legend goes, the falls were created centuries before their discovery by the force of a young Indian couple's love. Taroba, son of the chief of the Caigengue tribe that ruled the area between the Iguazú and Paraná rivers and Naipi, a blind princess, were inseparable. One morning as they were walking along the rivers in the Valley of the Butterflies, Naipi asked Taroba to describe the sights to her. Taroba complied with Naipi's request until they reached a small hill. Unable to bear Taroba's sudden silence, Naipi, bursting with curiosity, demanded that he tell her what he saw. Taroba described the Iguazú River "rounding the valley like a mighty warrior."

Stifled by her blindness, Naipi screamed in anguish. With a heavy heart, Taroba kissed Naipi's hand and moved to the edge of the river where he prayed to Mboi for Naipi's sight. Suddenly the river stopped and all was silent until a great roar came forth from the earth. An earthquake ripped the ground, leaving a deep gorge in its wake, which in turn diverted the rivers to create the Iguazú Falls. Naipi, now sighted, became the first person to see the falls. Unfortunately, her lover Taroba, lost his life in their creation. In a full moon the falls reverberate with the painful cries of Naipi pleading for her lover's return.

Tourism began to grow up around the falls at the turn of the century. In 1898, the first group of tourists visited the falls, traveling by mule from Puerto Iguazú. Two years later, a group made the trip in a wagon pulled by six horses, two in front and four behind. Machete-bearing guides blazed a trail. Development of the region was initiated by Victoria Aguirre who, upon being unable to reach them in an early expedition, donated 3,000 pesos for the construction of a road to the falls. Its construction was completed through the generosity of the Núñez y Gibaja family, who donated 15,000 pesos and all the equipment necessary to finish it.

Getting There

Aerolíneas Argentinas offers several flights daily between Buenos Aires and Puerto Iguazú. Flight time is one hour and 50 minutes and a roundtrip ticket costs approximately $370 (unrestricted fare).

It is also possible to make the trip by train, bus, or you can rent a car and drive there via National Route 12 north from Buenos Aires. Though significantly less expensive, bus or train travel takes much longer, making both alternatives rather impractical unless you have two travel days to spare. It is at least a 24-hour trip, regardless of whether you go by bus or train. Round-trip tickets are around $100. The **Expreso Singer**, Reconquista 866 (tel 31-5893) and **Tigre Iguazú** (tel 31-6850) bus lines offer two departures daily from the Plaza Once terminal at the intersection of Bartolomé Mitre and Ecuador. The **General Urquiza** train line, Avenida F. Lacroze 4181, covers the route between Buenos Aires and Posadas, where you must then catch a bus to Puerto Iguazú. Departures are on Wednesday, Thursday, Friday and Sunday mornings. Sleeping accommodations are available and must be reserved in advance (tel 553-5213).

If you are planning to spend one or two days in Iguazú and then return to Buenos Aires, we recommend that you leave the bulk of your luggage at your hotel in Buenos Aires and pack an overnight bag. You can do without sweaters and heavy clothing since it's hot and humid in Iguazú all year long. An umbrella or light rain slicker is a good idea if you're traveling during the summer.

Hotels

Since tourism is the primary industry in Puerto Iguazú and in its Brazilian counterpart Foz do Iguaçu, you'll find plenty of hotels in all price ranges on both sides of the falls. However, remember that rooms fill up quickly during the summer, December through March, and you'll need to make reservations.

If you look forward to falling asleep and waking up to the roar of the falls, the five-star **Hotel Internacional** located within sight of the falls in the National Park is for you. Besides a fantastic view of the falls, it has three tennis courts, a swimming pool, a nightclub, casino and three restaurants. You can make reservations in Buenos Aires at Avenida Madero 1020, ground floor (tel 311-4259). The four-star **Hotel das Cataratas** on the Brazilian side of the falls is a similar choice. For reservations call 0455 23-2266/fax 0455 74-1688 or contact Varig Airlines.

In fact, there are several fine hotels on the Brazilian side just outside the town of Foz do Iguaçú, on the road leading to the falls. The quaint **Hotel Bourbon**, Estrada das Cataratas, Km. 2.5 (tel 0455 76-1313 or fax 0455 76-1110) is an excellent five-star hotel 2½ kilometers outside Foz. It has extensive grounds, two swimming pools, tennis courts, athletic fields, and a fine restaurant and piano bar. The four-star **Hotel San Martín**, Estrada das Cataratas, Km. 17 (tel 0455 74-3030 or fax 0455 74-3207) is closer to the falls than the Bourbon and is in a country club-like setting.

If you're determined to stay in Argentina, the **Hotel El Libertador**, located in Puerto Iguazú, is a fine four-star hotel with a pool – a must here – and a restaurant. For reservations call 0757 20823. Also recommended is the three-star **Hotel Alexander**, Avenida Córdoba 665 (tel 0757 2249).

A fine selection of hotels, restaurants and nightspots in Foz de Iguaçu makes staying on the Brazilian side of the falls very worthwhile.

Restaurants

Fresh fish from the Iguazú and Paraná Rivers, prepared in a variety of ways, are the regional specialties. When scanning a menu, look for **Dorado**, **Surubí**, and **Sábalo**, or ask your waiter for a recommendation.

Neither Puerto Iguazú nor Foz do Iguaçú have any truly outstanding restaurants. If your hotel has one, you may do just as well there. However, there are a few worthwhile options on both sides of the border. In Puerto Iguazú, **El Tío Querido**, Pto. Moreno 345, and the more economical **Chaco**, Córdoba 106, both feature grilled meats (*parrillada*). **La Rueda**, at the intersection of Avenida Aguirre and Córdoba, is a reasonably-priced choice for pasta. For authentic *churrasco*, the Brazilian counterpart of the Argentinean *parrillada*, try **Churrascaría Buffalo Branco** at Rua Rebouças 530 or **Churrascaría Novo Mundo**, Avenida J. Kubitschek 3,550 in Foz do Iguaçú. Another fine choice on the Brazilian side of the falls is the **Galeteria La Mama**, Avenida das Cataratas 130, a popular all-you-can-eat restaurant which specializes in pasta and *galeto*, spit-roasted chicken.

Many of the wooden walkways, called pasarelas, on the Argentinean side of the falls were destroyed by a flood in 1983. They are slowly being rebuilt as finances allow.

Sunup to Sundown

"Argentina pone el espectáculo y Brasil cobra la entrada." (Argentina puts on the show and Brazil charges admission.) This popular saying is the key to seeing the falls. Since 85% of them are on the Argentinean side of the Iguazú River, the best views are from Brazil, while on the Argentinean side you will walk along paths and wooden walkways, known as *pasarelas*, occasionally feeling the spray of the falls. The falls are located in the national park which spans the two countries, the **Parque Nacional Iguazú** (Argentina)/**Parque Nacional do Iguaçú** (Brazil), and there is an admission charge at either entrance. If possible, you should allow yourself two days here, spending one in Argentina and the other in Brazil. This will probably leave you with some free time for lounging at poolside.

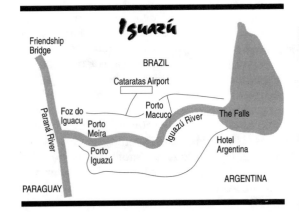

Iguazú Falls

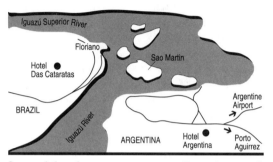

Several local tour operators offer trips to the falls, but there is no reason why you can't handle it on your own. Getting there is easy from both sides of the border. If you've rented a car, follow Route 12 to the falls if you're in Argentina, or the Estrada das Cataratas if you're in Brazil. Both lead to the entrance of the national park. Otherwise, there is bus service on both sides and your hotel will be able to provide you with an up-to-date schedule and rates. Departures are usually hourly.

The 275 falls are arranged in a semi-circle 2,700 meters long. Most are concentrated along the Río Iguazú Inferior, the lower portion of the Iguazú River. You'll pass various falls (*saltos*) as you wander along the paths and walkways, including the **Salto Alvar Núñez, Salto Adán y Eva** (Adam and Eve), **Salto Rivadavia**, and the **Salto Tres Mosqueterros** (the Three Musketeers), until you reach the most spectacular of them all, the **Garganta del Diablo** (Devil's Throat) where the Iguazú Superior crashes into the Inferior 70 meters below. Shared by Argen-

Although often overlooked by visitors, the flora and fauna of the park, which actually encloses a tropical jungle or rain forest, are just as amazing as the falls themselves and will be covered in the chapter on National Parks.

tina and Brazil, the omnipotent Devil's Throat spans the 150-meter width of the Iguazú River and it is the deafening roar of its waters that you'll hear ever-increasing as you make your way through the park. You may even feel its vibrations as you walk along.

A truly exciting way to see the falls is to rent a canoe at Puerto Canoas (on the Argentine side) and paddle along the Iguazú Superior to the crest of the Garganta del Diablo. You can also fly over the falls via helicopter ($30 US per person).

Itaipú

Another must-see is the **Itaipú Dam** 20 miles north of the falls on the Paraná River between Brazil and Paraguay. As high as a 62-story building and nearly five miles long, Itaipú is the world's largest hydroelectric dam. The hydroelectric plant has 18 turbo generators that supply 75 million kilowatts of electricity an hour. Amazingly, just one-third of one generator would fulfill all of Paraguay's electric needs! The dam's 390-meter-wide spillway can discharge over 62,000 cubic meters or eight trillion gallons of water per second. The reservoir created by the dam holds over 29 trillion liters of water.

Construction of Itaipú was a joint undertaking by Brazil and Paraguay as the result of a treaty signed by the two nations in 1973. Brazil financed most of the $25 billion required for its construction, and as many as 40,000 workers were employed during peak periods. A company town was established nearby which could accommodate 9,000 residents.

There is a visitor's center at the dam. Four tours are given daily, Monday through Saturday, each preceded by a short film. Inquire at your hotel regarding transportation to Itaipú. You may want to consider hiring a driver and requesting that he also take you to the **Tres Fronteras**, the point at which the Iguazú and Paraná rivers converge. You can see Argentina, Brazil and Paraguay from here. Each country is marked by a monument in the colors of its flag on its riverbank: blue and white for Argentina; red, white and blue for Paraguay; and green and yellow for Brazil. The Iguazú runs between Brazil and Argentina, while the Paraná separates Brazil and Paraguay. This is also a good vantage point for a view of the **Tancredo Neves Bridge** that spans the Iguazú to connect Brazil and Argentina.

There are two museums in Puerto Iguazú which you may find interesting. The **Museo de Imágenes de la Selva** features a collection of local woodcarvings inspired by the native wildlife. You can study the flora and fauna of the region at the **Museo Regional de Ciencias Naturales.**

Iguazú After Dark

You won't find much in the way of nightlife here. There is a **casino** in the **Hotel Acaray** in Ciudad del Este, Paraguay, just across the Río Paraná from Brazil via the Ponte de Amizade (Friendship Bridge). However, unless you're content to watch rather than gamble, a trip here is not recommended. Most games are stacked against the client, and your chances of winning are extremely slim.

The **Teatro Praça Foz**, Km. 726 on Highway BR-77 on the Brazilian side (tel 73-4370), features traditional drama highlighting the folklore of Brazil Argentina and Paraguay. Shows usually begin at 10:30 p.m. Many of the larger hotels on the Brazilian side have discos, including the **Salvatti**, Rua Rio Branco 67, and **Skorpius** in the Hotel Internacional. Additional nightclubs in Foz include **A Taberna**, Avenida República Argentina 500, **Wiskadão**, Rua Alma Barrosa, and **Sambalão** on Avenida J. Kubitschek. Since places come and go frequently, it's a good idea to ask for recommendations at your hotel before venturing out.

The receptionist or concierge at your hotel is your best source for up-to-date recommendations.

Shopping

Unless Iguazú is the only destination on your entire Argentine itinerary, there is really no need to shop here, except to pick up postcards or a little souvenir. The best shop in Puerto Iguazú is **Macarman** at Avenida Brasil 370. Nor will you find great shopping in Foz do Iguaçu. However, if you're determined to bring back something from Brazil, there is a branch of **H. Stern Jewelers** in the shopping arcade of the Hotel das Cataratas. **Artesanato Três Fronteiras** on Estrada das Cataratas in Foz sells local candy, ceramics, copper pieces and other souvenirs.

Iguazú A-Z

AIRLINES: Aerolíneas Argentinas has an office at Avenida Aguirre 404 (tel 20168). **Austral** is at Avenida Aguirre 429 (tel 20644). **Varig,** the Brazilian carrier has an office in Foz do Iguaçu at Avenida Brasil 821 (tel 74-3344).

CURRENCY EXCHANGE: You can change money at the **Banco de la Nación**, San Martín 525 in Puerto Iguazú.

POST OFFICE: The Post Office is on Avenida San Martín in Puerto Iguazú and at Avenida Getulio Vargas 72 in Foz do Iguaçu.

TOURIST OFFICE: The **Oficina de Turismo** is at Avenida Victoria Aguirre 396 in Puerto Iguazú.

Mar Del Plata

Mar y Sierra, Argentina's vacation coast, is the 30-mile stretch along the Atlantic between San Clemente del Tuyo and Mar del Plata. Here tranquil beaches and often placid seas are interspersed among towering cliffs and rocky shores that are continuously beaten by crashing waves. Argentina's summer playground extends from the Atlantic coast inland, covering an area of 1,460 square kilometers of shore line, rolling hills and pastures, lakes and lagoons. This is the General Puerrydón district of the province of Buenos Aires. Its capital is Mar del Plata, "La Perla del Atlántico" (The Pearl of the Atlantic), 250 miles south of Buenos Aires.

Argentina's most famous beach resort.

Prior to its development, sea lions (*lobos marinos*) inhabited much of the Atlantic Coast, especially the beaches south of Mar del Plata, which today are among the most exclusive of the region, and the zone was known as *La Lobería*. There are even references, dating as far back as 1885, to carriage rides from the Hotel Bristol to look at the sea lions. Unfortunately, the sea lions attracted hunters as well as nature watchers and their numbers began to decline quite rapidly. Nowadays, the sea lions are protected and visitors to Mar del Plata can again observe them in their "natural environment" at the *Reserva Natural Barranca de los Lobos* or catch their show at the Mar del Plata Aquarium.

Sea lions and beaches aren't the only draw for the four million visitors who flock to Mar del Plata from all over Argentina every summer (remember, it's December through March in the southern hemisphere) and on weekends too. You can watch the fishing boats set off for a day's work as the sun rises over the Atlantic, and then spend the rest of the day playing golf or tennis; fishing from one of the jetties along the shore or at a nearby lake; horseback riding in the Parque Camet or biking along the shoreline, stopping at beaches whenever the mood strikes you; or hiking in the surrounding countryside. Not surprisingly, windsurfing, sailing, water skiing, surfing, kayaking, swimming and, of course, sunbathing are also widely practiced.

If all that sounds like too much work for a vacation, never fear. Mar del Plata has a very strong creative community and offers much in the way of culture. You'll find museums, art galleries, exhibit halls, and artisan fairs throughout the city, along with concerts and great theater during the summer. Afternoon tea is *de rigeuer* here (remember, dinner is not until 11 p.m.) and a great way to catch up on the latest trends. You can people-watch from an outdoor table on the pedestrian-only Avenida San Martín while sharing a plate of *alfajores marplatenses*. After this late afternoon break you'll feel refreshed and ready for a night on the town. You can gamble the evening away at Mar del Plata's renowned Casino Provincial, take in a show, dance until dawn at the city's many discos, or spend a quiet evening at a pub or *confitería*.

When it opened in 1939, Mar del Plata's Casino Provincial was the largest in the world. Though that position has since been usurped by its counterparts in Las Vegas and Atlantic City, it is still quite impressive.

History

In 1581, one year after founding Buenos Aires, Juan de Garay landed in what is now Mar del Plata. However, little in the way of development occured in the area until 1746 when the Jesuits founded the region's first mission, La Reducción de Nuestra Señora del Pilar on the shores of what was then called the Laguna de las Cabrillas. They intended to convert the nomadic Indians who inhabited the region to a sedentary Catholic lifestyle, but were forced to abandon the mission in 1751 following an Indian attack. The lake was renamed Laguna de los Padres in their honor.

The current building on the Laguna de Los Padres is a reproduction of the original reducción. It was built in 1968 using straw and adobe as required by tradition.

In the mid-19th century, the region began to develop economically. In 1856 Coelho de Meyrelles, representing a consortium of Portuguese businessmen, set up a factory on Avenida Luro between Avenida Santiago del Estero and Avenida Santa Fe to salt leather prior to its shipment to Europe. He also built the iron dock on Punta Iglesias.

In 1860 Meyrelles sold a 32-league tract of land, including several *estancias* such as Laguna de los Padres, San Julian de Vivoratá, and La Armoniá de Cobo, to Peralta Ramos. This proved a pivotal event in the history of Mar del Plata.

Quite a visionary, Peralta Ramos recognized the region's great potential as a summer resort for families and dedicated himself to its development. The town was officially founded on February 10, 1874 by a decree signed by the

Governor of the Province of Buenos Aires, Mariano Acosta.

Pedro Luro took over the salting house in 1877. His son, Dr. Pedro Olegario Luro, developed the Mar del Plata harbor, officially founded in 1923 as the "Puerto de Ultramar en Mar del Plata." Today, it is Argentina's most important fishing port. In fact, 70% of the city's income is generated by the fishing industry.

At first, Mar del Plata was an exclusive summer resort attracting members of the high society of Buenos Aires, including rich cattle magnates, businessmen, and noblemen from Europe. The inauguration of the Hotel Bristol in 1888 made it a social "must" to summer in Mar del Plata. In the early years of the 20th century, through the 1920's and 30's, the very wealthy built elegant summer homes in a style known as *pintoresquismo,* an eclectic mix of several styles, including Tudor, New England, California, Mediterranean, Basque and *Anglonormando.* Many of these homes remain today.

With the rise of the middle class in the 1940's, Mar del Plata lost its aristocratic airs. The number of hotels in all price ranges grew by leaps and bounds, along with vacation complexes for middle class families. The number of summer visitors skyrocketed. Mar del Plata was no longer the exclusive resort it once was and Punta del Este, Uruguay replaced it as the summer playground of the Argentine jet set.

Climate

Located in a temperate zone, the average annual temperature is around 55°F. The summer months (December-February) bring daytime temperatures in the 80's. The maximum summertime temperature is 95°F. Temperatures drop down to the 40's in July, the coldest month of the year.

Getting There

Mar del Plata is a 45-minute flight from Buenos Aires and there are several flights daily. National Routes (RN) #2 from Buenos Aires and #226 run into Mar del Plata, as does Provincial Route 11. Several bus companies cover the route from Buenos Aires to Mar del Plata. The trip takes around 5½ hours and most buses are deluxe tourist coaches with video, bar and music. The Roca train line makes the trip in the same amount of time.

Arrival

The small Aeroparque Camet airport is located seven kilometers northwest of center city. There is a hotel reservation service in the airport, as well as car rental agencies and souvenir stands. A *remis* or taxi into Mar del Plata should cost around $10. Both the train and bus stations are located in town.

Orientation

The commercial center of Mar del Plata is not very large and can easily be explored on foot. The focal point of the downtown area is **La Rambla**, the huge beachfront plaza dominated by the city's largest hotel, the **Provincial**, and the largest entertainment complex, the **Casino Provincial**. The pedestrian promenade, **Avenida San Martín**, home of some of the city's finest shops and cafés, runs into the Rambla. A few blocks north of San Martín and parallel to it is **Avenida Constitución**, where you'll find much of our recommended nightlife. You may want to take a cab here in the evenings.

The **Bulevar Marítimo** runs along the beach and is officially known as **Avenida Peralta Ramos** while it crosses much of the city, then changes its name to Avenida M. de Hoz after passing the port not far from the southern border of the downtown area. Other major avenues include **Avenida Luro** and **Avenida Colón**, running parallel to San Martín, and **Avenida Independencia**, which runs north to south.

Hotels

You'll find no shortage of hotels in Mar del Plata, ranging from four down to two stars. We've selected what we consider the city's finest four-star hotels. Although there are no five-star hotels at present, the city's first, the Hotel Costa Galanda, is currently being built on the Playa Grande. If it is open when you visit and you do stay there, please don't hesitate to drop us a line and give us your opinion.

HOTEL PRIMACY Aparthotel
Santa Fe 2464, corner of Gascón
Tel (023)91-3600
Fax (023)91-3205
59 apartments
Pool, exercise room
Expensive

Alive Price Scale
Deluxe: $175+
Expensive: $100+
Moderate: $60-100
Inexpensive: $35-60
Budget: under $35

If we were asked to recommend just one hotel in Mar del Plata, it would be the Primacy. This 10-story aparthotel features tastefully furnished suites with kitchenette for up to six people. All suites have television, piped-in music, individually controlled heat and air conditioning, and a safe. The hotel has a cafeteria and restaurant, and offers room service. Baby sitters can be arranged. A few blocks from the center of town, it is quieter than many of the more centrally located hotels.

TORRES DE MANANTIALES Aparthotel
Alberti 445
Tel 51-99216
Fax 51-8789
145 apartments
Exercise classes, tennis court
Breakfast included
Expensive (more expensive on the weekends)

This 28-story apart-hotel with one- , two- , and three-bedroom suites seems to cater especially to vacationing families. There are special activities in the gym and pool nearly every day. Parents can head up to the 28th-floor Las Nubes bar in the evening for drinks and soft music in the evenings while kids are at the more raucous disco gym (over 18 not allowed unless accompanied by children). The hotel also has a game room for both young and old and offers closed circuit video movies (requests are welcome).

With advance notice, baby sitting is available in the evenings. Most suites have balconies. There are some two- and three-bedroom duplexes.

GRAN HOTEL PROVINCIAL ☆☆☆☆
Bulevar Marítimo 2300
(Las Ramblas)
Tel (023) 91-5949
Fax 91-5894
1,100 rooms
Tennis courts, weight room, sauna
Expensive

Size alone makes this hotel one that you've got to see to believe. Built by Perón in 1946, its overwhelming presence on the ard Marítimo brings back memories of Argentina's glory days. If we had to use just one word to describe all the facilities here, "huge" would have to be it. The lobby, decorated with enormous murals, is huge. The restaurant is huge. The hotel beach, with its never-ending rows of umbrellas and chairs, is huge. The swimming pool is huge. The hotel's many banquet halls and convention rooms are huge. If you're looking for intimate surroundings, you won't find them here. It can literally take you 20 minutes to walk from your room to the hotel beach.

HOTEL CASINO SASSO ☆☆☆☆
Martínez de Hoz 3545
Tel 84-0031
Casino, swimming pool, beach

A lovely beachfront location on Punta Mogotes is one of the best reasons for staying at the Sasso. The casino is another if you're a gambler. Otherwise, this is a fairly standard four star. All rooms are air conditioned.

GRAN HOTEL IRUÑA ☆☆☆☆
Av. Juan B. Alberdi 2250/70
Tel 2-4037
Fax 9-1183
110 rooms/5 floors
Expensive

Elegance is a high priority at the Gran Hotel Iruña, to the extent that guests may forget they are at the beach. Perhaps that is why this is a popular choice among convention planners and business people. The Iruña offers a wide range of business services including simultaneous translation, typing and shorthand, along with conference facilities. Decor, rooms included, is traditional and on the formal side. Rooms have either an ocean or city view. If you have a preference, make it known when reserving. Only common areas of the hotel are air conditioned.

HOTEL PRESIDENTE ☆☆☆☆
Corrientes 1516
Tel 2-8810
Fax 2-8537
50 rooms/8 floors

The Presidente is less formal than its sister hotel, the Iruña. It is also smaller. Yet it does offer the same business services and the same first-class attention. Only common areas of the hotel are air conditioned.

HERMITAGE HOTEL ☆☆☆☆
Bulevar Marítimo 2657
Tel 51-9081
Fax 51-7235
200 rooms/5 floors
Casino
Expensive

A block away and across the Bulevar from the Hotel Provincial, the Hermitage is much smaller. If you want to stay in the thick of the action and are a real night owl, this may be a good choice. Since there is no air conditioning, you will probably opt to keep your windows open at night, letting in both the breeze and street noises. There is a small casino, open weekends during the winter months and every day during high season. Be prepared to pay more for a room with an ocean view.

GRAN HOTEL DORA ☆☆☆☆
Calle Buenos Aires 1841
Tel 91-0033
Fax 91-0772
113 rooms/6 floors
Moderate
Consistent with her sister hotels in Córdoba and Buenos Aires, the Hotel Dora offers comfortable accommodations and excellent service at a reasonable price. The location is hard to beat, just steps from the casino and the beach.

ESTANCIA SANTA ISABEL
Ruta Provincial 11
Tel (0291)21000
10 rooms
Expensive
If you're torn between staying at an *estancia* or going to the beach, the Estancia Santa Isabel is the perfect solution. Definitely a very special place, this fully modernized yet elegantly colonial manor is surrounded by gardens and offers plenty of trails for solitary rambles or horseback riding. You can lounge beside the pool or head to the beach, where there is a fine seaside spa as well as chairs and awnings. For nightlife, Mar

del Plata is just a drive away, but if it's quieter times you're after this is the perfect place.

Restaurants

Seafood, of course, dominates most menus. Many of the best seafood restaurants are in the **Centro Comercial del Puerto** where they range from extremely informal to a little more than casual.

Alive Price Scale
(per person)
Expensive: $40+
Moderate: $25+
Inexpensive: under $20

This does not mean that beef has lost its place here. You'll find *parrillas* throughout the city, as well as restaurants specializing in Italian, Spanish, French, German and, as of late, Middle Eastern cooking.

One absolute must is the *alfajores marplatenses*. Although most would swear otherwise, these chocolate or caramel-filled pastries are what keep vacationers coming back to Mar del Plata year after year. More than just a tradition, afternoon tea is a ritual here. Mar del Plata probably has more *confiterías* per block than any other Argentine city and every afternoon, especially in high season, each and every one of them is crowded, with a plate of *alfajores* at the center of the table.

RESTAURANTE LA MARCA
Almafuerte 253
Tel 51-8072
International
Moderate
Located near the La Loma cemetery, La Marca would easily fit in among the restaurants in La Recoleta in Buenos Aires. Wood dominates the

simple decor of the large dining room, along with animal hides on the walls. Salads, *parrillada*, and pastas are featured dishes. Slightly out of the way, but worth the cab ride.

RESTAURANTE SORTILEJA Y ZABALITOS
Alem and Pringles, Playa Grande
Tel 80-2442
International
Open: 12:30-3:30 p.m.; 8:30 p.m.-1 a.m.
A favorite for more than a quarter of a century, this large restaurant manages to create elegance with Old West decor. The large, fancy bar attracts a crowd night after night. Pasta is the specialty.

RESTAURANT VERDI
Rejón 3656
Tel 73-4670
International
Moderate
One of the most elegant restaurants in Mar del Plata, Verdi would be a good choice for a special night. Fine artwork highlights the decor while fresh seafood dominates much of the menu. The *trucha* or *salmón ahumado* (smoked trout or salmon) appetizers were strongly recommended to us and rightfully so. Salads, very fresh, are also quite good. For main courses, you won't be disappointed by the *frutos del mar* (the seafood platter) or the *supremo de pollo a la cereza* (chicken supreme with cherries). Just one block off Avenida Constitución, dinner here is a great way to start an evening out.

LOS WAGONES
Avenida Constitución
Pizza
You may remember the days when they were used as diners. Well in this case, Los Wagones has put an old train car to good use as a pizzería. Definitely a fun place.

Other Options:

Restaurants abound and you should have no problem in finding one to your liking. Additional suggestions include seafood at **La Taberna Baska**, 12 de Octubre 3301 (tel 80-0209) or **Atalaya del Mar** at the Escollera Club de Pesca (tel 3-1713). The **Trenque Lauquen** on the corner of Mitre and Garay (tel 3-7149) is an excellent *parrilla*. The policy is *tenedor libre* or "all you can eat" at **Gran Parrilla** on San Martín. **Pizza Lola** and **Pumper** nearby are also quite good and reasonably priced.

Confiterías

There's virtually one *confitería* after another on the *peatonal* San Martín. For a late night café, we're especially fond of the **Bolshoi Café** on the corner of Leonardo Alem and Alma Fuerte. It reminds us of the traditional coffee houses in New York's Greenwich Village. The second-floor **Sir Thomas Confitería** at the corner of Santa Fe and San Martín is also a fine choice. Sunset is the perfect time for the **Torreón del Monje**, where the views are spectacular. If you go to the Bosque de Peralta Ramos, be sure to stop in at **La Cabaña del Bosque**.

Sunup to Sundown

Doubtless you'll find plenty of ways to occupy the daylight hours here. Of course, one of the main attractions of Mar del Plata is its beaches, 47 kilometers of them, often set against rocky cliffs. Most, especially those in town, have lifeguards and offer umbrella and chair rentals. Some even have changing cabanas. The busiest are also the most centrally located, **Bristol, La Perla** and **Playa Grande**. The best known beaches are those south of Cabo Corrientes, while the beaches north of the city, once fairly deserted, are becoming increasingly popular.

But there is more to life (and to a vacation) than just beaches. Following are a walking tour of the city and additional sightseeing suggestions.

Walking Tour

To give you a real feeling of being at the seashore, we'll start our walk at the **Exposición de Caracoles y Arte Nacár** (Exposition of Seashells and Mother of Pearl Art) at San Luis 1771 on the corner of San Martín. This collection of over 50,000 seashells was gathered by Señor Sisterna, an avid world traveler.

We hope you walked up the pedestrian-only Avenida San Martín to get here, admiring the many interesting shops along the way and perhaps even spending a little time at one of the sidewalk cafés.

The seashell museum is right on the **Plaza San Martín**. Christened Plaza América when it was first built in the 1930's, it was later called the Plaza Luro for Avenida Luro which bisects it, and was subsequently renamed Plaza San Martín. Interestingly, at the plaza's center is a statue of the General, not on horseback but in his older years, dressed in civilian clothes and supporting himself with a cane. Cast in bronze by the sculptor Luis Perlotti, it was donated to the city in 1956 by Roger Ballet. Benches all around make the plaza a favorite meeting place for friends and young lovers in the evenings, while others come here to feed the pigeons and the sparrows. Concerts are occasionally held in the small bandshell.

While still on the plaza, be sure to check the date on the city calendar, which keeps residents and guests up-to-date using flowers to spell out the month, date and year. Take a few minutes to visit the **Catedral de los Santos Pedro Y Cecilia** (Cathedral of Saints Peter and Cecilia). Built between 1893 and 1905, its neogothic style is reminiscent of the 12th and 13th centuries. Outstanding features include its enormous stained glass windows, a central chandelier which once hung in the city's original hotel, the Bristol, and the bell tower with its five bells. The crypt below the main altar supposedly contains the remains of 1st- and 2nd-century martyrs and a small piece of Christ's Cross.

An artisans' fair/hippie market is held most evenings on the **Diagonal Pueyrredón**, just off the western side of the plaza. Not far from the plaza at Yrigoyen 1627 is the **Municipalidad de General Puerrydón** (Town Hall). Built in 1938, it was designed by Alejandro Bustillo to resemble a 16th-century Florentine palace. Also on Yrigoyen at 1675 is the **Teatro Colón y Club Español**, built in 1924 by the architect Angel Pascual.

Walk through the center of the Plaza San Martín and continue along Mitre one block off the plaza to 25 de Mayo. At 2751 you'll pass the city's first public school, **Escuela N1 Pascuala Mugaburu**, which dates to 1917. Then take the the diagonal Alberdi towards the beachfront. The **Universidad Nacional de Mar del Plata** at 2695 houses the university's administrative offices, as well as the Humanities, Law, Science and Social Science departments. The **Monumento a los Caídos en Malvinas** (Monument to the Fallen of the Falklands Conflict) is between Córdoba and Santiago del Estero. Designed by Eduardo Lodi, it was dedicated on December 16, 1986 to honor those who perished in the Falklands War.

Continue along Alberdi until it ends at the Bulevar Marítimo Patricio Peralta Ramos and the **Monumento al Pescador** (Monument to the Fisherman), at the site of the original port where salted leather hides were once loaded onto cargo ships. Heading right you'll shortly find yourself on **Las Ramblas**, the focal point of Mar del Plata. Presided over by two sea lions, the promenade, which runs along Bristol Beach, was rebuilt several times, most recently in the 1930's by Alejandro Bustillo. Of course, you can't miss the **Hotel Provincial y Complejo Casino Central** which, in addition to its many gaming rooms, features several auditoriums, the largest of which is the **Teatro Auditorium**. The **Ente Municipal de Turismo** (Municipal Tourist Office) is located here at Bulevar Marítimo 2267.

At this point you can continue the walk, or take a time out and visit the beach, picking up the rest of the walk later. Beaches extend in both directions from here. You may even want to catch a bus or cab, or bike it to one of the locations outside the center of town (see below).

Bordered by Avenida Buenos Aires and Colón across from Las Ramblas is the **Plaza Colón**. Flowers, many of them in pots, dominate the plaza along with a children's playground. Continuing along the boulevard, there is a statue of **Patricio Peralta Ramos**, the city's founder. The **Paseo Jesús de Galíndez**, a beachfront garden walk extending from Cabo Corrientes to Las Ramblas, was added in the 1980's. **Cabo Corrientes** was originally named Cape Lob (for the large population of sea lions spotted there) by Sir Francis Drake on his way to the Straits of Magellan.

As you have probably already noticed, the beach front **Torreón del Monje**, built in 1904 by Ernesto Tornquist who donated it to the city, was designed to resemble a medieval fortress. Today it hosts special exhibits and is home to *confiterías* and tea rooms. The Jesuit belltower is a fine vantage point for views of the ocean and the city.

Nearby at Avenida Colón 1189 is the **Villa Ortiz Basualdo**. Built in 1909 and remodeled in 1919 by the Italian-born engineer Alula Baldassarini, it is one of the best examples of picturesque architecture and art nouveau in the city. Today it is home to the **Museo Municipal de Arte Moderno Juan Carlos Castagnino**. In addition to the city's collection of more than 450 paintings, photographs and sculptures by national and local artists and a salon dedicated to the painter for which it is named, the museum also contains the home's original furnishings, which were imported from Belgium by the Ortiz Basualdo family. A few blocks from the Villa, the 48-meter-high **Torre Tanque**, at Falucho 993, supplies the city's drinking water and great views of the coast.

One block from Viamonte is Almirante Brown where at 1074 stands the **Capilla Stella Maris**. This simple chapel is home to a beautiful neo-classic image of the Virgin Mary. You are now at the border of **Los Troncos**, Mar del Plata's most traditional residential district and home to the city's finest examples of picturesque architecture. It is named for the **Casa de los Troncos** at Calle Urquiza 3454, between Rodríguez Peña and Primera Junta. Built in 1938 by Cornejo Saravia, an affluent businessman from Salta, this house was built using trunks of quebracho and lapacho wood transported via railroad from Salta, and it is the epitome of colorful architecture. Other noteworthy examples include the **Chateau Frontenac** at Almirante 2010, which was built in 1905 and remodeled in 1925 under the direction of Alejandro Bustillo. A replica of its namesake in Quebec, it is currently a hotel. The **Villa Normandy**, Viamonte 2216, was designed by Gastón Mallet in 1920 and is now home to the Italian Consulate. Equally fine are the **Villa Blaquier** (1905) at Alvear 2138; the **Villa Unzué de Cobo** at Bolívar (1910) 1159; **Saint Michael** (1930) at Mendoza 2047 which was designed by Alula Baldassarini; the **Villa Unzué de Casares** at Olavarría (1920) 2154; and the **Villa Perés** (1930) at Alvear 2390.

Continue heading away from the beach on Avenida Colón or Alberti (five blocks south of Colón) and make a left onto Las Heras. Follow Las Heras until Matheu and turn right. At 1851 is the Belle Epoque-style **Centro Cultural Victoria O'Campo Villa Victoria**. One of the first

Downtown Mar Del Plata

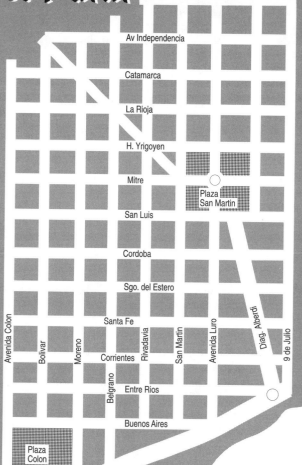

Av Independencia

Catamarca

La Rioja

H. Yrigoyen

Mitre

Plaza San Martin

San Luis

Cordoba

Sgo. del Estero

Santa Fe

Corrientes

Entre Rios

Buenos Aires

Avenida Colon

Bolivar

Moreno

Belgrano

Rivadavia

San Martin

Avenida Luro

Diag. Alberdi

9 de Julio

Plaza Colon

Casino

homes of its kind in this upper class neighborhood known as **Divino Rostro**, this prefabricated house was imported from England by the great aunt of the writer Victoria O'Campo in the first years of the 20th century. Many important figures from the world of arts and letters, including Jorge Luis Borges, Igor Stravinsky, Waldo Frank and Gabriela Mistral, spent time here. Upon her death, Victoria O'Campo donated the building to the city. Today, as the city's cultural center, it is a frequent host of music festivals, art exhibits, dances and courses.

History aficionados may want to stop at the **Museo Archivo Histórico Municipal Villa Emilio Mitre** at Calle Lamadrid 3870. This small museum traces the history of Mar del Plata and the General Puerrydon district with over 5,000 photos, clippings and documents. It also houses a library of books by local authors.

Follow Lamadrid to Formosa, then Las Heras and finally Alma Fuerte. The **Capilla Divino Rostro**, the chapel for which this neighborhood is named, was built in 1937 by a wealthy resident, Angiolina Astengo de Mitre, in memory of her husband Emilio Mitre. The main alter was brought from Peru and features a replica of the face of Christ from the shroud of La Veronica in Turin, Italy. Noteworthy homes here include the **Villa Santa Paula** (1909) at Garay; the **Villa Alula Baldasarrini** at Sarmiento 2508, which was built by the architect in 1905; and the **Villa Mayón** (1905) at Almirante Brown 1154.

Walk down to the port on Avenida Juan B. Justo. Most of the city's sweater shops and factories are concentrated along this street, earning it the nickname "Avenida del Pullover." Just before reaching the port you'll cross Calle Alem, home to many restaurants, *confiterías*, pubs and shopping arcades. If it's sea lions you're interested in, late afternoon when they sun themselves along the piers is a great time to visit the port. While there is always a lot of activity here, peak times are early morning when the fishing boats are just going out or noon when they return. The **Centro Comercial del Puerto** features many fine restaurants and cafés, as well as shops selling canned and fresh seafood. A few favorite restaurants include **La Caracol**, **El Viejo Pop** and **Santa Rita**.

From here you can head back to the center of town along the Bulevar Marítimo or head to the beach. We always like to relax with a cold drink and watch the goings-on at the port. On your way back to the center, walk through the **Parque San Martín** in front of **Playa Grande**. Flowers are interspersed among the rocks here creating a beautiful garden setting. This time San Martín is once again on horseback.

Other Sights

Hardcore walkers may opt to visit some of the next sites on foot. For those less inclined to walk, many are easily biked to and we've also included bus routes. Of course, you can always "cab it."

Grota de Lourdes

This reproduction of the Grotto of Lourdes in France is built into a quarry surrounded by lots of greenery. Inside, you'll find a beautiful image of Our Lady of Lourdes, along with miniatures of Bethlehem and Jerusalem, complete with moving figures and several small waterfalls. To get here follow 12 de Octubre from the port and turn left at Magallanes or take bus #522 which runs past the port.

Laguna de los Padres & the Reducción de Nuestra Señora del Pilar

Among the interesting rock formations the area was first known for, some new residential developments are beginning to pop up here and with them cafés, restaurants, and shops selling regional items. There is also a golf course. The lake is a popular place for picnics and there are several *asadores* (barbecues) here. Rowboats are also available for rent and fishing is popular. A reproduction of the Reducción de Nuestra Señora del Pilar was built here in 1968. While here you should visit the **Museo Tradicional-ista José Hernández**, which features arms used by the Army of the Desert, antique money and riding gear.

El Faro Punta Mogotes

Following the beachfront Avenida Martínez de Hoz a few blocks further south from the Port, you'll come to Punta Mogotes and the Punta Mogotes Lighthouse. First built in 1891 and modernized in 1975, it was once one of the most modern lighthouses in South America. Also on Punta Mogotes at Avenida Hoz 5600 is the **Aquarium Mar del Plata** (tel 3-3173; open seven days a week, 9 a.m.-8 p.m. No tickets sold after 2 p.m.). All the usual attractions are here, including dolphin shows, sea lions, water skiing demonstrations, aquariums and water games. Admission is $12 for kids and $15 for adults.

Barranca de los Lobos

Continuing south along the coastal highway #11, just under five miles outside town you'll reach the Barranca de los Lobos (Sea Lions Ravine). These 45-meter cliffs afford a great view of the neighboring cliffs along the coast. The beaches below are a popular spot for fishing and many also come here to explore the small coastal caves within the cliffs. The government-run **Chapadmalad** hotel complex, which belongs to the Secretary of Tourism, is about six miles further south from here. Open to the public, it has its own beaches, playgrounds, watersports facilities and a coffee shop and restaurant. Bus routes #717 and #221 run here.

Miramar

Founded in 1888, this lovely seaside resort is known for its wide, peaceful beaches, quiet residential streets, and beachfront hotels. Many of the older homes here resemble those in Mar del Plata. The calm atmosphere is ideal for biking and there are plenty of bike rental shops in town. Though there is not a great deal of nightlife, there is a casino and a golf club. The **Vivero Dunícolo Florentino Ameghino** at 105 meters above sea level, is the highest forested dune in the country. To get here follow Route 11 south 15 miles beyond Punta Mogotes.

Bosque de Peralta Ramos

Not far from Punta Mogotes, the Bosque de Peralta Ramos was once the estate of the city's founder Pedro Peralta Ramos. Now it is an exclusive residential area of magnificent homes hidden within tree-filled gardens. Groves of eucalyptus, acacias, and cypresses afford residents lots of privacy, while the silence is often broken by birds singing. You'll find several bike paths, playgrounds, artisan shops and outdoor cafés. To get here, follow Route 11 south to the Diagonal Norte or take bus #526.

Parque Camet

This large recreation area has polo and rugby fields, riding stables and a ring equipped with jumps and an obstacle course, plus sports fields galore. There is a forested park with picnic areas, complete with *asadores* (barbecue spits). The park is four miles north of town on Route 11. Buses #221 and #541 run here.

Santa Clara del Mar

For great beaches continue north on Route 11 for about 30 minutes to Santa Clara del Mar. The most famous are **El Arroyo, La Hermosa, El Viejo Contrabandista, La Sirena, Las Corvinas** and **La Posta del Angel**, which is home to a well-known center of Latin American handicrafts – **El Centro de Artesanías Américanas**. Several hotels and restaurants are in the area. You can take bus #221 to get here.

Mar Chiquita

Not far beyond Santa Clara, you'll reach Mar Chiquita and its 40-plus miles of beautiful beaches bordered by coastal forests. They surround an *albufera*, a large inlet or lake formed by the ocean. Fishing is very popular here, with eels, flounder, and small sharks likely to be among the day's catch. There is also a reserve for migratory birds. Windsurfing, regular surfing, canoing and water skiing are also popular.

Balcarce

Located in the sierra 40 miles north of Mar del Plata, Balcarce is probably best known for its famous resident, five-time world champion of auto racing, Juan Manuel Fangio. Most come here to visit the **Museo del Automovilismo**, which was donated by Fangio. In addition to displaying 10 of the driver's cars, along with numerous trophies and awards, it traces the evolution of the automobile. The **Autodromo Juan Manuel Fangio** is another popular attraction.

The natural beauty of the area is another popular reason for visiting Balarce. Traveling Route 226 north, you'll pass scenic ranches, farms and rolling hills. The town is in an area known as the **Cinco Serros** for the series of five hills there, including **Serro El Triunfo**, a naturally formed amphitheater.

Other Options

Harbour Cruise

Although we would not necessarily classify it as a party boat, the *Anamora "Yate Fiesta"* offers a one-hour cruise through the waters just off shore. Featured on the itinerary are Cabo Corrientes, the Club Nautico, Isla de los Lobos (an offshore island that doubles as a sea lion preserve), Playa Grande, the Torreon del Monje and, of course, the port itself.

The cruise lasts at least an hour and costs $10 for adults and $5 for kids under 10. There is a bar and cafeteria on board as well as a small dance floor. The *Anamora* has several departures every day, as well as sunset cruises. For schedule information call 89-0310.

Rent a Bike

Except for much of the downtown area, Mar del Plata with its parks and coastal roads is a great place to explore by bike. Bikes can be rented on the Plaza Mitre at the intersection of San Luis and Almirante Brown, and on the Plaza Pueyrrdon at the intersection of Dorrego and Chacabuco. Hours are from 9 a.m. to 12 noon and 2:30 p.m. to 7:30 p.m. and all day long on the weekends. Always check the condition of a bike before renting it, making sure that brakes, gears and tires are in working order.

Aquasol Water Park

Waterslides, toboggans and pools galore make for a fun day or afternoon. A great place to take the kids, it's open all day. Two-hour, full-day and multi-day tickets are available. For information call 60-0119. It's just north of the city on Route 2. Park buses leave from Avenida San Martín and Córdoba or take bus #542.

Granja La Piedra Educational Farm

A day or afternoon visit to the Granja La Piedra is a delightful alternative to the beach crowds at Mar del Plata. "Bucolic" best describes the setting, with its modern yet rustic main building and barns, organic orchards and herb gardens, pine trees filled with singing birds, and grazing sheep and goats. You'll learn about cheese making and organic gardening, and enjoy freshly baked *empanadas* and breads. There is also an artisan exhibit. Lunch or dinner is included in the cost of admission. For information and reservations call 64-2546. The Granja is located on Route 88 not far from the Chapadmalal vacation complex. You can take buses #715 and #720 to get there.

Mar del Plata After Dark

Culturally speaking, Mar del Plata is no run of the mill beach town, where summer theater means amateur summer stock performances. Quite the contrary, in a tradition started in the 1950's and 60's, Argentina's finest stars of stage and screen (i.e., the TV screen) not only summer in Mar del Plata, they perform in first-run theater productions that often travel to other cities across the country and continent after premiering here. When we were last in Mar del Plata, Neil Simon's latest play "Lost in Yonkers" (*Per-*

didos en Yonkers) was being performed at the Auditorium in the Casino Provinicial. Works by Eric Bogosian and Marc Camoletti were also on stage. The concierge in your hotel should be able to direct you to the most popular shows in town, or check the listings in the Summer Guides published by the *Diario La Capital* newspaper and the tourist office.

A Few of the Better Theaters:

Auditorium, The Casino Provincial, La Rambla. Tel 3-7786.
Alberdi, Alberdi 2455. Tel 2-0021.
Atlas, corner of Luro and Corrientes. Tel 4-5001.
Colón, Irigoyen 1665. Tel 4-8571.
Corrientes, Corrientes 1766.

Mar del Plata also has a number of cinemas. Check the daily paper, *Diario La Capital* ,for listings.

Gambling

Besides theater, gambling is another of Mar del Plata's traditional after-dark activities. When it first opened in 1939, the **Casino Provincial**, with its 36 roulette tables, was the largest casino in the world. Although that honor may very well have been usurped by its counterparts in Las Vegas or Atlantic City, the casino, though perhaps slightly faded, is no less grandiose and the crowd that gathers here no less pretentious than when it first opened. Amid its several gaming rooms, which offer roulette, blackjack, punta y banca, craps and poker, are several restaurants and a theater. There is a $5 admission fee for the casino and the minimum bet is

$20. It is open from 3:30 p.m. to 5 a.m. weekends only during the winter, and 6 p.m. to 5 a.m. all summer long. If the stakes are too high here, there is a smaller casino in the **Hotel Sasso**.

Bingo is also quite fashionable and popular with the common folk. There are several bingo salons around town including the **Del Sol** at Independencia 1752; the **Marplatense** at Sarmiento 2157; and the **Puerto** at Juan B. Justo 400.

Pubs & Discos

Mar del Plata does not want for discos. Most are concentrated on Avenida Constitución. **Chocolate**, at Avenida Constitución 4445, which opens its doors to kids-only in the afternoons, attracts a crowd 18 to 30 years old in the evenings. **Sunset**, a combination disco and pub at Constitución 5096, admits singles on Friday while observing a couples-only policy on Saturdays. Other popular choices include **Sobremonte** at Constitución 6690, **Go**, and **Dug**, which are also on Constitución. Tango lovers will find their niche at **Del 40**, Constitución 5205.

A little outside the center of town. You will probably want to take a taxi to get here and should definitely take one for the trip back to your hotel.

For a more sedate, romantic atmosphere, head to **Café Satchmo**, Constitución 6708. **Café Frac** at Almafuerte 249, which is really more a pub than a café, is another fine choice if you're not in a disco mood. The **Bolshoi Café** at the corner of Leonardo Alem and Almafuerte is a delightful spot for a late night coffee.

Shopping

Once the season has ended and the last tourist gone home, many year-round residents of Mar del Plata literally go back to their knitting. In fact, besides its beaches, theater productions and casino, Mar del Plata is known for the beautiful handknit sweaters and other woolen articles, featuring original designs in all the colors of the rainbow, produced by its residents during the off-season. You really shouldn't go home without one.

Your best buys will probably be in one of the factory shops on Avenida Juan B. Justo, commonly referred to as **La Avenida del Pullover**. Shops around the city, some with branches in Buenos Aires, include **Forlí Sport** at San Luis 1836; **Tejidos Pagliardini** at Alberti 2217; **Creaciones "Duly"** at San Martín 9604; and **Kangas**, with two locations, Avenida Colón 1722 and Rivadavia 2760.

Another must are the **Alfajores Marplatenses**, delicious pastries filled with chocolate or caramel (*dulce de leche*) or, even better, filled with caramel and covered in chocolate. You can pick up a box of these at almost any *confitería* on Avenida San Martín.

Mar Del Plata A-Z

AIRLINE OFFICES: Aerolíneas Argentinas has an office in the shopping arcade in the Hotel Provincial, tel 2-8725 or 2-5014. **Austral** also has an office on the Rambla, Tel 2-3085.

AIRPORT: For flight information call 73-0029, ext. 128.

AUTOMOBILE CLUB: The **Automovil Club Argentino** is at Avenida Independencia 3675, tel 72-3059.

AUTOMOBILE RENTALS: Avis has an office at Bulevar Peralta Ramos 2451, tel. 3-7850. Local agencies include **Móvil Rent** at Avenida Luro 2240, local 10, tel 2-6489, and **Rambla Tour** at Corrientes 1847, 3A, tel 9-0950.

BUS STATION: The Bus Terminal is at Alberti 1602, tel 51-5406.

CURRENCY EXCHANGE: You can exchange dollars or travelers cheques for pesos at **Jonestour**, San Martín 2574 (tel 2-0674) and Avenida Luro 3185 (tel 4-9103) or **Noroeste Cambio**, San Martín 2534 (tel 2-2820).

EMERGENCIES: In case of a medical emergency, dial 107. For the police, dial 101 or call the **Federal Police** at Sarmiento 2551, tel 51-6425.

GOLF & TENNIS: There are several tennis clubs and golf courses in the area. Most are listed with phone numbers in the City Guides. The concierge at your hotel should be able to help you make arrangements.

PEDICURES: After days and endless miles of sightseeing, your feet deserve some extra attention. There is an office of **Dr. Scholl** at Santa Fe 1768, tel 2-0755.

SUPERMARKET: Pick up all sorts of terrific picnic fixings at the **Autoservicio Inés,** Edison 498 or at **Elefante,** Avendida Juan B. Justo 2367.

TAXIS: To phone a cab, call **Central Taxi** at 72-4798 or 73-5466; **Del Plata** at 91-4069 or 91-6540; or **Teletaxi** at 72-3688 or 72-0949.

TELEPHONE OFFICE: To avoid high hotel surcharges on long distance phone calls, head to a *telefónica.* The **Playa Grande** office is at Avenida Juan B. Justo 2901 and the downtown office is at Avenida Luro 2554.

TOURIST OFFICE: The Municipal Tourist Office is on La Rambla at Bulevar Marítimo 2267, tel 2-1777.

TOUR OPERATOR: Excursiones Lorentur offers various bus tours of the city and outlying communities. For information call 3-0732. For a bird's-eye view, make arrangements with **Aero Club Mar del Plata,** tel 64-2151.

TRAIN STATION: The General Roca Norte Train Station is at Avenida Luro 4599, tel 72-0813.

Ushuaia/Tierra Del Fuego

shuaia is a long way from home. It's even a long way from Buenos Aires – 1,500 air miles. So why are most of the planes coming here filled to capacity in the Argentine summer (November-March) and tight even in the winter? The lure is not the town itself, although it is picturesque enough. It's because Ushuaia is the perfect base for exploring the wonders of nature on the island of Tierra del Fuego and the tiny islands south of it in the Beagle Channel that are largely Chilean and uninhabited. The town is also a great get-away point for trips to Argentinean Antarctica.

Ushuaia is 600 miles north of Argentine Antarctica. At this writing most trips to Antarctica leave from the Chilean port of Punta Arenas.

You'll want to explore stunning Tierra del Fuego National Park, cruise almost close enough to touch a 30,000-year-old glacier and visit a tiny island inhabited only by penguins. In the winter you can ski, downhill or cross country, on fresh white snow. You can do all of these things and more from Ushuaia where there are many options of the land and sea variety. All are readily accessible and well-organized. Tourism is big business at the tip of the Americas, but don't expect to meet your next door neighbor – not yet anyway. If you enjoy experiencing new travel horizons, you should definitely consider a stop at Tierra del Fuego, which one of her native sons called "The Uttermost Part of the Earth."

Some Background

Unless your history teachers were far better than ours, you learned little about this southernmost inhabited region of the earth. So you'll be surprised at the important role this area played in world history. Ferdinand Magellan, Charles Darwin and Jemmy Button, major players here, will become part of your travel vocabulary.

Reading materials to enrich your trip are listed in the Potpourri section of this chapter.

Tierra del Fuego (Tee-air-uh del Fuey-go) is a large irregularly-shaped island off the southern tip of South America. It was part of the continent until the final Ice Age when the waters separating it from the mainland broke through, stranding several native tribes. The meandering body of water was later named the "Straits of Magellan" for the Portuguese explorer who was the first to traverse it. The strait forms Tierra del Fuego's western and northern boundaries. Magellan is also responsible for the island's name – "Land of Fire." When he sailed by in the 1520's he spied fires on the island. These, lit by local Indians, were not beacons of welcome, for in this case the natives were definitely not friendly.

Magellan christened the island "Land of Fire" for the Indian bonfires he spotted on the shore.

The island is shared by Argentina and Chile. Chile governs the western portion of the island as well asthree-quarters of the land. The Argentine portion, which is triangular in shape and covers approximately 8,000 square miles, abuts Chile to the west and the Beagle Channel to the south. More people (about 72,000) live in Argentine Tierra del Fuego, with 35,000 in each of the two major towns, Ushuaia and Rio Grande. Island residents are called Fuegians (Foo-jee-ins).

Porvenir is the only major town in Chilean Tierra del Fuego.

History

In the 2nd century A.D., Egyptian navigators sailing eastward exploring the Indian and Pacific Oceans are thought by some to have sighted Tierra del Fuego and noted it on their maps. A later map indicated the western opening of a strait to the north of the island. In 1428, an Italian cartographer drew a map showing the island and the waterway which was used by two Portuguese ships in 1514. They sailed into the strait but soon retreated, not realizing that it was a through passage connecting the two oceans. Magellan persevered in 1520 and was soon followed by other European explorers, particularly British and Dutch. Driven by their search for wealth and spices, they had no desire to settle the land.

The Dutch braved the open sea route around the Cape and named it for the town they came from, Cape Hoorn.

It wasn't until 1830 when Robert Fitzroy (English) and his party anchored offshore to chart the coast and nearby islands, that Europeans encountered the island natives. Four distinct tribes lived on Tierra del Fuego but two were dominant. The Onas, who lived inland, survived by hunting, primarily for *guanacos*. They ate the meat and used the skin to cover themselves and their rude huts. The Yahgans were canoe Indians who lived along the southern channel and hunted and fished for their food. It was likely Yahgan fires that Magellan saw and it was Yahgans who were involved with the

British explorers and Anglican missionaries. Extremely primitive, the Yahgans were surprised to find Europeans on shore and were none too friendly. They threatened and stole many of the supplies brought ashore. Fitzroy was furious and in response he caught four Yahgans and carried them back to England. He hoped to educate them, teach them to use modern tools and to worship God, then return them to their tribes to educate others. One of the Yahgans was a young boy whom the crew named Jemmy Button, since that was the price Fitzroy paid for him.

The Beagle Channel was named for this voyage. Darwin developed his Theory of Evolution based in part on his findings gathered in Tierra del Fuego, although the Galapagos Islands provided more evidence for his theory.

Two years later Fitzroy returned with three Yahgans (one had died) and released them near the spot where they had originally been captured. Also aboard Fitzroy's ship, *The Beagle,* was the naturalist Charles Darwin. Assigned to survey the eastern coast of South America and the southern islands, the voyage lasted five years and their findings formed the basis for Darwin's Theory of Evolution.

The desire to bring the word of God to the natives of Tierra del Fuego brought a group of Anglican missionaries led by Alan Gardiner. They set up camp on Picton Island in December 1850. Indians stole much of their food while storms destroyed the rest, and this first group starved to death. Later attempts were also largely unsuccessful. Ironically, one group was ambushed and killed by a mob allegedly led by Jemmy Button.

Undeterred, a group of missionaries settled on Keppel Island (Las Malvinas/The Falklands) and tried to reach out to the Yahgans. One of the group was a young man named Thomas Bridges who used his time to learn the Yahgan language. He and his wife set up a mission on the site of Ushuaia in 1869, compiled a Yahgan dictionary and raised a family whose descendants still live on Tierra del Fuego. It was Bridges' son Lucas who wrote the definitive story of early life on Tierra del Fuego, "The Uttermost Part of the Earth."

Bridges' descendants live on Estancia Haberton which you can visit.

A conflict between Chilean and Argentinean interests in Tierra del Fuego and the islands nearby led to a war of words and almost of bullets. The boundaries were settled in 1984. Tierra del Fuego, with its beautiful lakes, glacier-capped mountains and strangely diverse flora and fauna, is one of the last natural frontiers.

Most islands are uninhabited but Navarino Island (Chile), south of Ushuaia across the Beagle Channel is inhabited.

Getting There

By Air

Although Ushuaia is remote, it is easily reached by air from Buenos Aires and other towns in Argentine Patagonia as well as from Punta Arenas, Chile. Ushuaia's small airport is located on a causeway across the bay from the waterfront. Until recently it had a very short runway. Combine that with the strong, erratic winds and you can see how several planes have been forced to ditch in the bay, including one carrying the governor of the state. Needless to say, funds were quickly found to lengthen the runway and landings are far less dramatic these days. A new airport is under construction.

Aerolíneas Argentinas, Austral, and **LADE** have several flights into Ushuaia each day from other parts of Argentina. At this writing, Aerolíneas has two flights from Buenos Aires to Ushuaia with intermediate stops at Trelew and Rio Gallegos. Flight time is about eight hours. Make reservations well in advance, particularly for December, January, and July.

Flight reservations should be made well in advance, especially if you plan to travel in December, January and July.

Overland/Ferry

If you have lots of time and patience you can reach Tierra del Fuego by car or bus, and a ferry. Argentine buses from all parts of the country head south on National Route 3 (NR 3) which winds its way along the coast to Rio Gallegos, a town at the southern tip of the mainland. The road continues into Chilean territory to Punta Delgada, which is a 30-minute ferry ride across the Magellan Strait from Tierra del Fuego. No local buses meet this ferry. The more popular route is to make the three-hour crossing from Punta Arenas, Chile to Porvenir, the largest town in Chilean Tierra del Fuego. Porvenir is a seven-to-10-hour bus ride from Ushuaia but buses do meet this ferry. At this writing, the ferry operates twice a week.

Cruising to Ushuaia

The *M/V Terra Australis*, a luxurious ship, makes sailing the Straits of Magellan and the Beagle Channel a fun-filled learning experience. The ship leaves from Punta Arenas, Chile each Saturday from October through March. It reaches Ushuaia on Wednesday, where it picks up additional passengers, and returns to Punta Arenas the following Friday evening. Enroute it

November - March the Australis visits the penguin refuge on Magdalena Island, Chile.

anchors near stunning icy-blue glaciers and carries passengers ashore on small Zodiac motor boats. On one day passengers climb the small mountain on Picton Island for a peek at a string of snow-topped mountains and the Beagle Channel. Another day is spent on Navarino Island. Sailing hours are spent watching informative videos or relaxing on board. This is a unique experience and a highlight of many a Patagonian adventure. Contact Lan Chile Airlines for more information.

Orientation

At first glance, from the airport or from a ship in the Beagle Channel, Ushuaia looks like a Swiss village. Surrounded by mountains, some snow-capped all year round, the commercial center of town spreads out along the channel, with the bustling municipal dock at its core. Many buildings, including government offices, are built of wood and in chalet-style, while the higher altitude residences are more contemporary in style. The residential areas, built on the hillside, are connected by a series of wooden staircases.

Buildings near the waterfront are painted in pastel shades.

The name Ushuaia comes from the Yahgan language, Yahmana, and means "port at the end." Home to 35,000 Argentineans, the city is *arguably* the most southerly in the world. Chile accounts for the "arguably" by pointing out that Puerto Williams, a Chilean settlement, is on Navarino Island, which is clearly south of Ushuaia across the Beagle Channel. To our way of thinking, however, Puerto Williams, with only 2,000 residents (most are Chilean Navy families) is too small to qualify as a city.

Despite Chile's claim to the contrary, Argentina boasts that Ushuaia is the southernmost city in the world.

Ushuaia is the capital and seat of government for the Argentine province known as Territorio Nacional de la Tierra del Fuego, Antartica y las Islas del Atlántico Sur (National Territory of Tierra del Fuego, Antarctica and the Islands of the Southern Atlantic).

Avenida Maipú is the street that faces the waterfront. Facing town, the numbers rise from right to left. Several hotels are on Avenida Maipú, as is the historical museum.

Malvinas Argentinas is the continuation of Avenida Maipú as it circles the bay and leads to the airport.

Avenida San Martín, the second street from the waterfront, is Ushuaia's main street. It has many restaurants, shops, airline offices and government buildings.

Cerro Martial is the snow-capped glacial mountain that overlooks Ushuaia. The resort hotels are located on it, as are the ski facilities.

Climate

Since Ushuaia, like most of South America, is in the southern hemisphere, seasons are opposite those of the northern hemisphere. The summer solstice falls in December when the city is bathed in daylight for 17.5 hours (December 20-23). At the winter solstice (June 20-23), daylight lasts for just seven hours. Contrary to what you may be thinking, winters here are not unbearably cold. There are two climate zones on the island. The southern area around Ushuaia gets lots of rain and clouds, while the northern area near the town of Rio Grande is drier. Temperatures rarely fall below 6°F (-21°C) and can reach the low 80's (29°C) in December. The average temperature in Ushuaia is 50°F, but the wind blows constantly year-round, which makes it feel colder than it actually is. The winds are strongest in spring and summer. Most importantly, the weather changes frequently and unpredictably, with wide variations in one day. Be prepared with waterproof gear and lots of "layerables" no matter when you visit.

Hotels

Ushuaia's accommodations vary from five-star resorts on the glacial mountain that overlooks the town, to charming in-town waterfront stops. For the most part, hotels are small and not many rooms are available. Things can get tight in the Argentine summer (November-March) and again in the ski season. If possible, reserve your accommodations in advance. All of our selections have rooms with heat and private baths, accept major credit cards and include breakfast in the rate. Rates are highest in December.

Alive Price Scale
Deluxe: $175+
Expensive: 100+
Moderate: $60-100
Inexpensive: $35-60
Budget: under $35

LAS HAYAS RESORT HOTEL ☆☆☆☆☆
Camino Glacial Martial, Km. 3.5
Phone (901) 30710
102 rooms
Deluxe
Las Hayas is Ushuaia's premier stop. Set on the mountainside overlooking town and the Beagle Channel, its five acres permit cross-country skiing, horseback riding, and hikes through a beech forest and past fast-running creeks.

Rooms are contemporary and have plush carpets. The public areas, complete with roaring fireplaces, resemble a chic ski lodge. A well-stocked gym and indoor heated pool, plus several excellent restaurants make this a greatplace to stay.

HOTEL DEL GLACIAR ☆☆☆☆☆
Camino Glacial Martial, Km 3
Phone (901) 313-4923
100 rooms
Expensive
Hotel del Glaciar has recently undergone a thorough renovation, upgrading both the guest rooms and the hotel facilities. More formal than Las Hayas, it resembles a country manor house. Its 100 rooms are decorated with dark woods and muted tones. Guests enjoy cross country skiing and hiking in the woods nearby.

HOTEL ALBATROSS
Avenida Maipú
Phone (901) 22504
Expensive
Under the same ownership as the Hotel Del Glaciar, the Albatross sits on the waterfront facing the port of Ushuaia, where the cruise ships dock and many of your daytrips will originate. The Albatross is nicely maintained, with modern furnishings and a friendly staff.

LAS LENGAS ☆☆☆☆
Goleta Florencia 1722
Phone (901) 23366
Expensive
Slightly off the beaten track, Las Lengas is on a quiet residential street. Rooms are clean and

neatly, if plainly, furnished. The front desk staff tries to be helpful, but few speak English.

HOTEL USHUAIA ☆☆☆☆
Laserre 933
Phone (901) 30671
Expensive

In the heart of the commercial center of town, an easy walk to the port and our restaurant selections, the Ushuaia is a comfortable choice. Most guests are Argentineans who come for skiing. Rooms are good-sized and furnishings, while well worn, are maintained.

CANAL BEAGLE ☆☆☆
Avenida Maipú (at 25 de Mayo)
Phone (901) 21117
Moderate

A bustling choice, the Hotel Canal Beagle sits on the waterfront facing the channel for which it is named. Rooms are good-sized and neatly, if basically, furnished. The dining room serves all three meals and is crowded with tour groups at lunch.

Should the selections above be full, the town and its environs have several two-star stops that are acceptable. Clean but with no frills. These include:

Hotel Cabo de Hornos, Avenida San Martín, Tel (901) 22187.

Hotel Tol Keyen, Calle Rio Pipo (three miles east of town), Tel (901) 22637.

Restaurants

Clustered along Avenida San Martín, the eateries of Ushuaia are a heterogeneous bunch. Whether you feel like sampling the local *centolla* (king crab), a freshly grilled Fuegian lamb or a hearty bowl of chowder, you'll find a restaurant to suit your mood. Restaurants are informal both in decor and dress code. If you dine in one of the resort hotels, your clothing should be casually chic. In Ushuaia, as in most of Argentina, dinner is served late, with restaurants empty until 9 p.m. Because it stays light much later in spring and summer, the streets are crowded well after midnight. Prices are a bit higher for comparable food than in other parts of Argentina since costs involved in bringing foodstuffs here get passed down. You'll need to make reservations at our top choices during high season.

Large crabs and gigantic mussels are caught in the Beagle Channel.

MOUSTACCHIO
San Martín (300 block) at Calle Godoy
Tel 23308
Lunch and dinner
Closed Monday
One of the top spots in town. It has a diverse menu serving pastas as well as grilled meats.

TANTE ELVIRA
San Martín (200 block)
Tel 21982
Another popular dining choice and known for its seafood, Tante Elvira is the place to sample local crab served both hot and cold.

IDEAL PIZZERIA
San Martín (400 block) at General Roca
This fine pizzeria is housed in a whitewashed building with a blue tin roof. The tables are covered with snowy-white clothes and the pizzas are the best in town. They come with a variety of toppings. Ideal also serves pastas, salads and *empanadas*.

PARRILLA DON JUAN
San Martín (500 block)
Tel 22309
A typical Argentine steakhouse complete with *gaucho*-attired waiters and a charcoal grill front and center. Courses include generously-filled *empanadas*, tomato and onion salad, garlicky sausages and, of course, grilled meats. Lamb is very popular here since it's local.

EL NUEVO CAFE
San Martín (400 Block)
Crowded with locals at breakfast time, you'll find this an equally good choice for lunch or dinner. Fare runs from eggs to burgers to light platters.

TANTE SARA
San Martín (1,000 block) at Don Bosco
A longtime favorite, Tante Sara is best known for her hearty sandwiches and delicious ice cream. A good lunch or coffee break choice.

Other Dining Options

If you'd like to dine in sophisticated surroundings, head to Las Hayas Hotel on Cerro Martial, a five-minute drive from town. Choices here include **La Martial**, which serves seafood and locally-caught shellfish, and **El Asador**, a restaurant that specializes in grilled meats including local lamb.

A popular daytrip from Ushuaia is a visit to a local *estancia* (ranch) for a typical lunch and the best grilled lamb in Ushuaia. The restaurant in the **Hotel Tol Keyen** on the road to the National Park (about three miles from town) is top notch. You can combine the meal with your visit to the park. Expect to spend about $20 for more than you can eat.

Tierra del Fuego National Park is covered below. See page 408.

Sunup to Sundown

If you have come to Ushuaia in the Argentine spring or summer, you'll be grateful for the long days. You'll want to spend those daylight hours exploring the town, its small but fascinating waterfront museum, nearby Tierra del Fuego National Park and the islands of the Beagle Channel. You can hike or mountain bike along the park's marked trails or fish in the rivers and lakes. Catamarans whisk you to islands in the channel inhabited by penguins or to the oldest *estancia* on the island. Local tour operators offer scores of daytrips. Most are well organized. Shop around for those that most interest you and for the best prices as well. What follows are concise descriptions of major sights near Ushuaia and some ideas for visiting and exploring each.

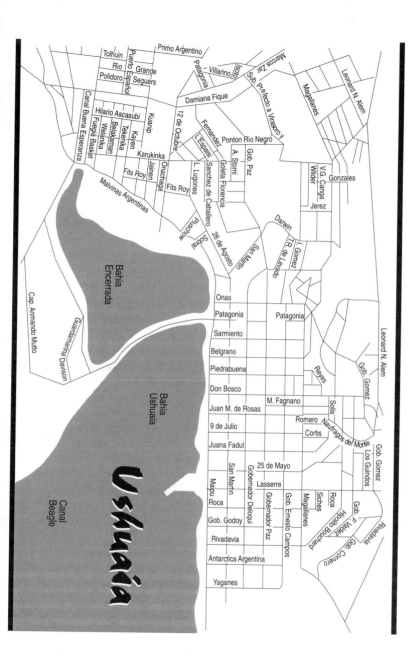

Estancia Haberton

In 1870, Thomas Bridges and his wife, Mary, established a mission on Tierra del Fuego on the site of present day Ushuaia. They were the first Europeans to live on the island. Bridges had come to the area as a teenager with his adoptive parents and worked with the Yahgan Indians on the Islas Malvinas (the Falkland Islands). He learned their language and gained their confidence so he was able to succeed where other missionaries had failed. In 1886 he asked the Argentinean government for and received a parcel of land on the Beagle Channel, 85 kilometers from Ushuaia. He lived the last 12 years of his life as a sheep farmer here and his family has continued to live on the land ever since. The *estancia* is open to the public and guided tours are conducted in English and Spanish by Bridges' great grandson, Thomas Goodall, and his American-born wife, Natalie. A stroll through the area offers views of nearby islands, a visit to the sheep shearing facility and the boathouse where Despard Bridges' boat, built in 1901, is housed. Tea is served in the original farmhouse, the oldest house on the island. Pick up a copy of Lucas Bridges' book, *The Uttermost Part Of The Earth* ,here as well as Natalie's book, *Tierra Del Fuego*.

The road to Haberton is only partially paved and is a difficult drive so it's best to visit by boat. You can combine a visit here with stops at Beagle Channel islands.

Museo del Fin del Mundo
Avenida Maipú 177
Summer hours: Mon.-Sat. 3-8 p.m.,
Sun. 4.-8 p.m.
Winter hours are curtailed, so check by calling 9-1863.
Small but worth a visit, exhibits focus on Indian life, exploration of the area and artifacts from

the earliest settlements. There is also a library. Do buy some "End of the World" stamps as mementos of your visit and have your passport stamped here as well.

Beagle Channel Island Hopping

Islands dot the Beagle Channel along the Argentine coast. Most are tiny, Chilean and uninhabited except for colonies of sea lions, penguins, cormorants and many types of birds.

Catamaran and motorboat tours leave daily from the dock area. They follow the routes of ancient sailors as they hug the coastline, passing snow-capped mountains, lagoons and tiny islands.

Half-day (2½-hour) cruises sail to **Faro Les Eclaireurs**, called the "Lighthouse at the End of the World." Many a ship has foundered here. The last went down in 1930 even after the lighthouse was built. The cruise returns by sailing near **Isla de los Lobos** (Sea Lion Island) and **Isla de los Pájaros** (Island of Birds).

Full-day cruises (9 a.m.-7 p.m.) follow the same route but pass the small islands and lighthouse enroute to **Isla Martillo** – home to a colony of Magellan penguins. Enroute you pass quite near **Puerto Williams**, the Chilean settlement on Navarino Island. A stop at Haberton Estancia and lunch at nearby Almanza completes the trip. An option here is to return to Ushuaia by bus.

Other daytrips go to **Lapataia Bay** and the *estancia*. These trips, and a 3½-hour crossing from Ushuaia to Puerto Williams, are available only from November through March.

Local Tour Operators

Rumbo Sur at San Martín 342 (tel 21139) is the largest agency running maritime excursions. Other reliable tour operators are **All Patagonia** (ecological tours by bicycle) at 25 de Mayo 31, Office A (tel 24432), and **Antartur** at San Martín 638, Local 14 (tel 23240). There are scores of tour operators in Ushuaia. It's a buyers market.

Other Outdoor Activities

Horseback riding, fishing and cross country treks across the Martial Glacier are also daytime possibilities. Tours are organized at Las Hayas Hotel and by the organizations listed above.

Winter Activities

If you have a sudden craving for snow on July 4th weekend, head for Ushuaia where you can ski downhill or cross country. You can also go snowmobiling, wind skiing and snow catting or explore the countryside while snuggling on a dog sled. Five ski areas are located on Glacier Martial near Ushuaia. The closest to town (about 20 minutes) is the **Andean Club Ski Slope**. Resort areas with hotel facilities include **Tierra Mayor**, 21 kilometers from town, and **Las Cotorras**, five kilometers further. Both offer downhill and cross country skiing. Equipment can be rented.

After Dark

If you still have energy to burn after a late dinner and a long day of outdoor activity, head to one of Ushuaia's discotheques. **Barny's**, Antártica Argentina 196, draws a young crowd and is packed till the early morning hours on Friday and Saturday nights. Tourists head for **El Estadio** on San Martín at 9 de Julio or **Extasis**, a block downhill at Maipú. Pubs are popular late-night hangouts. **Saint Christopher Pub**, near El Estadio is crowded, particularly on winter evenings, while **Cervecería Inselburg** on Leandro N. Alem 966 is the "in" spot on warm evenings.

Chilean Patagonia (Magallanes)

At this narrow tip of South America, Chile and Argentina are intertwined so it is common to visit both. Punta Arenas, a city of 130,000 people on the Straits of Magellan, is the capital of Magallanes. Much like Ushuaia, Punta Arenas is a kick-off point for exploring this region. Many cruise ships headed to Antarctica stop here. The major lure is **Torres del Paine National Park**, which lies 150 miles north. This huge park has several glaciers within its borders, as well as the stunning glacier-studded Paine Tower mountains. There are scores of hiking trails, *refugios*, a maze of connecting lakes for boaters and well-organized treks. Punta Arenas is the starting point for daytrips to islands in the Magellan strait and the Beagle Channel. Unlike Ushuaia, Punta Arenas does not have ski facilities and is not a winter destination.

Magallanes (Magellan) is Chile's southernmost province.

Hotels

Hotel José Nogueira, Bories 959. Fax (061)24-8832. 52 rooms, good restaurant.
Hotel Cabo de Hornos, Plaza Muñoz Gamero 1039. Tel (061)24-1321. Oldest hotel in town, with over 100 rooms.

Restaurants

Asturias, Lautara Navarro 998 and **Sotitos Bar**, on Bernardo O'Higgins, are the best dining spots in town. There are pizza and fast food stops as well.

Ushuaia A-Z

AIRLINE OFFICES: Aerolíneas Argentinas is at Avenida Roca 156 (tel 21218). **Austral** is at San Martín 657 (tel 21945). **LADE** is also on San Martín at 564 (tel 21123).

AUTOMOBILE CLUB: The **Automovil Club Argentino** is on the corner of Malvinas and Onachaga (tel 21121).

BACKGROUND READING: If you have some time before leaving or want a book to bring along, we recommend *The Uttermost Part of the Earth* by Lucas Bridges, *Three Men of the Beagle* by Richard Lee Marks, and *Darwin and the Beagle* by Alan Moorehead. If you prefer more contemporary impressions of the area, Bruce Chatwin's *In Patagonia* or *The Patagonian Express* by Paul Theroux are both excellent.

BUSES: Transporte Los Carlos at Juan Manuel de Rosas 85 (tel 22337) and **Transporte Techni-Austral** in the Hotel Canal Beagle offer service between Ushuaia and Rio Grande. Service between Rio Grande and Porvenir is provided by **Transporte Sencoria** at the Avenida Belgrano Terminal (tel 0964/21339) and **Transporte Pacheco** also out of the Belgrano Terminal (tel 0964/23382). Service between Rio Gallegos and Buenos Aires is provided by **Transporte Don Otto**, whose office is in the Retiro Terminal in Buenos Aires (tel 313-3580).

Buses from Ushuaia to Porvenir make a stop in Rio Grande. The same is true on the trip for Porvenir.

CAR RENTAL: A reputable agency is **Tagle** at the corner of San Martín and Belgrano (tel 22744).

CHILEAN CONSULATE: Is at Malvinas Argentinas 236 (tel 22177). Office hours are 9 a.m. to 1 p.m., Monday through Friday.

FERRIES: Primera Angostura (tel 56-6121 or 56-8100) offers ferry service, both autos and passengers, between Rio Gallegos and Tierra del Fuego (30 minutes) and Porvenir and Punta Arenas (three hours). If you're transporting a car, it is probably a good idea to reserve ahead.

HOSPITAL: The **Ushuaia Regional Hospital** is at the intersection of Avenida Maipú and 12 de Octubre (tel 22950).

NATIONAL PARK OFFICE: For park information, the office is located at San Martín and Patagonia (tel 21315).

POLICE DEPARTMENT: Police headquarters are at the intersection of Deloqui and Laserre (tel 21335).

POST OFFICE: Located at Avenida San Martín and Governador Godoy, hours are Monday through Friday 8 a.m. to 6 p.m. and Saturdays from 8 a.m. to 1 p.m.

TELEPHONE DIAL CODE: 901.

TELEPHONES (LONG DISTANCE): Long distance phone calls can be made from the telephone offices **Telefónica Abaco** at San Martín 133, which are open from 8 a.m. to 2 a.m., and **El Locutorio del Fin del Mundo** at San Martín 957 (7 a.m. to 12:30 a.m.).

TOURIST OFFICE: For maps and brochures, and perhaps some guidance, the local tourist office is at San Martín 660 (tel 22455).

Outdoor Argentina

In this section we offer a potpourri of active vacation options for those who enjoy them. Skiing is first rate here and there are several world-class resort areas. Since seasons are reversed, you can plan a vacation that allows you to ski in July. The country also has 18 national parks. We have detailed seven distinctive parks. Within the parks and in the picturesque towns nearby you can climb volcanoes or glacier-studded mountains, trek, bicycle, kayak, fish, sail or hunt. You can visit a penguin rookery and hobnob with sea lions and seals. Local tour operators have organized these activities and their services have been honed over many years. Also in this section, we have detailed Argentina's unique *estancias*, some of which now operate as guest ranches, as well as cattle and sheep ranches.

Skiing

It has only been within the last decade or so that the potential for terrific skiing offered by the Andes Mountains has been developed. Now avid North American and European skiers are joining the ever-growing number of Argentines who take to the slopes during the Argentine winter. In recent years, ski centers here have even hosted competitions organized by the International Ski Federation, further attesting to the quality of skiing in the Southern Hemisphere.

While facilities vary, the ski centers we've listed offer slopes to satisfy skiers of every level, from beginner to expert, all in breathtaking surroundings. All offer equipment rental, instruction, and medical attention. **Las Leñas** is the most luxurious, featuring four- and five-star accommodations, fine dining and plenty of après ski activities, including tennis, swimming (in a heated indoor pool), a casino and discotheque. **Cerro Catedral**, just outside Bariloche, though smaller and not quite as luxurious, is a similar choice. **Cerro Chapelco** and the somewhat more isolated and smaller **La Hoya** are especially fine choices for beginning and intermediate downhill skiers as well as cross country enthusiasts.

Ski packages can be arranged through travel agents in Buenos Aires. You can also contact or visit the Provincial Tourist Offices for more information.

LAS LEÑAS
Malargüe, Mendoza Province
Tel in Buenos Aires: 312-2121
Maximum altitude: 11,319 feet
33 slopes
Alpine & Nordic
Ski season: June 15-November 15

LOS PENITENTES
Mendoza Province
Maximum altitude: 10,540 feet
21 slopes
Alpine & Nordic
Ski season: June 15-October 15

CERRO CATEDRAL
Bariloche, Río Negro
Maximum altitude: 7,590 feet
Alpine & Nordic
Ski season: June 15-September 30

CHAPELCO
San Martín de los Andes, Nequén Province
Maximum altitude: 6,528 feet
Alpine & Nordic
Ski season: June 20-September 30

LA HOYA
Esquel, Chubut Province
Maximum altitude: 6,930 feet
Alpine
Ski season: July 1-October 9

National Parks

As noted previously, Argentina is over 2,000 miles long. Within those 2,000 miles there is tremendous diversity – rainforests, spectacular waterfalls, glacial lakes and soaring mountains – as well as a wide variety of climatic zones. Much like the United States and Canada, Argentina started to feel concern for its natural areas around the turn of the century. In 1904 President Roca enacted legislation creating Argentina's first national park, the *Parque Nacional*

Moreno's nickname "Perito" was given to the glacier and national park in Southern Patagonia. "Perito" means expert.

del Sud. It was the first national park in all of South America. Most of the land for the park had been donated to the Argentine government by the famed Patagonian explorer, Francisco Pascasio Moreno. It was officially inaugurated in 1934 and was called **Parque Nacional Nahuel Huapi.**

At the same time, Argentina created a National Park Service *(Servicio de Parques Nacionales),* which maintains local offices in towns throughout the country. Staffed by friendly, helpful people (but rarely English speakers), their offices have good maps and printed materials, though virtually none are in English. Within the parks themselves, there are *guardaparques* (park rangers) who maintain and protect the environment, while helping visitors.

Today, Argentina maintains 18 national parks and nine natural reserves (some within the confines of parks). The parks protect 1% of Argentine territory. Provinces have also created provincial parks and reserves.

Argentine parks, perhaps because they have fewer visitors, are pristine.

Argentina's parks are naturally stunning but are not nearly as developed as U.S. parks. There are far fewer visitor facilities and organized activities are arranged in nearby towns rather than in the parks themselves. Local clubs, such as the Club Andino for hikers, organize various activities and maintain "refugios" and campgrounds.

Your decision to visit a national park may depend on geography (most are located in Patagonia), but it may also depend on your interests. Each park has unique features. Trekking, horseback riding, river rafting, kayaking, mountaineering, birdwatching, photo safaris, hunting and sport fishing are all active vacation options that tour operators organize.

Contact the Argentine National Park Service at Avenida Santa Fe 690, Buenos Aires (tel 54-1 311-1943). There are two books that you might find helpful as well. *South America's National Parks* (Mountaineer Books) and *Adventure Travel in Latin America* (Wilderness Press) should be available at your local bookstore. You can order them (and other publications about hiking and skiing in Latin America) from The Complete Traveller Bookstore in New York (tel 212/685-9007).

Concise Comments on Our Favorite Parks Follow:

Iguazú National Park

Iguazú National Park is the most visited national park in all of South America by foreign visitors. It is home to Iguazú Falls, one of the continent's best known tourist attractions. Only a tiny percentage of those visitors realize that the falls are located in a highly accessible rainforest which has over 2,000 species of plants, 400 species of birds and 500 species of butterflies.

Higher than Victoria and much wider than Niagara, Iguazú Falls is a memorable sight. You hear its roar and see its foggy spume long before reaching the river bank. Often a rainbow will straddle the falls. Because most of the cataracts are on the Argentine side of the Iguazú River, the views are better from the Brazilian park, which is much larger than the Argentine one. Rent a slicker and cross under the falls at the "Garganta del Diablo" (Devil's Throat). There are walkways on both sides of the river.

Leave your machete at home and explore the rainforest along a series of well-maintained trails. Although it is always hot and humid here, the rainforest is cool. Towering trees, some reaching well over 100 feet, form a dense green ceiling. Colorful flowers are everywhere and large ferns and shrubs create a dense lower level. Stick to the trails because some plants are armed with stinging nettles, spiky thorns and burning oils.

Blinds have been set up in the park for bird-watchers. Toucans, trogons, parrots and hummingbirds are among the most common. Animals are more elusive. Many are nocturnal or make their homes high in the trees. To spot them, you'll have to get up early in the morning, tread quietly and go alone or in a very small group. South America's largest jungle animal (often over 700 pounds), the tapir makes its home here, as do the peccary (wild pig), the paca (a huge rodent), the howler and capuchín monkey and, most elusive of them all, the jaguar.

Take your swimsuit along. You'll appreciate a refreshing swim on a humid afternoon. And don't forget your bug spray. There are picnic facilities in the park but no camping within the grounds. Campgrounds do exist near the entrance.

See "Iguazú"in "Around Argentina" for accommodations and dining options near the park.

Parque Nacional Lanín

Fishing and trekking are the most popular pastimes enjoyed by visitors to Lanín National Park, which extends across Northern Patagonia's Lake Region in the province of Nequén. The perpetually snow-capped, 12,000-foot-high Lanín Volcano keeps vigil over the park's 24 lakes and three nature reserves from its position on the border with Chile.

Tourist facilities are available in Junín de los Andes and San Martín de los Andes. Many visitors opt to camp right in the park.

Largely undeveloped, the park is home to several endangered species, including the tiny deer known as the *pudú*, the *gato huiña*, the *puma potrillero* and the *huemel* or Andean deer. Hunting of the more common varieties of deer and *jabalí* (wild boar) is permitted at certain times and strictly regulated. Several species of birds make their home here, including the great white heron, the Patagonian thrush, parrots, the condor, and a host of others. Common to the park is the unusual and rare monkey puzzle tree, also known as the *araucaria* or the *pehuén*. Shaped like a huge umbrella, its seeds, rich in carbohydrates, were a staple of the diet of the Araucan Indians. Other native trees include the cypress, the *lengua*, the *coihue*, and the *ñire*.

The volcano can be climbed. Contact the Club Andino in Junín de los Andes.

Lanín is a favorite destination of sports fishermen who come to fish for Patagonian pejerrey, salmon and trout in the crystal clear water of its glacier-fed lakes. The largest and best known is *Lago Huechulafquen*, which boasts the biggest brown trout in the world, some as large as 30 inches in length. The majority of campsites within the park are located alongside the lakes; the loveliest is on the banks of Lago Quillen.

Local tour operators in Junín de los Andes arrange trekking and fishing trips.

Another park highlight is the therapeutic thermal baths, *Termas Lahuen Co*. Water from hot springs is piped into a bathhouse, which is open to the public from December through April. Space here is limited and you will need to make arrangements ahead of time at the park office in San Martín de los Andes. There are campsites nearby.

Getting There

You can easily drive to Lanín from Bariloche. Just head due north. If you're coming from Chile you would enter Argentina through the Tromen Pass (Argentine summer only). Travelers coming from Buenos Aires should fly into Chapelco Airport, midway between San Martín de los Andes and Junín de los Andes. Buses connect San Martín or Junín with other towns in the area.

Nahuel Huapi National Park

From skiing in the winter to summer music festivals, trekking, mountaineering, rafting horseback riding and fishing, Nahuel Huapi offers visitors an endless array of activities. The oldest and largest of Argentina's national parks, it extends from the continental divide to the plains of Patagonia in the provinces of Río Negro and Nequén. Within its boundaries are numerous lakes and rivers, mountains and glaciers; and well-marked hiking trails wind through the park.

The park's dominant feature is the lake which shares its name, Lago Nahuel Huapi. The name means Tiger Island in the Mapuche Indian language and originally applied to the island at the lake's center, now called Isla Victoria. Nahuel Huapi, the largest of the park's six big lakes (there are countless smaller ones) extends 60 miles, covering an area of 200 square miles.

Argentina's famed resort, Bariloche is at the lake's southern shore. Tourist facilities and accommodations are discussed in the chapter on Bariloche.

The rare, myrtle-like *arrayán* tree grows on Isla Victoria and is easily recognized by its pale orange bark and white flowers. They bloom in January and February and then bear fruit. Other trees on the island include the Ponderosa pine, Douglas fir, sequoia and the Monterey cypress. Unique to the island are the lake cormorants which, although normally saltwater birds, have adapted to freshwater and make their home on its western shore. The *Valle Encantado,* Enchanted Valley, is east of the lake on the banks of the Río Limay, or Crystal River in Mapuche, where you'll find a series of unusual limestone formations with names such as *Castillo* (Castle), and *Dedo de Díos* (God's Finger).

It is possible to travel to Chile via the lake.

Tiny Los Arrayanes National Park on the Quetrihué Península within Nahuel Huapi National Park was organized to protect these trees.

There are camping facilities on Isla Victoria. You can make arrangements or pick up information at the Tourist Information Center in Bariloche.

The park's most popular attraction is the *Cerro Catedral,* whose 7,000-foot peak offers terrific views of Bariloche and the surrounding countryside during the summer and great skiing in winter. You can also ski or hike nearby *Cerros Otto and López,* although they aren't quite as high.

There is a cable car to take you to the top. Inquire at the Club Andino for trekking and mountaineering information.

El Tronador, the Thunderer, at 11,722 feet, is the park's highest peak, actually three peaks in one. Ice frequently falls off the many glaciers on this extinct volcano to create the loud rumblings that account for its name. Several different species of deer make their home in the park, including the miniature *pudú* and the relatively rare *huemul* or Andean deer, along with mountain lions, foxes, weasels and river otters. There are fewer species of birds here than in other parks but Magellanic woodpeckers are common.

Getting There

See Bariloche in "Around Argentina."

Perito Moreno National Park

Unless you're a rugged outdoor type, you should skip right over Perito Moreno National Park, Argentina's most remote park. No public transportation serves the park and it is over 100 miles from the nearest town, Gobernador Gregores, which is not exactly a metropolis. Needless to say, the park gets few visitors - so few that the park service does not station park rangers here. There are a few sheep *estancias* near the park whose owners distribute maps, hot *mate*, a bed and trekking advice.

Why go? Perito Moreno is a terrific place to see the barren yet stunning landscapes that exemplify Patagonia and the park is filled with interesting fossils and Indian artifacts.

South America's Continental Divide traverses the semi-circular park. A series of snow-capped mountains run along its borders, almost surrounding the eight interconnected lakes at its center. Seven of the lakes drain into the Pacific, while the eighth empties into the Atlantic. Due to their differing depths and sizes and the stage of erosion of the limestone in the mountains surrounding them, the lakes are a rainbow of grays, greens and blues. Yet their waters are invariably cold. Cerro San Lorenzo, at 12,160 feet the highest peak in Patagonia, is just north of the park.

Very little wildlife inhabits this barren landscape. Among the rugged animals that do are guanacos, European hares, armadillos, ibis, rheas, southern lapwings, flamingoes, and condors.

Only experienced hikers, trekkers and mountain climbers should head here since you will be truly isolated. The park is accessible from December through March, but don't expect warm weather even in those months. Bring plenty of supplies and heavy clothing.

Getting There

Your best bet for getting to the park is to fly to the town of Perito Moreno, 200 miles north of the park. LADE flies there. Rent a four-wheel drive and don't make the trip solo.

Glaciers National Park

Los Glaciares, home to some of the most fantastic glaciers in the world, is at the southern tip of Argentina in the province of Santa Cruz. Declared a national park in 1937, it has soaring mountains, vast lakes and, of course, the glaciers themselves.

Make arrangements to visit the park at Calafate.

Los Glaciares covers an area of some 2,300 square miles and is actually two parks in one. If you want to see glaciers, then stick to the southern portion of the park. Lago Argentino is its heart. At 600 square miles, it is four times as big as Lago Nahuel Huapi. It was discovered in 1873 by Francisco P. Moreno. The glaciers at the western end of the lake cut into the Andes. It is their run-off which is responsible for the lake's green or turquoise color. The 30-mile-long Upsala, located at the northern end, is the lake's largest glacier and sends huge blue icebergs tumbling into the lake.

The park's best known glacier is the Glacier Moreno. Unlike most of the world's glaciers, which are receding, Moreno is still growing. At last measure, it was three miles wide and rose 200 feet above the surface of the lake. You can reach the Glacier Moreno by road, but pay careful attention to the signs warning of falling ice.

Other than glaciers, Lago Argentino also offers fine fishing and even swimming on especially warm days. Birdwatchers should visit in the spring and summer when torrent ducks, eagles, condors, austral parakeets and buffnecked ibis make their home in the park.

The northern section of the park is less accessible and a visit here should only be attempted by serious hikers and climbers. Top attractions include the glacier-fed Lago Viedma, over 400 square miles in size, and the infamous Mt. Fitzroy. Climbers have lost their lives attempting to scale it, but there have been several successful attempts. The peaks surrounding Mt. Fitzroy are known as *torres y agujas* (towers and needles). Not as high as Mt. Fitzroy, they are, as their name suggests, extremely treacherous.

Several hiking trails wind through this section of the park.

Getting There

The best way to get to the park is to fly from Buenos Aires to Río Gallegos and catch a connecting flight to Calafete. The second leg of the journey can also be made by bus. It is a six-hour ride and a great way to see the countryside.

Valdes Península

Wildlife enthusiasts will find a trip to the Valdes Peninsula especially worthwhile. Penguins, sea lions, seals, elephant seals, guanacos, whales, dolphins, rheas, maras, tinamous and a host of birds spend the summer months on this Atlantic peninsula midway between Buenos Aires and the Straits of Magellan.

Not a national park but rather a national reserve.

Weatherwise, spring and summer are the best seasons to visit. Seal and sea lion enthusiasts should plan on visiting during the breeding season in November or December when the *lobería,* or breeding grounds, at Punta Pirámides are in full-swing. The best months for penguins, and hence the most popular months for visiting, are October, November, February and early March. Penguins gather in the thousands at the penguin rookeries at Cabo dos Bahías and Punto Tombo.

Accommodations and restaurants are available in Puerto Madryn, the town nearest the park. Tours can be arranged here as well. There are campsites within the Península.

While overzealous tourism once threatened the birdlife here, the establishment of the *Reserva Isla de los Pájaros* is slowly but surely ensuring their return. Birdwatchers are not permitted to enter this six-acre preserve just off the entrance

The Automovil Club Argentino runs a motel at Punta Pirámides.

to the park. However, the park service has set up powerful field glasses at key vantage points. Birdwatching is best from November to February.

Getting There

The Valdes Peninsula is in Chubut Province. It is best to fly to Trelew Airport from Buenos Aires and then travel by bus to Puerto Madryn.

Tierra Del Fuego National Park

Created in 1960, the world's most southerly national park is also Argentina's only park with a seacoast. Five of the park's 300 square miles front the Beagle Channel. The southernmost accessible part of the park is only 12 miles west of Ushuaia. Most of the park is not readily accessible. Rugged, steep mountain ranges that run in parallel lines from northwest to southeast form barriers to exploring. They've also created isolated valleys, glacier lakes, and rivers. Only 10 miles of paved road exist in the park and you can cover them in half a day if you just want to look. But you'll want to do more than that.

Hiking trails have been created throughout the park and the most popular ones are self-guided. Two easy trails are: **Sendero Laguna Negra** (Black Lagoon Trail) and **Sendero de los Castores** (Beaver Trail). They lead to scenic overlooks, from which you can see the Beagle Channel and Lapataia Bay. It is at this bay that National Route 3 (NR 3) ends – the southern terminus of the PanAmerican Highway.

The landscape is both stunning and stark, yet has more trees than one would expect. Many are evergreens of the beech and lenga variety. Cinnamon trees with white flowers stand out. In the early part of the 20th century, local prisoners cut down trees and more are being cut down today, this time by beavers. Imported to fill some long-forgotten need, the beavers have created havoc by cutting down trees and building dams that change the waterflow. Another imported pest, rabbits can be seen everywhere. Red foxes, guanacos, condors, and even an albatross call this park home.

If you want to hike the more difficult trails that go into the mountains, join a group.

While no longer in operation, the old prison can be visited.

Lago Roca, the most accessible lake in the park, has a small restaurant and campground. The *hostería* nearby had been damaged by a fire and was not open at this writing.

Visit the Yahgan village campsite, which is marked by mounds of mussel shells. A reconstructed Indian village is near Rio Lapataia.

Campers can pick up supplies here.

Lago Fagnano is the park's most spectacular lake. Carved by a glacier, it is seven miles long and surrounded by mountains. Organized bus trips go to the lake, but it is too long a trip for one day. Fagnano extends into Chile.

National Park Offices

Iguazú National Park
3370 Puerto Iguazú
Provincia de Misiones
Tel (759) 20382

Lanin National Park
8300 San Martín de los Andes
Provincia de Nequen
Tel (972) 27233

Nahuel Huapi National Park
(and Los Arrayanes National Park)
Avenida San Martín 24
8400 San Carlos de Bariloche, Rio Negro
Tel (944) 23111

Perito Moreno National Park/
Los Glaciares National Park
Lago Argentino 9405
Calafate, Provincia de Santa Cruz
Tel (902) 91005

Tierra del Fuego National Park
Avenida San Martín 395
Ushuaia, Tierra del Fuego
Tel (901) 21315

Estancías

For a truly unique experience and a different view of Argentina, visit an *estancia*, an Argentine ranch. While many continue to operate as cattle and sheep ranches, others raise thoroughbred horses, and some combine those activities while entertaining a small number of guests. Since virtually none have more than 18 rooms (and some as few as three), service is always personal and extremely friendly. Accommodations range from super-luxurious to simple and rustic.

Scattered throughout Argentina, most are in breathtaking locations and offer a variety of outdoor activities as well as a glimpse of life on an *estancia*. Facilities vary, but may include swimming pools, tennis and paddleball courts, access to nearby golf courses, fishing and hunting trips, horseback riding, polo lessons, rafting, birding and photographic safaris.

Some no longer operate as estancias but rather as unusual resort hotels.

Some *estancias* are close enough to Buenos Aires so they can be visited on a daytrip. You can watch the *gauchos* in action, tour the colonial-style mansions and lunch at a typical *asado* (barbecue). You can also arrange for an overnight stay.

We'll detail a few of the country's finest *estancias,* but for more information and to make reservations, you should contact **Círculos Mágicos**, an organization that represents over 100 *estancias* and unique hotels throughout Argentina. Their offices are at Uruguay 864, 3rd floor, office 305/306, 1015 Buenos Aires (tel 54-1/42-0206 or 815-2803; fax 54-1/814-3344).

In Buenos Aires Province

ESTANCIA LA MARTINA
Vicente Casares
11 rooms
Activities: Horseback riding, polo, tennis, paddleball, swimming, and golf
This modern, colonial-style mansion was one of the first in the world to offer polo clinics. Daytrips as well as overnight stays can be arranged.

ESTANCIA LA CANDELARIA
Lobos
19 rooms
Activities: Horseback riding, polo, carriage rides, birdwatching, tennis, swimming, and golf
Accommodations are in a magnificent mansion that looks like a medieval castle. Beautiful landscaping replaces the moat.

2½ hours from Buenos Aires by car.

ESTANCIA ACELAIN
Tandil
14 rooms
Activities: Polo, horseback riding, carriage rides, tennis, paddleball, swimming, fishing, hunting, golf, windsurfing
Whitewashed buildings topped by red tile roofs that would look at home in Seville overlook a landscape of singular beauty in the sierras west of Mar del Plata.

Has a local commuter airport. Approximately 210 miles from Buenos Aires.

ESTANCIA EL RINCON
25 de Mayo
4 rooms
Activities: Polo, horseback riding, paddleball, tennis, carriage rides, birdwatching, fishing, hiking, small game hunting, photo safari
Top-notch polo and excellent horses are the calling cards of this fine *estancia*, which also specializes in cattle breeding. You're bound to run into a *gaucho* or two here.

Has a local commuter airport. Approximately 220 miles from Buenos Aires.

In Cordoba

CORRAL DE LOS COCOS
Los Reartes, Valle de Calamuchita, Córdoba Province
6 rooms
Activities: Swimming, tennis, horseback riding, fishing, trekking, sailing, windsurfing
Rustic best describes this ranch nestled between the hills of the pampean sierra.

In Patagonia

PRASHANTI
San Martín de los Andes, Nequen Province
5 rooms
Activities: Horseback riding, birdwatching, fishing, trekking
A contemporary family home surrounded by the majestic Andes and rivers and lakes. Very rustic and peaceful.

PUERTO LUSSICH
Lago Quillén, Nequén Province
17 rooms
Activities: Horseback riding, fishing, hunting, kayaking, rafting, windsurfing, trekking, sailing
This traditional Patagonian *estancia* on the shores of a lake in the heart of the Andes takes "getting away from it all" quite seriously.

GÜER AIKE
Rio Gallegos, Santa Cruz Province
6 rooms
Activities: Fishing

With six miles of river running through its property, Güer Aike is a fisherman's paradise. Brown trout are the major catch.

ALTA VISTA
El Calafate, Santa Cruz Province
7 rooms
Activities: Horseback riding, photo safaris
A contemporary *estancia* with lots of grounds to explore overlooking the Perito Moreno Glacier.

NIBEPO AIKE
El Calafate, Santa Cruz Province
4 rooms
Activities: Horseback riding, fishing, photo safaris
Located within the Glaciers National Park, this intimate *estancia* is a working sheep farm.

Hable Español!

As languages go, Spanish is relatively easy to learn. Your ability to understand and pronounce a few key phrases will enhance your enjoyment.

TIPS ON PRONUNCIATION

Vowels – These are always pronounced in exactly the same way, that is a (ah); e (eh); i (ee as in deep); o (oh); u (oo as in spoon).

Consonants – These are pronounced similarly to English, with these major exceptions:

double l as in llama is like "y" (yama)
ñ as in niño equals "ny" (neenyo)
j as in jabón (soap) equals "h" (habón)
c before e or i equals "s" as in "central" (sentral)
g before e or i equals "h" as in "general" (heneral)
h as in "hablar" (to speak) is silent (ablar)

DAYS OF THE WEEK

lunes	Monday
martes	Tuesday
miércoles	Wednesday
jueves	Thursday
viernes	Friday
sábado	Saturday
domingo	Sunday

MONTHS OF THE YEAR

enero	January
febrero	February
marzo	March
abril	April
mayo	May
junio	June
julio	July
agosto	August
septiembre	September
octubre	October
noviembre	November
diciembre	December

NUMBERS

uno	one
dos	two
tres	three
cuatro	four
cinco	five
seis	six
siete	seven
ocho	eight
nueve	nine
diez	ten
once	eleven
doce	twelve
trece	thirteen
catorce	fourteen
quince	fifteen
dieciseis	sixteen
diecisiete	seventeen
dieciocho	eighteen
diecinueve	nineteen
veinte	twenty

veintiuno	twenty-one
veintidos	twenty-two
treinta	thirty
cuarenta	forty
cincuenta	fifty
sesenta	sixty
setenta	seventy
ochenta	eighty
noventa	ninety
cien	one hundred
cento uno	one hundred one
doscientos	two hundred
quinientos	five hundred
mil	one thousand
mil uno	one thousand one
dos mil	two thousand
un millón	one million
mil millónes	one billion
primero	first
segundo	second
tercero	third
cuarto	fourth
quinto	fifth
sexto	sixth
séptimo	seventh
octavo	eighth
noveno	ninth
décimo	tenth
undécimo	eleventh
duodécimo	twelfth
último	last

CONVERSATION

¿Cómo está usted?	How are you?
Bien, gracias. Y usted?	Well, thanks, and you?

Buenos días.	Good morning.
Buenas tardes.	Good afternoon.
Buenas noches.	Good evening/night.
Hasta la vista.	See you again.
Hasta luego.	So long.
¡Buena suerte!	Good luck!
Adios.	Goodbye.
Mucho gusto de conocerle.	Glad to meet you.
Felicidades.	Congratulations.
Feliz cumpleaños.	Happy birthday.
Feliz Navidad.	Merry Christmas.
Feliz Año Nuevo.	Happy New Year.
Gracias.	Thank you.
Por favor.	Please.
De nada/con mucho gusto.	You're welcome.
Perdóneme.	Pardon me.
¿Cómo se llama esto?	What do you call this?
Lo siento.	I'm sorry.
Permítame.	Permit me.
Quisiera...	I would like...
Adelante.	Come in.
Permítame presentarle...	May I introduce...
¿Cómo se llama usted?	What is your name?
Me llamo...	My name is...
No sé.	I don't know.
Tengo sed.	I am thirsty.
Tengo hambre.	I am hungry.
Soy norteamericano/a	I am an American.
¿Dónde se puede encontrar...?	Where can I find...?
¿Qué es esto?	What is this?
¿Habla usted inglés?	Do you speak English?
Hablo/entiendo un poco español.	I speak/understand a little Spanish
¿Hay alguien aquí que hable inglés?	Is there anyone here who speaks English?
Le entiendo.	I understand you.
No entiendo.	I don't understand.
Hable más despacio por favor.	Please speak more slowly.

Repita por favor.	Please repeat.

TELLING TIME

¿Qué hora es?	What time is it?
Es la una.	It's one o'clock.
Son las...	It's...
... cinco.	... five o'clock.
... ocho y diez.	... ten past eight.
... seis y cuarto.	... quarter past six.
... cinco y media.	... half past five.
...siete menos cinco.	... five of seven.
antes de ayer.	the day before yesterday.
anoche.	yesterday evening.
esta mañana.	this morning.
a mediodía.	at noon.
en la noche.	in the evening.
de noche.	at night.
a medianoche.	at midnight.
mañana por la mañana.	tomorrow morning.
mañana por la noche.	tomorrow evening.
pasado mañana.	the day after tomorrow.

DIRECTIONS

¿En que dirección queda...?	In which direction is...?
Lléveme a... por favor.	Take me to... please.
Llévame alla ... por favor.	Take me there please.
¿Qué lugar es este?	What place is this?
¿Dónde queda el pueblo?	Where is the town?
¿Cual es el mejor camino para...?	Which is the best road to...?
De vuelta a la derecha.	Turn to the right.
De vuelta a la isquierda.	Turn to the left.
Siga derecho.	Go this way.
En esta dirección.	In this direction.

¿A que lejos está...? — How far is it to...?
¿Es este el camino a...? — Is this the road to...?
¿Está... — Is it...
  ... cerca? — ... near?
  ... lejos? — ... far?
  ... norte? — ... north?
  ... sur? — ... south?
  ... este? — ... east?
  ... oeste? — ... west?
Indíqueme por favor. — Please point.
Hágame favor de decirme dónde está... — Please direct me to...

  ... el teléfono. — ... the telephone.
  ... el baño. — ... the bathroom.
  ... el correo. — ... the post office.
  ... el banco. — ... the bank.
  ... la comisaria. — ... the police station.

ACCOMMODATIONS

Estoy buscando un hotel.... — I am looking for a hotel that's...
  ... bueno. — ... good.
  ... barato. — ... cheap.
  ... cercano. — ... nearby.
  ... limpio. — ... clean.
¿Dónde hay un hotel, un pensión, un hospedaje? — Where is a hotel, pensión, hospedaje?
Hay habitaciones libres? — Do you have rooms available?
¿Dónde están los baños/el servicio? — Where are the bathrooms?

Quisiera un... — I would like a...
  ... cuarto sencillo. — ... single room.
  ... cuarto con baño. — ... room with a bath.
  ... cuarto doble. — ... double room.
¿Puedo verlo? — May I see it?
¿Cuanto cuesta? — What's the cost?
Es demasiado caro! — It's too expensive!